MEDIEVAL AND RENAISSANCE MUSIC
A PERFORMER'S GUIDE

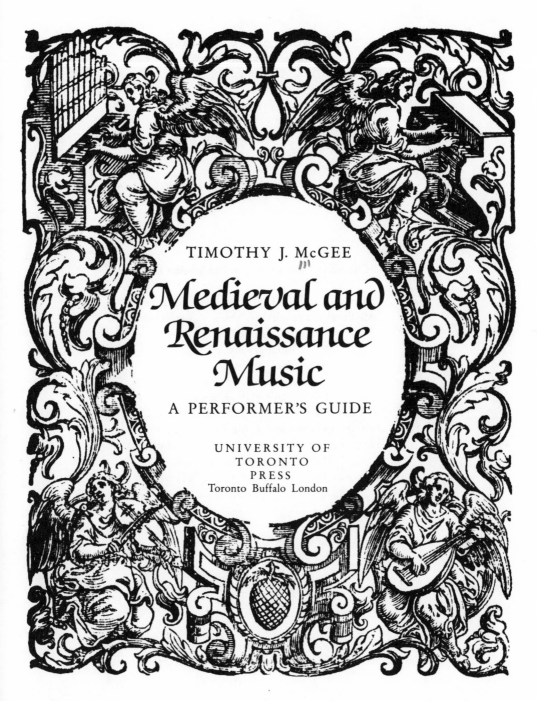

TIMOTHY J. McGEE

Medieval and Renaissance Music

A PERFORMER'S GUIDE

UNIVERSITY OF
TORONTO
PRESS
Toronto Buffalo London

© University of Toronto Press 1985
Toronto Buffalo London
Printed in USA

ISBN 0-8020-2531-5

Design: William Rueter RCA

Canadian Cataloguing in Publication Data

McGee, Timothy J. (Timothy James), 1936–
Medieval and renaissance music : a performer's
guide
Bibliography: p.
Includes index.
ISBN 0-8020-2531-5
1. Music – Interpretation (Phrasing, dynamics, etc.)
2. Music – Performance. 3. Music – 500–1400 –
History and criticism. 4. Music – 15th century –
History and criticism. 5. Music – 16th century –
History and criticism. I. Title.
MT75.M23 1985   781.6'3   C84-099530-X

Publication of this book has been assisted by the Canada Council and
the Ontario Arts Council under their block grant programs.

TO EGON F. KENTON

CONTENTS

ix Contents

ILLUSTRATIONS

MUSICAL EXAMPLES

TABLES AND CHART

PREFACE

HIS BOOK is addressed to those who are interested in performing early music – by which I mean the music of Western Europe before about 1600 – as it was performed when first composed. Over the last few decades enough information has come to light to allow us to believe that we are able to approach the historical performance practices with a degree of authenticity, and it is to that end that this work has been undertaken. There is much more work to be done in many of the areas, as will become evident, but enormous strides have been made since the first recorded performances of early music in the 1930s. As we listen to those old recordings now we may be aware of this or that inaccuracy, but whatever improvements we are able to make today are a direct result of the work and imagination of the pioneers in the field during the earlier decades of this century. With any luck, the performers of a few decades from now will be able to smile at our own efforts.

I have attempted to summarize the subject at its present stage of development as I perceive it. The information here is based on the most complete and accurate sources available, both scholarly and practical, but the attitudes, the information selected, and especially the way in which it is presented are the product of my personal approach both to the subject and to teaching. I have intentionally avoided the temptation to give a single solution to any problem. The information and principles on which the solutions should be based are stated here, but the final choice is left to individual performers.

For those topics on which there is general agreement, the accepted facts are set out; where there is controversy I have attempted to present all possibilities; and where sufficient evidence is not available I have given my opinion based upon the known evidence and upon practical experience. The various kinds of information – fact, controversy, and opinion – are clearly identified so that the reader will understand the strength and nature of the statements.

Regrettably I have been unable to pursue the largest single repertory of early music – chant. Thousands of manuscripts have been preserved containing monophonic material for the Mass and Daily Office, and although it is early music by definition, it is outside the scope of this book because the topic is so vast. Discussion of chant items will be limited to those types which can be found in connection with Liturgical Drama (chapter 6). Discussions of the transcription of early notation and tablature and systems of tuning have also been omitted because of their complexity. These subjects are covered in detail in a number of the sources mentioned in the bibliography.

Although this book is devoted entirely to historically authentic interpretation, I do not insist upon that as the only approach to the early music repertory. Much early music can be performed successfully in the style of later centuries, and performing musicians should feel able to play the music of any century with or without concern for period style. Authentic performance of the music of another era is mostly a product of the twentieth century; previously the music of earlier periods was always performed on the instruments and in the style that was current. Even today pianists feel free to present Bach and Mozart on an instrument that has a completely different sound from the one those composers knew, and performances of Handel's oratorios are most frequently heard today with ensembles far larger than those for which the composer originally conceived the works. The result may not be what the composer himself had in mind, but if it is presented musically there is no need for criticism. It is unfortunate that performers do not feel free to approach the early repertory with the same free spirit allowed for the rest of the repertory. Is the music of Machaut or Lasso so lacking in intrinsic beauty, so much more fragile than Bach or Vivaldi, that it cannot survive a musical but stylistically inauthentic performance? I think not, and this book is not intended to support the view that there is only one way – the historical way – to present early music.

My objective is to present information that will permit historically accurate performance of the early repertory, and for those who share my interest in the subject it should be of some assistance. But the primary attraction is the music itself, and performers interested in the music rather than in historical performance practice should feel free to present the repertory in whatever way their musical instincts dictate. There is an aspect of music that transcends style and period, and the early repertory is much too worthwhile to be considered the exclusive performance property of the few.

ACKNOWLEDGMENTS

IT IS MY PLEASANT DUTY to thank the many people who helped in this endeavour: my wife, Bonnie, for having typed several drafts of the entire manuscript; Ann Wall of Anansi Press for initiating the idea; Geoff Gaherty for continued support of several kinds; the Ontario Arts Council and the Canada Council for financial assistance. I am indebted to Garry Crighton, Jessie Ann Owens, Keith Polk, and Andrew Hughes, who read the entire manuscript and offered many helpful suggestions; Ross Duffin, John Nadas, and several others, who read sections of the typescript and offered their comments; Marcy Epstein, who provided information concerning language and symbolism; the library staff at Villa I Tatti and the Edward Johnson Library at the University of Toronto, who helped in a number of small but important ways; the many students at the University of Toronto and the Scarborough College Early Music Workshop, who allowed me to experiment and develop my theories; my colleagues in musicology and performance, who unselfishly shared their views and ideas; Ron Schoeffel for his enthusiasm and encouragement; David Harford for photographic assistance; Margaret Parker, who edited the text; Will Rueter, who designed the book; and John Fodi, who copied all musical examples not reprinted from published editions. I would especially like to thank the members of the Toronto Consort, whose needs kept me searching for possible solutions and whose penetrating questions and suggestions provided a needed forge for many of the ideas; they were at once my students, my experimental group, and my teachers.

1 'Chapel Choir,' from *Practica musicae utriusque cantus
excellenti Franchini Gaffori ...*
(Venice 1512) title page

2 Matthias Grünewald, 'Angel Concert,' from the Isenheim Altarpiece
(ca 1512)
Used by permission of the Musée d'Unterlinden, Colmar (photo by O. Zimmermann)

3 Hans Burgkmair, from *Triumph of Maximilian the Great*

4 M. Wohlgemuth, 'Minstrels at a Banquet,' from *Der Schatzbehalter* (1491)

5 Jean Dreux, 'A Tourney,' from Brussels, Bibliothèque Royale Albert 1er,
MS 9017, fol. 240r.
Copyright Bibliothèque Royale Albert 1er, Bruxelles. Used by permission

6 Cristoforo de' Predis (or school of), 'Influenze di Venere,' from Modena,
Biblioteca Estense, MS Lat. 209-α.x.2.14: *De Sphaera* (fifteenth century)
Used by permission (photo by Roncaglia)

7 Hans Muelich, 'A Chamber Concert at the Court of Bavaria,' in Munich,
Bayerische Staatsbibliothek, Mus. MS A II
Used by permission

PART ONE

The Materials

Approaching Early Music

Introduction

IDESPREAD INTEREST in the performance of early music is a rather recent phenomenon. Although serious interest in the field dates back to the turn of the century, notably to Arnold Dolmetsch, for the first half of this century performance of pre-baroque music was mostly confined to relatively few specialists, who went about their business with perseverance and dedication and without much public attention. For those first interested in the field each step presented problems: they had to research the performance practices of the early centuries, edit the music themselves, and locate instrument makers who would copy museum instruments.

In recent decades this situation has changed. Concerts of early music are a regular event in cosmopolitan centres, colleges, and universities in Europe and North America, and a representative portion of the repertory is available on recordings. A number of factors have contributed to the current popularity of early music, and chief among these have been the exciting performances by groups of talented musicians who have brought out the vitality, charm, diversity, and innate quality of the early repertory. When brought to the attention of the public at large by competent performers the music reveals itself to be of the highest quality – a fact known to the specialists for some time.

The public success of the performing ensembles has caused renewed activity in both the scholarly and commercial worlds: scholars in significant numbers have newly addressed themselves to problems of early performance practice, and it is now possible for interested musicians to obtain some of the required materials for early music performance with relative ease. Good historical instruments are offered for sale by a surprising number of makers, and obtaining quality modern editions of most genres of music from before 1600 is no longer an obstacle; indeed, for some of the repertory there is even a choice of several good editions. Anthologies and collected works are readily available in many libraries, and a large amount of music can be obtained from booksellers and from societies established to promote early music.

The single problem that remains is access to information concerning the actual performance practices of the early centuries. The primary sources – theoretical treatises, iconographic and archival material, and written accounts – are becoming increasingly available in scholarly editions, and much has been written on the subject of performance practice in recent years. But the primary material and the commentary by scholars are not collected in any one place, and modern performers are hindered in their search because both are written in a variety of languages, the publications are not always accessible, and the writing is frequently on a technical level requiring a specialist's background to understand it.

This book is therefore intended to distil and present the current state of knowledge concerning the performance of music written before 1600. The sources drawn upon are all those mentioned above, combined with the results of performance and experimentation by myself and others. Needless to say, a field so vast is not near to being understood completely, but there is now sufficient information to allow modern performers a certain amount of security in the faithfulness of their historical re-creation.

That there is no single 'right way' to perform a composition of any era is one of the beauties of the art. At any point in history one can find substantial variations in the interpretation of the repertory, and this is as true of the early centuries as of any other era. Within certain limitations artists are always expected to express the music as they see it, and to bring out the elements they believe should be communicated. But the key phrase is 'within certain limitations,' since the freedom enjoyed by performers always lies within the bounds of contemporary performance style. The objective of this book is to provide information about those limitations and boundaries during the medieval and Renaissance periods – the various components of style and technique and the kinds of freedom expected of a performer during that time.

There was not, however, one single performance custom for the early centuries, but several. Although change took place comparatively slowly during those years, customs did change, and a particular performance ensemble or style of ornamentation popular in one century was replaced by something new in the next. Further, the relative isolation of the various centres encouraged the development of individual tastes and regional differences in the customs of performance. Thus interested performers today are confronted with the task of learning not one but a number of different performance customs if they wish to re-create the music as it was originally intended. They must be aware that the instrumentation or articulation correct for the music of one century must be modified when performing music of the next, and that even within the same time period, Paris, Rome, and Munich would have had somewhat different performance traditions.

Because of the newness of the early music revival, few current performers, either professional or amateur, were originally trained for this music. They are mostly converts from training programs developed for the repertory from 1700 forward – a repertory with somewhat different musical and technical demands. Chapters 4 to 10 of this book are directed, therefore, towards expanding the techniques of trained modern performers to encompass the requirements of the early repertory as it was originally performed. Chapters 1 to 3 are devoted to an equally important goal – expanding the attitude of modern performers so that they will be ready to approach the early repertory and its techniques from a historical point of view and helping them to rethink the music and their own roles in order to approach the music from the right direction. Finally, chapter 11 is intended to aid in the search for repertory.

Historical perspective

In order to re-create the music of the early centuries as it was originally intended, twentieth-century performers must develop an attitude towards the music that approximates that of the people of those centuries. This includes a knowledge of the place and purpose of the music and the musicians, an awareness of the various styles and techniques, and most of all a basic respect for the art and artists of that time.

To begin with, a knowledge of the historical period is especially helpful in understanding the music. We are here concerned with the five hundred years between the beginning of the twelfth century and the end of the sixteenth, the period usually referred to as the Late Middle Ages and the Renaissance, a time of great change in Europe. During this period the arts, including music, underwent a number of changes that reflected the changing societies in which they were practised. The arts of any period are inseparable from the rest of the society; they are shaped by the changes in the society, and at the same time they participate in causing the changes. A basic knowledge of the history of the early centuries is therefore useful in understanding the music. This book necessarily presents only a partial view of the subject and should be supplemented by general histories of the early centuries and studies of the history of music.

Many performances of early music are hampered by a lack of respect for the musicians from those centuries; it is frequently believed that, just as each new form of animal is higher than its predecessor, so too each new generation of artists is better, and the artwork of a higher level than before. This is especially a problem in our technological society. Since we are constantly told that this year's automobile is better than last year's, it seems to follow that the same is true in the arts, and that by simple extension the most recent artist and artefact is superior to that of several centuries ago. No one is foolish enough to believe this entirely, but a surprising number do believe that music of the early centuries is inferior to that composed after 1700 since it lacks the harmonic colour of Wagner, the tonal tension of Bach, the drama of Beethoven, and the technical demands of any of them.

The same attitude is not usually found in connection with the other arts. The Gothic cathedrals of the late Middle Ages are accepted as never having been surpassed; the paintings of Giotto, the altar pieces of Memling, the sculpture of Michelangelo, and the woodcuts of Dürer are still viewed with the highest respect, and the *Roman de la Rose, The Canterbury Tales*, and the *Decameron* are read today and enjoyed as masterpieces of literature. Since these works and many more are still considered to be of the very highest level of artistry, how is it possible to assume that in music the standards or the achievements would have been any lower?

There is no doubt that early music does not emphasize harmony and drama in the same way as the music of later periods. Instead, its ingredients are used far more subtly than in later centuries, and include delicate modal and harmonic contrasts, sophisticated text portrayal on several levels, and a variety of rhythmic complexities, both linear and vertical – ingredients that required a high level of sophistication on the part of composers, performers, and listeners. As far as the apparently lesser technical demands of the music are concerned, it must be remembered that, whereas in the other arts all of the product is always visible, in the music of the early centuries often only the basic outline was written by the composer. Thus, although the music looks less demanding on paper, what is seen is only part of the product; the remainder was to be added by the performer, who was, in a sense, a partner to the composer in the realization of the total artefact.

It is important to assume that what was performed in the early centuries was the best possible musical representation of the culture, and if we are fully convinced of this there should be no temptation to 'improve' it for a modern audience, any more than we would be tempted to 'improve' paintings or architecture. If the music really is worthy of presentation to a modern audience it will demonstrate its quality when performed in its original form. Once we have decided that the artists of the early periods were our equals we must also assume that they knew best how to display their art. In music this means that in our performances we should avoid such non-historical 'improvements' as a large ensemble presentation of a composition that was originally chamber music, or the addition of 'colour' to a performance by using as many of the most exotic sounding instruments as possible. Early musicians had a musical purpose for their conventions and traditions. They chose certain instruments or voices for a performance because they wished to support the composition, not detract from it. The instruments they developed matched the music, and it is wrong for us to 'improve' a woodwind by adjusting the finger holes to yield a more tempered scale or 'improve' a medieval string instrument by rounding its bridge. The workshops of the Middle Ages had tools that were accurate, and the instruments they produced were exactly as intended. Rather than try to improve their workmanship and adjust their designs, we must attempt to understand their particular spacing of the finger holes and why they wished to play with flat bridges.

We must thus seek out the traditions and artistic objectives of the early artists and respect them as highly as we do those of any other age. To bring the music of the early centuries back to life we must understand the musical intentions of the composers, learn the skills of the musicians of the time, and perform with the highest standards of technical proficiency available. One can hardly offer less in order to match the quality of all the other arts that continue to provide proof of the extremely high level of accomplishment in the early centuries.

It is taken as a basic premise throughout this book that the full charm and beauty of any composition is best presented when the intentions of the composer are realized in the performance. For early music this means determining the instruments, voices, ornaments, tempo, and so on that the composer originally had in mind. This is not to say that there is a single correct presentation for every work and that all other performances are incorrect to the extent of the difference. What I mean is that composers usually had a specific presentation in mind when writing a composition, and that it is possible to determine many of those details. Further, in the various centuries and locations there were particular performance traditions which would have suggested several possible presentations of any composition, and these also can be determined. There is not a single correct performance of any given work, then, but a number of them, and by studying the historical evidence and looking closely at the music we can be fairly confident of our ability to present most compositions in a way that would have been in keeping with the traditions of the time.

Present-day musicians who wish to be thorough in their re-creation of early music may be surprised by the amount of work required. There are a number of factors that must be considered, such as reading the rhythmic flow as it was originally intended, determining the tempo, and selecting performance ensembles that are within the bounds of the various traditions. In addition, there are new skills of ornamentation and improvisation to be learned and a historical style of articulation to be applied.

In the musical tradition of the early centuries the composer assumed that the performer had the proper skills to convert the page of notes into music. What was written down was the composer's share of the creation, but for the performer merely performing the written notes was not sufficient, and it is therefore insufficient for historical re-creation. Virtually every aspect of music must be rethought in terms of the performance practices of the early centuries.

It is sometimes difficult to think of the people of the distant past in terms of practical, life-like situations, but this is exactly what we must do if we hope to enter into the spirit of the music, to solve the musical problems as they would have, and to re-create the music correctly. The early repertory we have represents people of many classes and reflects the wide array of emotions and occasions that were a part of their daily lives. To perform the music faithfully we must look at each composition as part of a living situation so that our performance can take on the attitude and spirit of that occasion. The key to the skills and the information is provided on the following pages, but to convert that into an attitude that will re-create the true spirit of the music requires a great amount of effort on the part of each performer.

If early music is approached as the highly refined art product of an age as sophisticated as any other, the stage is set for a performance that brings the music back to life with the integrity it originally enjoyed.

Reading the Edition

The music

HE MOST OBVIOUS PLACE to begin is with the printed music most of us use. Everyone knows that the music notation in modern editions is changed in some way from the original. It is important for modern performers of this music to understand what the original looked like and what the transcriber has done in changing the piece into modern notation. Understanding the problems and the amount of editorial choice involved enables us to assess the kinds of information given in the original and therefore the flexibilities allowed to performers. In this chapter the differences between the contemporary and modern versions are discussed – not on the assumption that many will want to retranscribe the music, but to provide information for minor re-editing if performers wish.

Throughout this book we will continually return to the idea that the music itself contains far more information for performers than is usually assumed, and we will look to the music and its notation for the solutions to some of our performance problems. In the early writings about music there is frustratingly little information about the practical kinds of things needed to re-create a historically accurate performance. This is undoubtedly because the conventions of performance were so well known that it would not occur to anyone to write them down. In addition, most of the early writers of treatises were concerned with the theoretical and intellectual aspects of music, and it was not until late in the fifteenth century that the more practical performance topics were considered. Many of the performance conventions of the early centuries will never be recovered, but some of them are plainly visible in the music itself, which will yield its message if only we ask the right questions.

The development and peculiarities of a music repertory and its notational form are mutually influential. The notation is developed in order to express the artistic desires of the composers, but once constructed it also has a life of its own. Its capacities, limitations, and possibilities suggest musical ideas to the composer, who then finds his thoughts confined or expanded by the possibilities of the notation. An understanding of early music therefore requires an understanding of its notation, for the notation itself contains the answers to some of our questions. Much of the subject-matter of this chapter and the next concerns the problems created when one attempts to represent the musical thoughts of earlier centuries in modern notation. For help in understanding early music we must look upon the original notation as the ideal method of expressing the information the composers wished to communicate and must attempt to see in the modern edition the information included in the original.

Original notation and modern editions

The extent of the difference between the original and the modern edition depends on any number of variables: what the original looked like; what kind of notation was originally used; how much alteration has been done by the editor in the transcription; and how much trouble the editor has gone to in transmitting the information in the original manuscript. There are many different kinds of editions that provide varying amounts of information, and to aid modern performers in dealing with the variety of editions, many of the examples in this book are reproduced in their published formats.

All differences, no matter what their cause, are the result of some compromise, some distortion of the original music. If we are to understand what the composer intended it is necessary to know exactly what he presented to the performing musicians of his time, and in this way we can begin to overcome the transcription problems and attempt to regain the original music.

If we compare a modern transcription with the original, many changes in format, note shapes and groupings, clefs, and so on can be seen. Example 2.1a is from a fifteenth-century manuscript and example 2.1b is a modern transcription of it, in which the transcriber has indicated with special signs some features of the original notation. These are marked on the example by numbers and arrows:

1 *The incipit* We are shown here the actual appearance of the beginning of the original – the clef and its placement, the appearance of sharps or flats at the beginning (signature position), the number of staff lines, the shape and pitch of the first note of each part.

2 *Ligature marks* The bracket shows how many notes were connected together (ligated) in a single neume in the original (see example 2.1a).

3 *Coloration marks* The brackets indicate notes written in a different colour in the original (in this case black).

4 *Editorial accidentals* The sharps or flats written above the staff are editorial insertions and are not found in the manuscript.

5 Signum congruentiae This is a sign found in the manuscript that, in this instance, indicates that the parts should all come together at this point.

6 *Longa* The shape of the note in the manuscript calls for a note that is long but not necessarily of definite duration.

This transcription is quite helpful in that it tells us so much about the original. Although most of the transcriptions made in recent decades incorporate most of these signs, earlier ones do not: not all editors furnish ligature or coloration brackets; some choose to supply editorial accidentals on the staff in print slightly smaller than that used for the accidentals supplied in the manuscript while others do not differentiate. Fortunately, publications with 'silent editing' are being superseded by those which supply as much information as possible, which allows serious performers to make up their own minds on a number of important issues.

Very little is actually the same in the original and the transcription. The differences can be listed as follows:

Original	*Edition*
1 c clefs in all parts	treble clefs
2 no score	score
3 no bar lines	bar lines
4 no metre signature	metre signature
5 indifferent text underlay	specific text underlay
6 all notes of fairly long duration	notes of shorter duration
some long notes ligated (♭)	no long notes ligated (♩ ♩ ○)
no short notes ligated (♪ ♪)	some short notes ligated (♫)
7 few accidentals indicated	many editorial accidentals

These differences are important. Some can be dealt with easily, but several affect the very essence of the music and will be discussed more fully in chapter 3.

1 *Clefs* The change of clefs is the only change that does not bring with it any problems.

2 *Score* Very few pieces from the Middle Ages and Renaissance were written down in score. The formats usually found in the early centuries were: parts

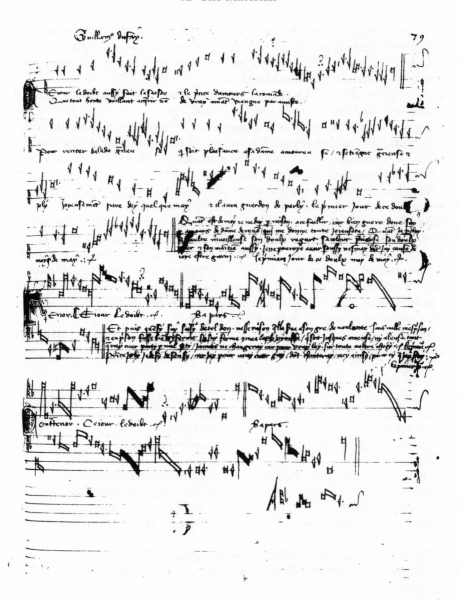

2.1a Guillaume Dufay 'Ce jour le doibt'
MS Canon. Misc. 213, f. 79ʳ. By courtesy of the Bodleian Library, Oxford

2.1b Guillaume Dufay 'Ce jour le doibt'

Guillaume Dufay *Opera Omnia* ed. Heinrich Besseler, vol. 6. © 1964 by Armen Carapetyan,
American Institute of Musicology/Hänssler-Verlag, D-7303 Neuhausen-Stuttgart (West Germany) No. 60.106.
Used by permission

written separately on a single page, as in example 2. 1a; so-called choir book format with the parts written out separately on facing pages – soprano and tenor on one side and alto and bass on the other; and part books, in which the performer could see only his own line of music. The score format of the modern edition has many advantages; for example, each musician can see what else is going on at any time, and it facilitates start-stop rehearsing. The change, however, does bring with it a distortion of the original, although fortunately one that is not too difficult to overcome. Because the early musician could see only a single line, all information needed for performance had to be included on that part alone. It was not possible to look at the other parts to locate a cadence, to see if a flat or sharp should be added to avoid dissonances or enhance a phrase, or to make the rhythmic flow of the line conform to that of the other parts. All this information had to be ascertained from the single line the performer could see, and we can re-create this situation by realizing what was and was not available in the original.

3 *Bar lines* The use of bar lines in modern transcription is one of the biggest distortions of early music. To the traditionally trained modern performer the bar line indicates a regular flow of rhythmic stresses which are to occur to the right of each bar line unless otherwise marked. Much of early music does not have regular recurring rhythms, and in compositions such as that in example 2. 1, the bar lines suggest a rhythmic flow which may be contrary to the intentions of the composer. In order to determine the rhythmic groupings in early music it is necessary to disregard the bar lines (not an easy thing to do) and look to the notes to find the rhythmic flow. This will be discussed in detail in chapter 3.

4 *Metre signs* The transcription gives the metre signature as 3/4 and 6/4 although in the original work there is no sign of any kind to indicate metre. The problem of metre has been implied in the discussion of bar lines – since there is no regular metre in much early music, no metric marking can be assigned. In some music, especially in the sacred repertory, there was an indication called a mensural sign which performed a function similar to a tempo marking (see chapter 3), but much of the secular material before 1500, and even some of the sacred, lacked even this.

There was something in the original, however, that is absent from the transcription, and that is an indication of tempo. Tempo was apparently implied by the note values used; that is, unless otherwise indicated there was a commonly accepted tempo for certain note values, and if a composer wished to write a work that moved faster or more slowly he used larger or smaller note values. This, of course, is an over-simplification of an extremely complex problem that has not yet been fully explored and will be discussed further in chapter 3.

5 *Text underlay* The degree to which the text is underlaid (fitted to the notes) accurately in the early manuscripts differs from scribe to scribe, but for the most part it was fairly haphazard. This would suggest that the specifics of text underlay were often left to the discretion of the soloist, and since much of this music is soloist material, there would be little problem. The only real problems will occur when the members of a chorus attempt to underlay the text individually.

The editor of music in which there is no definite underlay in the original has much freedom in the edition, and in the case of 'Ce jour le doibt' it can be seen that the editor has made several kinds of decisions about underlaying the text. He has, for example, decided upon the placement of the last syllable in both the envoy (the first seventeen bars of music) and the main verse (see the scribal underlay in example 2.1a), and has also made important decisions concerning the melodic-rhythmic flow of the melody line by the placement of text. This is another subject that will be discussed at length in chapter 3.

6 *Note shapes* If we were to transcribe the original notes with only their present-day equivalents, the notes in the superius of example 2.1b would begin with four whole notes. A direct transcription would look something like the following: o o o o o. ♩ o o

To the modern reader these are the longest notes still in common use, and therefore they suggest a very sustained passage. In the fifteenth century, however, these notes called for fairly quick motion and were used with other longer values still commonly used at that time: the breve (□), two or three times the value of the semibreve (◇), and the longa (⊐), two or three times the value of the breve. The editor of example 2.1b, thinking of his modern reader, has rightly changed the value of the original, reducing it to note values that suggest faster motion. The problem that often arises from this has to do with ligatures; in early music only the notes of the longest values (⊐, □, ◇) could be ligated. The modern tradition allows for ligature only on the shortest levels (♫, ♪). But ligature suggests phrase groupings that are not indicated in the original; for example, let us consider the passage from 'Ce jour le doibt' given in its original form in example 2.2a. Example 2.2b gives the transcription as in 2.1b in which the editor has suggested both rhythmic grouping and text underlay by use of ligature. It is possible, however, that a different rhythmic grouping and text underlay, such as example 2.2c, would suggest itself to the performer if the editorial ligature were not present. To overcome this kind of problem modern performers must be aware that the grouping on small-note levels is entirely editorial, and before accepting any grouping they should look at the notes without ligature to see if another grouping suggests itself. No single

2.2 Guillaume Dufay 'Ce jour le doibt': a/ original passage;
b/ same passage as transcribed by Besseler (bars 33–4); c/ another reading

solution is proposed here, but as with the text underlay many solutions are possible and will be discussed further in chapter 3.

7 *Editorial accidentals or* musica ficta In modern editions, editorial additions of accidentals can usually be recognized easily because they are usually written above the staff. The indication of accidentals was only partially supplied by the composer in all early music, and the performer added the remainder according to personal preference within the confines of what must have been well-known rules. It is a source of constant frustration to modern performers that we have not been able to reconstruct these rules with anything resembling thoroughness. One can suspect that there must have been much room for flexibility within the rules of the time, and further, that the customs need not have been the same for each locality or century. There is ample evidence that theorists at the time did not agree on the application of accidentals and that musicians were frequently confused and uncertain.[1] What appears to be a logical guess is that the rules, whatever they were, must have been capable of being applied to only a single line of music (as opposed to a score), and that they were probably applied at sight. The reason for these conclusions is that the notation system already included the signs necessary to mark the copy accurately, but they were used inconsistently and only under certain circumstances. It would seem impractical in any age to require extensive score analysis in order to determine the chromatic alterations when they could easily have been written into the parts.

Needless to say, there are as many solutions to *musica ficta* as there are editors, and a corollary of this statement is that there are as many modern theories of *ficta* application as there are editors. Several good studies of the problem can be found, but many difficult problems still remain. Serious performers are encouraged to pursue the detailed studies.[2]

The problem of *musica ficta* has a fairly high profile in current scholarly investigation and debate, and perhaps before long the subject will be understood more thoroughly. Since so many fine scholars cannot agree on a solution, the problem must be extremely complex, and a complete solution will not be found on these pages. However, the following simplified discussion may help performers understand what the problem is. The

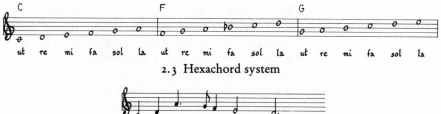

2.3 Hexachord system

2.4 Guillaume Dufay 'Ce jour le doibt,' bars 41–4

2.5 Guillaume Dufay 'Ce jour le doibt,' bars 13–17

basics of the theory as stated here will be seen to be quite straightforward; it is in the applications that the problems arise.

Early music was sung to six solfège syllables – a 'movable do' system that ordinarily had three possible starting positions: C, F, and G (example 2.3). Since the entire octave was not available in a single scale, the singer could mutate (jump) from one hexachord (six-note scale) to another according to what was indicated and necessary in the notes. To pick a simple example, let us refer to the melodic phrase in example 2.4. There is no problem in this example because all the notes lie within the C hexachord. The problems of mutation arise when the notes exceed the six available in a single hexachord. At the fifth note of example 2.5 the singer must change hexachords because the upper C is not available in the original C hexachord. He must therefore shift to a hexachord in which as many of the notes as possible can be handled without changing again; in this case both the F and G hexachords would cover the notes. I have chosen the G hexachord instead of the F because the passage ends with a long note on G, suggesting a tonal foundation on that pitch. The F hexachord would also cover all the remaining notes, but that hexachord includes a B-flat, and there would have to be some other indication that a B-flat would be important to the passage – for example a tonal ending or emphasis on F, a B-flat written into the music (as can be seen elsewhere in this composition), or some other such indication. (Would that all problems were this easy.) If we now consider the superius line in example 2.1b from bars 1 to 17, there is some question about the flats suggested by the editor. The entire melody of this section appears to be centred around G and therefore can be fully sung to the C and G hexachords; the F-sharp before the first phrase-end (bar 4) helps to strengthen this centre, and, in imitation of this, I would suggest a similar raising of the Fs before the ending of the complete section.

Many editors solve their accidental problems by playing over the music at the piano, from score. It must be remembered, however, that the early musician did not see a score (unless he was performing solo on lute or keyboard) and therefore some of the solutions to editorial accidentals derived from score reading were not available to him. He saw only his own line, and whatever his rules they must have been derived from the sight of the single line, aided in some cases by what he heard in the other parts. The F-sharp would have been added in example 2.1b, bar 16, because he could see that his line was cadencing – a long note on G with a rest following it – and the rules we do know allowed for, or sometimes insisted on, heightening the feeling of cadence by raising the note below the cadence note. In a similar way he would judge whether to mutate to the F or G hexachord by looking ahead to see where his line was going and deciding what the range was and which notes were emphasized by rhythm and melody. If a B-flat was indicated at the beginning of a work, he knew in advance that he should select the F hexachord and not G whenever possible – that was what the sign meant.

In addition to this principle of mutation, by the sixteenth century most theorists agreed on the following basic rules:

a In a melodic line in which the hexachord is exceeded by only the step above La, that note should always be sung as a half-step. Thus, in example 2.1b, bars 34 and 53, the B should be made flat even if it were not so marked in the manuscript since it exceeds the C hexachord by only a single pitch and then returns. If either passage had continued to C or higher, however, mutation to one of the other hexachords would have been necessary, and in that case the B would be natural or flat depending upon which hexachord were chosen, according to the discussion of mutation above.

b Linear tritones and diminished fifths should be changed to perfect intervals whenever possible. That is, direct intervals such as B to F should be altered by either lowering the B or raising the F – the choice depends upon context. If the two notes are separated by one or more notes, for example B, A, F, the alteration is possible but not as necessary, and therefore if alteration is not suggested by melodic or harmonic context (see next rule), it then becomes the choice of the performer.

c Vertical tritones, diminished fifths, and diminished octaves should be changed to perfect intervals whenever possible, although passing tones need not always be changed. Thus in example 2.1b, bar 57, the superius F should probably be raised because of the F-sharp in the tenor, but in measure 14 the B-F interval between superius and tenor need not require alteration of either line.[3]

For an interesting comparison of two different but acceptable views of accidental application I suggest that you attempt the first seventeen bars of 'Ce jour le doibt,' first as edited by Besseler in example 2.1b, and then in the form I have suggested, without any editorial flats but with sharps added to the superius in bar 16. As you will see, both versions are musical, although they have slightly different modal flavours.

It can be seen, then, that there are many differences between a modern edition and what was originally written. The editors do their best to represent the intentions of the early composers, but it is simply not possible to transmit the information exactly in modern notation. I am not suggesting that we abandon modern notation – far from it. For it is possible for modern musicians to use these editions and realize excellent and authentic musical performances. But to do so they must understand the differences between the two systems of notation, must be aware of the way in which the early composer expressed his music in notes, and must be prepared to expend the thought and practice time necessary to overcome the differences and misleading assumptions inherent in the notational changes. Once we have realized what the notational differences are, the next step is to approach the music on its own terms.

Basic Musical Problems

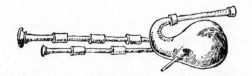

HE LOCATION of stresses within the flow of the melodic line, the placement of text to support this flow, and the tempo and style of the composition are all basic to the way in which a composition is performed. Unfortunately, of all the problems encountered by modern musicians wishing to re-create early music, these present the greatest difficulties. All four areas allow a high degree of individual interpretation and thus the discussions here should be considered to be more an exposition of general concepts, approaches, and guide-lines rather than a set of rigid rules to be applied without further subjective consideration. For the subjects of text underlay and tempo there are contemporary writings which provide us with some practical information on which to base our ideas, but there are no contemporary writings about either melodic-rhythmic flow or style; my discussions of those topics are entirely extracted from the music itself.

The four topics are discussed separately below, but in reality they are interdependent and should be considered as a single unit. For didactic reasons melodic-rhythmic flow and text underlay are presented in a more or less 'stylistically neutral' form. That is to say that the principles put forward are basic to all early music and can serve as a starting place for any composition, although they must be subjected to considerations of style before they can be applied correctly to any specific composition.

Melodic-rhythmic flow

In the discussion of bar lines in chapter 2 I stated that much early music does not involve a regularly recurring stress. A large amount of early music has as its major ingredient a sophisticated use of rhythms – both melodically in single lines and in rhythmic counterpoint between two or more parts – and it

3.1 Guillaume Dufay 'Ce jour le doibt,' opening phrase

is precisely this important element that modern bar lines tend to destroy. If we look at 'Ce jour le doibt' without bar lines or text underlay (example 3.1), the melodic and rhythmic flow will suggest a grouping quite different from that suggested by the bar lines in the published edition (example 2.1b). If we were to mark off the lines according to the rhythmic groupings visible in the music, they would be irregular and would produce rhythmic phrases for the first phrase of the superius:

Each of the phrases of this piece will yield irregular rhythmic groupings similar to this if we look at the music the way the early musician would have seen it.

The principles used in assigning the irregularly spaced unit markings above are quite simple; they are not mentioned in any writings of the period but would appear to be the only ones available to a musician reading a single line without bars:

1 Long notes indicate stress; short notes do not. That is, the rhythm flows from long to long, through the shorter values. This is supported by the

3.2 Guillaume Dufay 'Ce jour le doibt,' internal phrase, superius

natural rhythmic flow of Medieval European languages, which flow from long to long, not stressing short syllables. Since music is so closely aligned with text, this principle has been assumed for music in the absence of any direct theoretical commentary either supporting or contesting it. (But see the discussion of style below pp. 49–53.)

2 Even note patterns are divided evenly unless unusual melodic skips indicate otherwise. For example, the first four notes of example 3.1 can be considered to be a rhythmic unit of four (or two plus two). The fifth note is both long and a large skip, indicating that it is the first of a rhythmic group. It is considered the first of a group for both reasons, but either of these elements alone would have been sufficient reason to designate it as first; for example the eighth note of example 3.1 is first solely because of its length, and in example 3.2 the seventh note is considered to be first because of its position after an upward leap in spite of the fact that it is not of a longer duration.

It is important to note at this point that the division by unit markings above or the designation of any note as first in its rhythmic group does not imply accent. The word 'stress' would be a better way to express the function of first as long as it is understood to imply only that subtle kind of emphasis which marks off a melodic line into sub-units and causes the phrase to flow forward. The use of more obvious stresses or accents depends on other kinds of criteria such as text accent and representation of the spirit of the work.

To continue with the analysis of rhythmic units, if the above principles of rhythmic-melodic flow are applied to the second phrase of the superius, the following rhythmic groups will suggest themselves (compare with the pitch transcription in example 3.1):

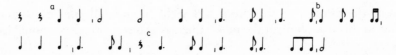

Most of the divisions or groupings indicated above are simply the result of straightforward application of the first two principles. There is also a new item involving short rests at points marked a and c in the above phrase which can be solved by application of the following rule:

3 Short-value rests (that is, shorter than a longa = o) indicate the absence of

the initial member(s) of a group, thus rendering the note or notes following the rest up-beat(s). As a result, the first two notes at point a are considered to be not a rhythmic group of two but the last two of a group of four, serving as up-beats to the next unit. At point c we are again faced with a group that could be taken as a down-beat except that the rest preceding the first note in this phrase renders the pattern an up-beat to the following group. This rule has been abstracted from the music itelf and has an exception: if the new phrase begins with an accented text syllable, the first note is considered to be the beginning of a group. It will be found, however, that in the majority of cases the new syllable will be unaccented. Experimentation has found rule 3 generally applicable to instrumental performances.

In the above phrase a number of different levels of rhythmic division can be seen. The first complete unit in the phrase can be considered to be a triple unit on the level of three half-notes, ♩ ♩ ♩ ♩ beginning on the third note after point a; the five notes at point b are on the level of the eighth-note, which renders that group 6/8; and the group of three that follows it is 3/4. Thus in a single line we have three different levels of note organization into triple rhythms – eighth, quarter, and half. If the rhythmic flow of each part is considered carefully according to the principles set out above, the natural beauty of a fairly complex phrase (complex both melodically and rhythmically) can be realized. It is far more difficult to perform than one that adheres strictly to regularly spaced bar lines, but the musical product is well worth the extra effort. If in addition the other two parts of the musical example are also marked off according to the same principles, the result is an attractive and variable rhythmic flow in the superius and an extremely sophisticated rhythmic counterpoint provided by the varieties of rhythms that result from the simultaneous sounding of the different parts. The rhythmic interplay of the three parts can be seen in the plot of the first phrase shown below.

A bar line gives a false message to modern performers because it signifies a regular recurring stress on the first beat of every bar. This is a product of the eighteenth and nineteenth centuries, in whose music rhythmic flow is usually quite regular and sophistication lies in other elements of the composition,

3.3 Claude Gervaise 'Branle,' bars 1–12, from Pierre Attaingnant *Second Livre* 1547
Avec l'autorisation de Heugel et Cie, Editeurs-Propriétaires pour tous pays

often the harmony. The polyphonic music of the earlier centuries, however, grew from the simple harmonies of the Middle Ages – simple because polyphony was begun as a 'dressing-up' of a single line. Early music therefore retains elements of its origin, the intricate rhythms of monophony, and the earlier the music, the more complex are the rhythms and the simpler the harmonies.

It is not true that all early music has an irregular flow of rhythms; any number of examples can be found in which regular bar lines will not do violence to the intentions of the composer. Much dance music falls into this category, although even in a four-part dance from the sixteenth century one of the parts will often have a rhythmic flow contrary to the regular units of the others. See for instance, example 3.3, in which the superius line contains a rhythmic flow that would suggest the following phrasing:

In example 3.4 from the fourteenth century, however, bar lines will not harm the flow of the music at all. But the best rule for modern performers is to approach each new piece of music on its own merits and allow the music itself

3.4 Ghirardellus da Firenze 'Per prender cacciagion,' bars 1–21
Nino Pirrotta, ed. *The Music of Fourteenth-Century Italy*, vol. 1. © 1954 by Armen Carapetyan,
American Institute of Musicology/Hänssler-Verlag, D-7303 Neuhausen-Stuttgart (West Germany) No. 60.801.
Used by permission

to decide the flow of the rhythmic patterns. If the patterns fall into regular groups a bar line transcription is acceptable; if not, the regular accents must be eliminated and the dictates of the musical line followed. Sometimes this means a complete rewrite and the use of *Mensurstriche* (bar lines marked between staves rather than through them, as in example 3.14). In any case, even in music which contains regular rhythmic units, the principle of allowing the music to flow from the long notes to the long notes and avoiding accented short values is a good one to follow. It can often be applied to advantage on a small scale within otherwise regularly barred music, as in bar 11 of example 3.4, which could be thought of as 6/8 + 1 rather than 4/4, yielding these rhythm patterns:

Text underlay

Once the regular and natural flow of the musical line has been established, it is possible to underlay the text so that it will fit the melody. When this is done properly the text and the melodic flow are mutually supportive: the placement of text syllables aids in the proper flow of the melody, and the melody at the same time reflects the correct pronunciation and natural stress of the text syllables. In modern transcriptions many of the problems of text underlay have already been solved by the editors. Nevertheless, it is a good idea to understand the principles and to check the transcriptions, since not all editors will have thought out clearly the principles of melodic flow.

Very few statements about text underlay come down to us from the early centuries. In fact, the first real information is found in four sixteenth-century treatises: one written by Giovanni Maria Lanfranco in 1533, another by Nicola Vicentino in 1555, a set of ten rules by Gioseffo Zarlino in 1558, based on eight by Lanfranco, and finally Gaspar Stocker's treatise of approximately 1570–80 adding refinements to Zarlino's rules.[1] Although these do not cover the many centuries considered here, they are at least a good starting point, and one from which we can attempt to move towards the earlier centuries.

THE SIXTEENTH CENTURY

Following the analyses and comparisons by Edward Lowinsky and Don Harrán,[2] the essential points of sixteenth-century underlay are these:

1 Long notes receive strong syllables; shorter notes are considered to be grouped with the longer ones and therefore should receive unaccented syllables. This can be seen to be the principle adopted in the previous section concerning melodic-rhythmic flow.

   a In evenly divided passages of equal-value notes the syllables should be divided in order to reflect the equal division. Thus, for example, in a passage of four equal notes with two syllables, the syllables are assigned to notes 1 and 3.

   b If a syllable must be assigned to a passage of fast notes, it is assigned only

3.5 Note subdivision. The whole note in the lower voice causes a dissonant interval. Therefore, if subdivision is necessary, do not assign an accented syllable in place of the dot in the upper part.

3.6 Adrian Willaert 'Veni sancte spiritus,' superius cadence

to the first note in the passage, and the first long note following that fast passage should not receive a syllable:[3]

♪   ♪♪♩   ♩

syllable   no syllable   syllable

An exception is noted for the last section of this rule: in French chansons syllables are sometimes assigned to middle notes of fast passages and to the first long note that follows the passage.

2 The first note of a composition and the first note following a rest receive a syllable.

3 The final note should receive the final syllable (but see rule 4).

4 A ligature receives only a single syllable, and that is on its first note. If the last note of a phrase is a member of a ligature the final syllable is assigned to the first note of the ligature. (Exceptions to this rule can be found.)[4]

5 If there are more syllables than notes the notes must be subdivided (but see rule 6).

6 A dotted note should not ordinarily be subdivided. If, however, this must be done care should be taken that the last value – the dot – is not unduly emphasized. This is especially true in cases where harmonic suspensions have been constructed, as in example 3.5. In this case the dissonance is in danger of over-emphasis if a syllable is sung in place of the dot.

7 Repeated notes on the same pitch must receive individual syllables.

8 If there are many notes left at the end of a phrase, the last note is assigned to the last syllable, and the remainder is sung to the second-to-last syllable. But if the second-to-last syllable is unaccented, the melisma is assigned to the third-to-last syllable, as in example 3.6.

9 In a passage involving the rhythm ♩. ♪ ♪ (♩. ♪♪) the short note does not
   receive a syllable, nor does the long note following it. However, if there
   are not enough notes to allow this, if the short note receives a syllable, then
   so must the note that follows it. In other words, ♩. ♪ ♪ is a rhythmic unit
   of 3/2 in which the stress falls upon the first of the unit.

Vicentino's example of good text underlay (example 3.7) illustrates most of
the above rules.

These rules were recommended for all music from the time of Josquin (about
1475–1521) until 1570–80, when Stocker wrote his treatise. Stocker mentioned some changes between the 'old' style (that is, the style of the Josquin
era) and the 'new' style (that is, post-Josquin). They can be summarized as
follows:

10 Notes as small as eighth notes in example 3.7 may receive a syllable,
   whereas formerly the smallest note commonly to receive one was the next
   larger. This reflects the tendency of music in the middle of the sixteenth
   century towards more syllabic setting of the text (that is, settings in which
   for the most part each syllable receives a single note) and rhythms more
   closely reflecting the rhythm of the text.

11 If there is space and notes enough to repeat the text, repetition should be of
   complete phrases rather than isolated words or half-phrases. This rule is
   stated in a way that suggests it was frequently broken in practice.
   Madrigals, especially, come to mind as a form in which single words and
   half-phrases commonly receive repetition for dramatic emphasis.

12 The portion of rule 1b concerning texting of fast passages is now reduced
   by one level, that is, only the first note of the passage should be texted and
   neither the middle notes nor the long note following the passage should
   receive text.

13 When a composition ends with a flourish of fast notes rather than with the
   usual longer notes, the final syllable should be assigned to the first note of
   the fast-note passage.

Writing in the last third of the century, Stocker called attention to the fact
that the modern music was more syllabic than the old and therefore less open
to complexity in underlaying text. He also acknowledged that not all
composers followed all the rules, and that this was true of both old and
modern composers.

The rules of the sixteenth-century theorists are fairly clear in reference to
the music from 1475 to the end of the sixteenth century. For music written
after that time, two other factors are equally helpful: the music is mostly syllabic, and therefore the problems are few, and greater care is taken in the
actual underlay of the text in the manuscripts and prints.

3.7 Nicola Vicentino: illustration of text underlay from *L'antica musica* cap. xxx

THE MIDDLE AGES

In the music written before 1475 there are many problems but only a single source of instructions: a short statement from ca 1440[5] that tells us only that rule 4 – text on only the first note of a ligature – existed in the mid-fifteenth century. For more detailed information about this vast repertory we must go to the music itself, keeping in mind the rules above, to which the earlier music gradually evolved, and the statement by Stocker that he believed that the rules for underlay existed prior to the old (that is, Josquin's) music, even though they were not issued as rules.

It is important to note that the rules from the sixteenth-century theorists cited above are, for the most part, the sensible kinds of practices that naturally follow the preceding discussion of melodic flow and phrasing. Because of this, I will assume that the same principles can be applied to the earlier centuries. It is always dangerous to attempt to apply practices of one century to the music of another, but in this case, lacking contemporary information of any kind, we shall proceed from the attitude that if all other things are equal, the text should not destroy or interrupt the rhythmic-melodic flow. We can find some assurance in the fact that when we finally have direct statements in the sixteenth century, they support this attitude. To expand on the sixteenth-century theorists' thought, the rules for good text underlay are those which fit with the best possible flow of the musical line. Whether they were written down or not, those rules are obvious.

Sacred and secular music of the twelfth and thirteenth centuries and even some from the fourteenth is often syllabic, thus offering no problem. Where the few melismas do occur in this music the solution is usually obvious, and modern editors, with few exceptions, underlay the text in a way that supports the melodic line. The problems arise, however, in works which are quite melismatic, and this repertory comes from almost all European nations beginning in quantity in the late thirteenth century.

Since this book is directed towards performers who must read modern transcriptions, we shall have to assume that the transcription to be used makes some distinction between original material and editorial addition and, further, that the editor has placed the text approximately where the manuscript suggests. (If these assumptions are not correct the only solution is to begin with the manuscript, and this involves familiarity with the notation, a subject which is outside the scope of this book.) The performer should check the underlay for its adherence to the following rules, which are derived from the desire to support the musical line.

1 The first note of the composition and that following a rest should carry a syllable. There is an exception to the first part of this rule in compositions that begin with an instrumental introductory phrase; this is discussed below (pp. 38–40). For the first note following a rest there is often a great amount of flexibility in a highly melismatic work. The performer must be careful, however, to recognize whether the note following the rest is an up-beat or a down-beat and then to select an unaccented or accented syllable accordingly. Further, in distributing the text in a phrase set apart by rests, an effort should be made to apportion the text so that the rest does not interrupt the text phrase.

2 Important words and strong syllables should be given relatively longer melismas. Unimportant words (for example, articles) should be placed under shorter, unaccented notes in less important positions in the phrase.

3 When possible, the last melisma is assigned to the second-to-last syllable (as in rule 8 in the sixteenth-century instructions) unless it violates rule 2 above, thus leaving the last syllable for the last note.

4 Ligatures are not to be broken, and the syllable is assigned to the first note of the ligature. (In most situations this would suggest that the ligature itself may have had a significance akin to the placement of rhythmic stress or grouping.)

Within these few rules there is much room for individual decisions. Example 3.8 provides three of many possible ways to underlay the text of a melismatic line from a mid-fifteenth-century chanson.

Thus, beyond the rules relevant for sixteenth-century music, the rules for the earlier centuries can also be stated as two prohibitions for the modern performer: avoid emphasizing a regular accent if none is apparent in the melodic-rhythmic flow; do not draw attention to short notes unless asked to do so by the composer/scribe, for instance by the linkage of short-long notes under ligature.

At this point a word should be added on subdivision of the written notes in order to accommodate syllables; rule 6 from the sixteenth century suggests

3.8 Anonymous 'La plus grant chiere,' opening section, superius

3.9 Anonymous 'Eya, martyr Stephane,' verse, lower voice, after *Musica Britannica* vol. 4, 9

some points in this regard. In music of the early centuries problems arise mostly in strophic settings of both sacred and secular music where the music is written for one verse and must be adjusted for another. In example 3.9 the music is laid out according to the textual needs of verse 1. Verse 2 of this same poem, however, suggests a slight adjustment to accommodate the textual accent, and the singer must be ready to add or subtract up-beats, combine or subdivide certain notes, and move text in order to preserve the flow of the music and the text. In this example the first note must be subdivided in order to accommodate the additional syllable in verse 2, so that the important word 'was' can be sung to the stressed note c. For the third phrase of the melody, verse 2 has the same number of syllables as verse 1, but the preposition 'in' has been shifted to avoid overemphasis of a relatively unimportant word.

Example 3.10 gives a similar kind of problem from a sacred work. In this

3.10 John Dunstable 'Ave Maris Stella,' superius

example quite a bit of difference is suggested in the underlay of the two verses shown in order to align the natural flow of text and melody and to place stress on the important syllables. The underlay proposed here is only one of a number of possibilities. These kinds of solutions must obviously be applied to all strophic situations from all centuries under discussion. When underlaying a second or third set of syllables to a French chanson, German Lied, or Italian villanella, these same principles boil down to a single rule: align the strong syllables with longer notes and weaker syllables with shorter notes, adding, subdividing, and combining notes wherever necessary.

Special texting problems

Mass settings
Missing text. The settings of the five (sometimes four or six) parts of the Mass Ordinary involve texting problems in addition to those discussed above. The parts of the Ordinary were sung every day, and therefore the singers could be expected to know the texts intimately. Thus when a phrase of text is omitted entirely from a particular manuscript, it is probable that the scribe was depending on the singers' knowledge of the standard prayer texts. The omission often signifies that the underlay was obvious and the scribe felt free to indicate only the place for the beginning of some phrases; the singer would immediately know how to add the missing words. Such a case is illustrated in example 3.11, in which the editorially supplied text is given in italics. Without

3.11 Josquin des Prez 'Credo' from *Missa: Ave Maris Stella*, bars 1–6
Josquin des Pres *Werken* ed. Albert Smijers, vol. 15. Used by permission of
the Vereniging voor Nederlandse Muziekgeschiedenis, Drift 21, 3512 BR Utrecht, Netherlands

3.12 Johannes Ockeghem 'Kyrie I' from *Missa: De plus en plus*
Johannes Ockeghem Collected Works ed. Dragan Plamenac, vol. 1,
American Musicological Society. Copyright 1959. Used by permission

the editorial additions the text would be incomplete, and this would obviously
be incorrect. But there are other cases which are not so obvious.
Repeated text. The problem of repeated text can be seen in its clearest form in
the text of the Kyrie eleison. The official prayer calls for a nine-fold invoca-
tion of the text, usually divided into three separate sections in polyphonic
settings:

section I	Kyrie eleison	(three times)
section II	Christe eleison	(three times)
section III	Kyrie eleison	(three times)

In some of the manuscripts, however, the text is given only once per section,
as in example 3.12. Should we invoke the common-sense rule that the singers

would have known to repeat the text three times per section, assuming that the scribe felt it necessary to indicate only the place of the first and last words? This is certainly possible, and many editors, such as this one, add the remainder of the words on that assumption. But we cannot make a general rule because three other possibilities come to mind in connection with the Kyrie: that in a polyphonic rendering of the prayer the repetition was deemed unnecessary, and the simultaneous singing of the words in several different voice parts was considered to be a substitute for repetition in any one line;[6] that the practice was to sing each section three times (there are indications that the Machaut Mass was intended to be sung in this manner); or that a practice known as *alternatim* was used. This refers to the alternation of polyphonic sections with monophonic chant sections, producing the following scheme in performance:

Kyrie 1	monophonic chant
Kyrie 2	polyphony
Kyrie 3	chant
Christe 1	polyphony
Christe 2	chant, and so on.

Except in cases where the manuscript clearly indicates either a threefold repetition of each polyphonic section or gives cues for the alternating chant, we simply do not know what the performance practice was for many of these sections. In Dufay's *Missa: Se la face ay pale* the text is actually written out three times for each section, thus making the texting clear. But in his *Missa: L'homme armé*, it is written but once for each section. In the latter the sections are so long that sectional repetition would seem impractical, but that does not tell us that the practice would not have allowed the performers to use solution 1 above.

In other movements of the Mass similar problems arise in regard to text repetition. There are sufficient notes after some or all phrases to allow text repetition, but does this mean that the singers were expected to repeat some of the text? From a study of the manuscripts of the fourteenth to the sixteenth centuries, some general rules can be derived in this regard.

The music of the fourteenth century tends to employ a substantial number of melismatic passages. Little effort is made to connect the text intimately with the melodic shape or rhythm, and sections of textless melody appear to be the style, as in examples 3.4 and 3.8 above. (These examples are secular, but the practice is also found in sacred music.) Everything in the music suggests that text repetition was not part of the style. These melismatic passages were

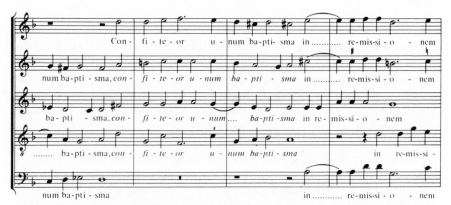

3.13 Orlandus Lassus 'Credo' from *Missa super 'Mon cueur se recommande à vous,'*
bars 137–44

Orlandus Lassus *Sämtliche Werke* ed. Siegfried Hemelink, vol. 11, neue Reihe. Bärenreiter-Verlag 1971.
Used by permission

reduced in length through the fifteenth century and eventually produced the
style of the mid-sixteenth century in which syllabic setting is emphasized in all
musical forms, both sacred and secular; repetition of text in sixteenth-century
music is often either present in the sources or indicated by sign. But
hand-in-hand with the sixteenth-century desire for syllabic setting went the
tendency to adapt the melodic-rhythmic shape to that of the text, and thus
works in which the performer is expected to repeat the text are fairly easy to
spot. In example 3.13 the phrase without text underlay in the original is
obviously of the same general shape as the previous one which received the

text. The performer can easily see that the text repetition indicated by the editor is desirable here.

The music of the fifteenth century represents a transition between the lack of repetition in the music of the fourteenth century and the repetition in that of the sixteenth, and so each fifteenth-century case must be considered on its own merits. Look at the edition to see if any text repetition was actually indicated in the manuscript. If the composer/scribe wrote out one or more of the repetitions (indicated in the transcriptions by repetition not in italics or brackets, depending on the edition), you can consider repetition part of the style. If there is no help in the manuscript, look at the melodic line to see if the melodic-rhythmic shape reflects a syllabic declamation of the text; if so, the work should probably be aligned with sixteenth-century rather than four-teenth-century practice.

Untexted parts

The text in a manuscript is often underlaid for only one or two parts and not for the others. In these cases an untexted part usually has at least the first phrase of text, which is inserted to identify the part as belonging to the others, but this does not necessarily indicate that the rest of the text should be underlaid by the performer. The question is: was the text omitted because the part was intended for instrumental performance, or because the scribe felt it unnecessary to write the text again?

During the centuries in question, the composer did not assign the parts; the musicians were free to choose voices or instruments as they pleased (but see a full discussion of this point in chapter 4). Therefore, whether a part was originally intended for voice or instrument, either is possible, and, given certain conditions, they are more or less equally acceptable.

In the case of secular music, the shape of the part itself will often suggest whether instruments or voice were intended for the untexted parts (see chapter 4). But for liturgical music the case is not so easily made. Strong evidence has been presented recently that instruments were not commonly used in a polyphonic liturgical context before the mid-sixteenth century.[7] It was undoubtedly done from time to time, but recent research suggests that it was not the usual mode of performance. Where all or part of the text is missing from some of the parts of a Mass it is usually fairly easy to supply the missing text. But not all lines will allow a full text to be underlaid with ease, as shown in example 3.14. In this Mass there is no text at all for the tenor, although its pre-existent melody is marked with the identifying label 'L'homme armé' at the beginning of the line. The tenor part is in much slower note values than the other three and does not share the common melodic-rhythmic motives found

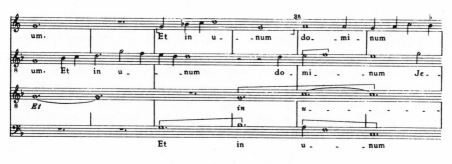

3.14 Guillaume Dufay 'Credo' from *Missa: L'homme armé*, bars 31–42
Guillaume Dufay *Opera Omnia* ed. Heinrich Besseler, vol. 3 © 1951 by Armen Carapetyan,
American Institute of Musicology/Hänssler-Verlag, D-7303 Neuhausen-Stuttgart (West Germany) No. 60.106.
Used by permission

in the other voices, which suggests that the composer intended to make this
one line stand apart from the others.

To add the entire liturgical text to the tenor line would require subdividing
nearly all the notes; to sing the secular 'L'homme armé' text along with the
liturgy would seem sacrilegious or at least irreverent; and thus two possible
solutions remain: vocal performance without text, using a neutral syllable, or
instrumental performance of the untexted line in spite of the evidence to the
contrary. There have been no definitive studies of this question to date, and
therefore modern performers are free to experiment and choose whichever
solution seems most musical. My own choice would be a vocal rendering of
the part without text; this choice is based on the earlier medieval practice of
writing motets over a sustained tenor that had only a few syllable changes.
Compositions in the mid-fifteenth century such as Dufay's Masses and
motets are possibly the last vestiges of that tradition.

There are similar cases in which modern performers of both sacred and
secular music will find it difficult to know whether to underlay a text, to sing
the part without text, or to play it. In these cases a sensible decision can be

made through experimentation. Try adding the text to the line to see if it fits without distorting the flow and lends itself to vocal performance (see chapter 5). Try it instrumentally to see if it falls more naturally into instrumental performance (see chapter 5) and whether an instrumental performance adds or detracts from the whole. In many cases one mode of performance will immediately emerge as superior. In cases where the solutions are equally satisfying, both are possible, and your choice should be determined by other criteria (see chapters 4 and 5).

Instrumental interludes

In both fourteenth- and fifteenth-century manuscripts there are texting practices that suggest possible instrumental interludes within a texted melody line. In examples 3.15a and 3.15b the transcriptions closely reflect the manuscript text underlay.

In the former the first word, 'Adieu', actually appears at the very beginning of the line beneath the long phrase which ends at a rest. The phrase following the rest begins with an up-beat, suggesting that the first syllable would be more appropriate here than the second. It is possible, therefore, that the word 'Adieu' appears at the beginning of the manuscript line merely for identification and artistic purposes, but that the line actually begins with an instrumental introduction, as the editor suggests; this subject is not yet fully researched, and until something more definite is known modern performers are free to experiment with both possible methods. If an entirely vocal performance is desired (and that is certainly a possible presentation), the first phrase should be sung to the first syllable, although it would be best to repeat it following the rest in order to reflect the rhythmic flow of the line.

At the end of the same composition a complementary situation can be found which suggests that the voice might end as underlaid in the edition and that an instrument could play the coda. If the voice does stop here and an instrument takes over, it is not always necessary for the singer to sing only the written value of the last sung note. Usually in these cases the harmony remains static for the equivalent of a bar or more of transcription, which would allow the singer to sustain the last note long enough to phrase off and provide an elision with the instrumental coda.[8] For a fully vocal performance, rule 8 on p. 27 should be followed.

Example 3.15b is an excerpt from a motet which begins and ends with text but has sections within the body of the composition which have no text and are so rhythmically different as to suggest an instrumental interlude; the text underlay in the manuscript supports this idea. In these cases too, vocal performance is a possibility, but it would seem in keeping with the style to

3.15a Guillaume Dufay 'Adieu ces bon vins de Lannoys,' bars 1–11, 24–33
Guillaume Dufay *Opera Omnia* ed. Heinrich Besseler, vol. 6 © 1964 by Armen Carapetyan,
American Institute of Musicology/Hänssler-Verlag, D-7303 Neuhausen-Stuttgart (West Germany) No. 60.106.
Used by permission

3.15b Guillaume Dufay 'Flos florum', bars 18–29
Guillaume Dufay *Opera Omnia* ed. Heinrich Besseler, vol. 1 © 1966 by Armen Carapetyan,
American Institute of Musicology/Hänssler-Verlag, D-7303 Neuhausen-Stuttgart (West Germany) No. 60.106.
Used by permission

sing the passages on a single vowel rather than either to repeat text or to alter the underlay in order to include the melismatic passage.

If a single theme emerges from the discussion of text underlay, it is that individual performers must stop to consider what they are doing and not blindly accept the transcription put before them. In many cases a careful investigation of the transcription will prove that the editor has been extremely sensitive to the music and the period style, and in those editions little, if anything, will need to be changed. But the thoughtfulness of all editors can not be guaranteed, and even in those works where performers agree completely with the editor, they will be much further ahead for having applied themselves analytically to the music.

Tempo

Once the rhythmic flow of the individual parts has been considered, it is necessary to determine the speed at which the entire composition moves. Once again we are dealing with a difficult topic which has been treated by several scholars but without total agreement. It would appear that even when we have finally understood the information that has come down to us we will have only general rules to which we can look for basic ideas. As in performances today, there were undoubtedly many factors that influenced the tempo of a given composition during the early centuries. The tempo of any work should be adjusted to accommodate the particular voices, instruments, and conditions of performance such as accoustics. My intention here is to obtain some idea of the norms of tempo during the early period so that modern performers will have somewhere to begin.

The music of the early centuries has no obvious indication of tempo – at least nothing as clear as our contemporary metronome markings and speed words (*allegro, lento,* and so on). The tempo was indicated by the shapes of the notes, and for some of the repertory this was further altered by mensural signs that indicated the relative value of certain notes and the pace of the composition. The system was complex but yielded the same amount of flexibility available in our modern system.[9] If the music is to be read in modern transcription, however, a different method must be used to determine tempo, because it is not possible to read from modern notation an element that exists only in the shapes of the original notes. The problem is further complicated by the lack of standardization in transcription practices: one editor may transcribe the breve as a whole note, another as a half note, and so on.

The method presented below for determining tempo has been chosen in order to help those who read only modern notation. It is admittedly imperfect and fairly general – there really is no totally satisfactory way to determine an early tempo without looking at the original. This system has resulted from first determining the tempo by reading the notation and mensural signs in representative compositions from the repertory, and then noticing those factors in modern transcription that appear to be reliable for determining tempo in a relatively high percentage of cases. What is proposed here will work for the majority of compositions, and with a bit of experience modern performers will sense when the solution is obviously not correct and something else must be tried. I will begin with a general description of some of the basic concepts of early notation in order to see the way in which that system achieved its flexibility.

EARLY NOTATION AND TEMPO

In the present century we have a fairly simple notation system involving notes that are easily divisible by two of the next lowest level, for example, $\quad$ ♩ = ♪ ♪, ♩ = ♫, and which can be divided otherwise by special signs, for example, $o = ♩ ♩ ♩$. For the speed of the basic unit of measure we use words and/or metronome markings, for example, Allegro, MM ♩ = 160.

The musicians of the early centuries had a far more complex system. There was a single generally accepted tempo that remained fixed throughout the period. This single tempo was assigned to certain note values, and in order to decrease or increase the speed one or more of the following devices could be used:

1 Choosing smaller or larger note values.
2 Changing the basic unit of measure; for example, instead of the beat falling on ❑ it could be changed to the next lowest value, ◊.
3 Alteration of the subdivision of certain note values. Changing the mensural sign from ℂ to ⊙ meant that the note value ◗ would be divided by three ❑ instead of two, and the value ❑ would be divided by three ◊ instead of two. Thus, to give a simple example of the system, if the beat were assigned to ❑, simply changing its subdivision to three ◊ instead of two, would make the music move one third faster as long as the notes were kept on the level of ◊ or smaller.
4 Using a system of proportional signs, for example, 3/1, which signified that in the next section three notes of a particular value would be performed in the place of one.

The result of these and many other devices was that the early musician had available the same infinite gradations of speed that are available to us, but in a different way.

The commonly used tempo during the early centuries was the 'pulse of a man at rest,' we are told by Ramis de Pareja in 1482;[10] and it would appear from earlier writings and from the music that with certain modifications this was true of the earlier centuries as well. In the absence of easily available time pieces, the most convenient pacing device was the heartbeat, which was not exactly the same for everyone but was as accurate a measurement as was needed. With an approximate beat established, the composer could use the notation to vary the subdivision or to assign the beat to various levels of notes. The basic note shape that determined tempo changed from century to century, always becoming one of lesser value: composers continuously wrote in ever smaller note values, which caused the pacing note to move more slowly until it was finally changed to a faster value, and this in turn encouraged them to write even smaller values. This apparently continued until the mid-sixteenth century, when note values became somewhat standard. At that point performers took even more liberties with the tempo, eventually destroying the system and leading to the use of speed words and finally metronome marks.

DETERMINING TEMPO IN MODERN TRANSCRIPTIONS

Many editors of early music indicate a tempo, which solves the problem for modern performers, but this is not true of all editions, unfortunately, and when no modern tempo is given the following method may be employed to obtain a general idea of speed. It is not foolproof, but it is generally correct and can be used when there is no other method available for determining tempo. Two different approaches are proposed here, one for heavily texted compositions and another for music which has little or no text. It will be seen later that they are two aspects of the same approach.

Tempo by text rate

For those compositions where there is a low ratio between the number of notes and the number of syllables, the rate of the text can be used to determine the tempo. There are two basic tempo ranges, one for text underlaid in duple division, the other for triple division. The basic tempo ranges can be stated as shown at the top of p. 43.

Tempo 1

In the simplest compositions the method can be applied without additional considerations. Tempo 1 can be applied easily to a composition such as

	common rate of syllables	occasional subdivision	tempo range
tempo #1	1 per unit (♩ or ♩.)	♪♪ or ♩ ♪	♩ (♩.) = MM 112–44
tempo #2	2 per 3 units (♩ ♪)	♪♪♪	♩. = MM 66–80

Note values written here symbolize duple or triple division. The value ♩ represents ♪, ♩,ₒ; the value ♩. represents ♩., ♩.,ₒ..

example 3.16, a monophonic work in which the text syllables appear fairly regularly at the rate of one syllable per unit of measure. The range for tempo 1 is given as approximately 112–44, and the specific tempo chosen depends on several factors. The rule of thumb is, the simpler and more straightforward the ratio of syllable to note, the faster the tempo. In terms of this fairly simple example, the rule would suggest a tempo near the faster end of the range. If, however, there were many complex rhythmic figures in the line, many subdivisions of the basic syllable unit, or a complex relationship of the texted line to other lines in a polyphonic composition, a tempo closer to the slower end of the range would be called for.

Example 3.13 is also syllabic with steady motion at the level of a half note and subdivision at the level of a quarter note. The tempo range of this composition would also be according to tempo 1, but because so many of the basic text units are subdivided the tempo chosen should probably be closer to the middle of the range, ca ♩ = 120–32. In polyphonic compositions the consideration of tempo is based initially on the fastest moving line with text. Once the basic rate is determined from that part, the other lines must be considered in order to determine if there are any reasons to adjust the tempo. In example 3.13 all parts contain the same kinds of text motion and there are no other complicating elements that would influence the tempo.

This method can also be extended to all compositions that have a steady rate of texting even though there are several notes per syllable. In example 5.4 many of the notes are subdivided, but the rate of text underlay for the superius line is generally one syllable per quarter note, with occasional subdivision at the level of a quarter and an eighth. Tempo 1, of ♩ = 112–44, is therefore also

Ka—len—da ma—ya   ni fuelhs de fa—ya   ni chanz dau-zelh ni flors de gla-ya

3.16 Raimbaut de Vaqueiras 'Kalenda Maya,' opening

indicated for this composition. Since the rhythms in all parts of this composition are quite regular and the lower two parts are actually simpler, a tempo nearer the faster end of the range is suggested.

Tempo 2

Steady texting at the rate of two syllables for three units of measure, tempo 2 above, can be seen in examples 3.15a, 5.2, and 5.6. Examples 3.15a and 5.6 begin with untexted sections, but when the text enters it moves at a steady rate. Because of the relative activity in all parts of these compositions, a tempo closer to the lower end of the range (ca 66) is recommended for 5.6, a medium tempo for 5.2 (ca 72), and a fairly quick tempo for 3.15a (ca 80).

A more complicated set of lines can be seen in example 5.3, in which the top line fits the description of tempo 1 – one syllable per note – and the other two lines match that of tempo 2 – two syllables per three units of measure. The solution here is a compromise, a tempo faster than ♩ = 144, but slower than ♩. = 66. At a tempo of ca ♩. = 56, all lines will move forward smoothly without causing the phrases to be too slow for breathing or too quick for clear enunciation.

For the repertory that has a regular rate of texting this method of determining tempo can be applied regardless of the century of the composition. If the music moves along at a fairly regular pace a tempo at the upper end of the range can be selected. If there are rhythmic complications in any of the parts a slower tempo should be chosen. A further influencing factor is the length of the phrases; the pace should allow the phrase to be sung without breaks that would harm the flow of the line. But this is the kind of musical factor that influences the tempo in all music, and performers should be prepared to make those kinds of decisions within the guidelines set out above.

Tempo for untexted music

For repertory with an uneven rate of texting or completely without text, the tempo must be determined by the flow of the structural rhythm of the melodic line. The basis of this method is the concept that the rhythm of most melodic lines can be analysed simply in terms of the basic units of measure which pace the composition, and that by identifying these we will be able to choose the general tempo range. The units of measure move within a relatively narrow range of speed, depending upon the basic organization of the line into either duple or triple division. Those organized in duple time have a tempo range corresponding to tempo 1, and those in triple time correspond to tempo 2. What is referred to here as 'basic unit of measure' is nothing more than what we have been measuring when considering the rate of the syllables above. To look back on the examples already considered in terms of tempo 1, example 5.4 has a duple division based on the value of a dotted quarter note, and example 3.15a has a triple division on the level of a quarter note. In example 5.3 we noticed two levels of texting, but the actual basic unit – the note level at which the music flows forward – is a dotted half note in all parts. In other words, if a composition has a regularly flowing rhythm, the recurring basic rhythmic unit is its unit of measure, and it is from this that the tempo is derived. The specific tempo selected depends upon the regularity of the motion and the quantity of subdivisions; the simpler the melody the faster the tempo.

This method can be applied successfully to a large portion of the transcribed repertory that is without a regular rate of texting because the editors have assisted us by presenting the music on the page according to the basic rhythmic divisions indicated by the notation. My earlier statement that regular rhythmic division is not an acceptable method of determining phrasing and flow of the line, is still true; the bar lines in the transcription do not tell us how to phrase the melodic lines, but they do give us the information we need about the basic pacing unit of the composition, and once we know this we can determine the tempo. Compositions with duple division fit into tempo 1 while those with triple division are in tempo 2.

To illustrate the point, we can see that examples 3.4, 5.7, and 5.15 all use duple division as their basic pace. The first two have a basic unit at the level of a half note and the third at the whole note. They are all, therefore, in the tempo 1 range of MM 112–44, with the specific speed determined by considering other factors, that is, phrase length and the amount of subdivision and rhythmic complexity in the composition as a whole. Tempo 2 would be applicable for examples 3.12, 3.14, and 7.9, all of which involve a subdivided triple pace, at the level of a dotted double whole note, a dotted whole note, and a dotted half. Again the particular speed selected within the tempo 2 range is determined by the relative complexity of the composition.

The method described above will not work in every case because some compositions have an amount of rhythmic complexity that all but defies an analysis into basic rhythmic flow. For those compositions performers can either guess based on general knowledge of the early repertory or perhaps avoid those few works and select repertory that either has been marked by the editor or lends itself to the method described above.

Change of tempo

A change of tempo within a composition is usually solved in one of two ways by a modern editor: either by marking note equivalents (for example, $\, \downarrow_{=o}$)

or by changing the level of the transcription and assigning smaller or larger modern values to cause the correct speed change. If neither of these has been done, or it is not clear what the editor has done about tempo change, the methods described above can be used to determine the new tempo.

The most common tempo-change problem encountered is the change to triple time within a composition. The question is always whether the composer intended a ratio of 3:1 or 3:2, or some other relationship. The mensural changes before ca 1470 are often quite complicated, and the specific relationship is therefore usually marked in the music. But after that time the change was often marked simply with a figure 3, leaving the modern editor and performer to wonder at which ratio the new section proceeds.

In some compositions the parts do not change all at once – that is, one part will still be in duple time while others change to triple – and in these compositions we can be certain of the ratio; otherwise we cannot be sure. There is no hard and fast rule to govern the situation, which must have been determined by custom in the early centuries, but my experience is that from about 1500 to near the end of the sixteenth century the ratio of 3:2 is the one most often correct when a simple 3 is found in the music; that is, the triple section proceeds with three of the new notes performed in the space of two of the old. In example 3.17, therefore, three half-notes are performed in the space of two, which means that one new bar of triple time is equal to one old bar of duple.

Although this will be found to be correct in most cases, especially in secular music, there are examples of the 3:1 ratio, and towards the end of the sixteenth century these instances increase.[11] If no help is provided by either composer or editor it is usually possible to find the answer by experimentation; one of the two tempos will seem uncomfortable.

The problem should be fairly simple, since in almost all cases the ratio refers to the semibreve; therefore if one knows which modern note represents the semibreve the possibilities are reduced to two tempos. In example 3.17 the transcription level is kept at ♩ = ♩ throughout the composition, thus allowing the performer to understand which notes are involved in the ratio. Unfortunately, not all editions keep the level of transcription constant, which can cause problems for the performer. A case in point is example 6.1, Giovanni Gabrieli's motet *In Ecclesiis*, written in about 1600, which contains sections of triple time at the ratio of 3:1. If the editor had maintained a constant level of transcription for the semibreve, performers would know immediately what to do in the triple sections, or at least they would know which notes are involved in the ratio and therefore which two tempos to experiment with. However, the transcription level is changed so that the semibreve, which is transcribed

3.17 Heinrich Isaac 'Alla battaglia,' internal phrase

as a whole note in the duple time ($\circ=\circ$), becomes a quarter note in the triple ($\circ=\downarrow$). The intention of the composer is quite clear in the original notation: three semibreves in the triple time (quarter notes in bar 118) are performed in the time of one semibreve of the duple (a whole note in bar 117). The editor has attempted to provide for the tempo change in the transcription (although the implied quarter note = quarter note would result in the incorrect ratio of 4:1), and has deprived performers of an understanding of the relationship. It is obviously important, therefore, for performers to understand the editorial procedures in each transcription. In many editions that information can be found in the critical notes or can be deduced by comparing the incipit to the first notes of the transcription.

Flexible tempo

The discussion above suggests that tempo was inflexible in the early centuries, but we do not know that to be true. The treatises do not mention whether the tempo, once established, was to be rigidly kept or observed with some degree of flexibility. We do have some information from the sixteenth century that in solo performance, both instrumental and vocal with single instrument accompaniment, liberties were taken with the tempo.

Luis de Milán stated in his vihuela book of 1536[12] that the performer must select the speed of a composition according to the spirit of the music, and he indicated that the fantasias in that collection were to be played with a fast or slow tempo as marked by the author. He also stated that a small pause should be placed on certain high points in the musical line.[13] Most of the compositions in Milán's book are fantasias which, like preludes and toccatas, were apparently performed quite freely in all centuries (see chapter 5), but he also marks some pavans and villancicos in that collection for fast or slow tempo, and those genres are not known to have been performed freely. It is not clear, therefore, how broadly Milán's directions should be applied. It would seem unlikely that he was referring to pavans played for dancing; from what is known about the nature of dance steps in the sixteenth century it is probable that each dance, including the pavan, had a tempo that could be varied only slightly from one performance to the next.

Two other writers refer to flexible tempo, but both do so in connection with repertory that did not have any tradition of a steady tempo: Girolamo Frescobaldi, in the preface to his toccatas in 1614, stated that tempo should be chosen in the light of the spirit of the music,[14] and Giulio Caccini seems to be advocating flexible tempo in his publication of 1601, in reference to the new style of vocal monody.[15] It can be seen, therefore, that as early as the first half of the sixteenth century, soloists felt free to select a tempo according to musical intuition, regardless of the tempo indications in the notation.

We do not know how widespread this attitude towards tempo was, but the music itself suggests that for the most part tempos were probably kept rather closely, inasmuch as the notation system allowed the composer to change the pace. The use of coloration, for example, which is found frequently in the music of the fourteenth and fifteenth centuries for short and long passages, brings with it a small change of pace. But the device would be worthless if the tradition had been to allow much flexibility in the tempo. We can suspect, therefore, that a tempo, once set, remained unchanged in most cases, with only those slight flexibilities and nuances that keep music from sounding mechanical in any age. The exceptions to this would be the music for soloists beginning in the sixteenth century, especially those forms for instrumentalists mentioned earlier that were traditionally played freely.

The only other repertory that would suggest a flexible approach to tempo is that of the early troubadours, trouvères, and Minnesingers. This repertory is mostly syllabic and musically quite simple – a musical heightening of the poetry. The rhythmic interpretation is currently in dispute, but no matter what the rhythms, it is likely that the tempo should be quite flexible in those compositions, according to the expressive demands of the poetry. (See the discussion in chapter 5.)

Style

After all the technical details have been applied, there remains one final consideration before a composition is ready for historical performance: style, by which I mean those elements, both large and small, that identify a performance with a particular performance practice. It is the specifics of style that narrow a performance from the large and rather gray area of 'early music' and bring it into sharper focus by identifying it with a single century and location. A chanson, for example, would not have been performed the same way in the fifteenth century as in the sixteenth, nor would it have been played in Vienna the same way as in Paris. There would have been differences in the application of a number of performance elements according to the current local practice. Many of the details of style are intangible and can be communicated only by actual performance; these, of course, are forever lost to us. But some of the information has been preserved and is included here under the various topic headings throughout the remainder of the book.

The differences in the style of music can be categorized broadly as having two dimensions: time and geography. Table 1 shows the general performance changes as music moved through the centuries. This information is treated in detail in chapters 5 and 6, where the music of each century is described in terms of its inherent characteristics, and in chapters 4 and 7 to 9, where the elements are singled out and described according to what we know of the changes in performance practice that reflected the changing demands of the music.

The matter of geographical style differences is tied to those changes outlined in table 1, with the additional consideration of national or regional temperament. Perhaps the clearest way to see this difference and its influence on music, both the compositions and the performance, is to approach it from the differences in languages. Since so much of music was written for a text, it should not be surprising that the peculiarities of a language would be reflected in much of the music, not only the texted but the instrumental music as well. The particulars of each language, therefore, should be kept in mind when determining both the rhythmic flow and the text underlay. The natural flow of a language will help when a choice must be made concerning how to emphasize various rhythmic figures or how to space the text over a long melodic phrase. Further, each geographical area also had its own practices of ornamentation, expression, and instrumentation which, when added to the language-related differences, would identify a performance with that particular locality.

The geographical areas covered in table 2 are quite broad, owing to the fact

TABLE I

Temporal changes in style

	1200	1300	1400	1500	1600
COMPOSITIONAL CHANGES	mostly monophonic	simple polyphony; 2 and 3 parts	increased use of polyphony; 3 and 4 parts	polyphony dominates; 4 and more parts →	
		harmonies dwell on 5th and 8ve	increased use of 3rds	mostly filled chords →	
		lines have independent contours and phrases		more integrated and similar lines →	
			some use of imitation	much imitation →	
	rhythms and phrases irregular and complex		becoming less complex and more regular →		
	national styles (secular) →			national and international styles →	
	mostly vocal music; instruments assist vocal music and play dances →			separate instrument repertory →	
INSTRUMENTATION	contrasting instrumental colours →			similar sounds and families of instruments →	use of continuo →
	separation according to loud and soft →			separation according to families →	
	drone and non-drone intermixed →		no drones →		
	much use of solo single-line instruments →		use of ensembles and polyphonic instruments →		
ORNAMENTATION	graces and short *passaggi* →		graces and longer *passaggi* →	national preferences →	
	all ornaments on highest part →		some on lower parts →	ornaments on all parts →	
	much rhythmic variety →		less variety →	variety by national style →	

TABLE 2
National style characteristics

	language	rhythmic flow	ornaments	other remarks*
ITALIAN	regular, accented; emphasis on vowels	regular, even, smooth motion; long phrases; accents	some graces; preference for *passaggi* in long and elaborate groups	near 1600 interest in dramatic stress and exaggeration of emotion
FRANCO-NETHERLANDISH	irregular; duration for stress rather than accent	irregular, complex; short and long groups; irregular phrases	preference for graces; short *passaggi*	emphasis on smooth line with complex rhythmic flow
SPANISH	accented, irregular; emphasis on consonants	irregular, short-long groups; very rhythmic mixture of short and very long phrases and rhythmic values	even mixture of graces and *passaggi*; much variety; *passaggi* not as long as Italian	near 1600 somewhat dramatic rhythmic variety
ENGLISH	irregular, accented	irregular, accented; short phrases and rhythmic groups	graces and *passaggi* in moderation; florid, even *passaggi* in instrumental music	more subdued expression; less interest in imitation
GERMAN	regular, accented; emphasis on consonants	regular, accented; mostly syllabic; short phrases	graces and *passaggi* in moderation; regular flow	rhythms accented and regular phrases regular

*For instrument preferences see table 3.

that syle is another of the subjects in need of much further research. There is no doubt that stylistic differences were far more refined than this table indicates; there may have been differences between practices in northern and southern Germany, for example, or between those in Paris and Burgundy, but little of that information has been brought to light. The categories shown here can only point the way for interested musicians to obtain detailed information concerning stylistic differences. The various statements are relative – more or less of each element as compared to the practices in another location – and they are very general.

Tables 1 and 2 can best be used as quick memory refreshers, but they are not meant to be a substitute for the more detailed discussions found elsewhere in this book. As with all the information presented here, you are urged to work directly with the music in order to convert the general and abstract ideas into detailed musical understanding. Once you are aware of the differences as outlined in the various chapters, you should then become acquainted with the repertory in order to see how the individual characteristics are realized in musical terms. After that, the tables and discussions can serve as reminders of those points of style that have been experienced in the music.

If, for example, you wish to understand the style of fourteenth-century France, tables 1 and 3 will guide you to a selection of probable instrument and voice combinations; table 2 suggests that you emphasize relatively long phrases and rhythmic intricacies without strong accents, and that you ornament using graces and short *passaggi* on structural notes. Relevant passages in chapters 4, 5, 7, and 9 will supply additional details on these matters. From this point you must go to the music in order to see how these elements and techniques can be applied so that you will establish in your mind a 'sound' for that repertory that causes it to stand apart from other centuries and other areas in the fourteenth century. Once this is firmly established, reference to the tables will bring to mind not just facts, but an impression of a unique musical style.

THE INTERNATIONAL STYLE

Many of the details of style mentioned above, especially the language-related points, are most pronounced in the traditional national forms. Throughout the Renaissance there was also an international style; a general style of writing that was used in all European countries for the more sophisticated compositions. It is usually referred to as the Netherlandish style after its probable origin and was used by most composers, regardless of nationality or training, for chansons, Masses, and motets. The basic differences between the two kinds of compositions are that the international style usually employs a high proportion of imitation, with the lines more or less melodically equal and similar, while the national styles are more homophonic, with a single line melodically dominant. (See the discussion accompanying examples 5.9 and 5.10 below.)

Although the imitative compositions are international, they stem from the tradition described in table 2 as Franco-Netherlandish, so an interpretation should begin with those style characteristics, and for as long as the composition remains basically in the imitative style the interpretation should stay close to those points. This is straightforward when the text is also in French, that is, in chansons. For Masses and motets there must be an adjustment to accommodate the natural flow of Latin which is more accented (similar to Italian). A further complication exists inasmuch as composers rarely felt the need to be 'stylistically pure' in these international works, and one can frequently find sections in the national styles. In the midst of an otherwise imitative composition, Josquin des Prez, for example, occasionally inserts a short homophonic section in triple time resembling sections found in Italian songs. In order to recognize these changes of style it is necessary to have a fairly wide acquaintance with the repertory and to be aware that a mixture of styles is always possible in the sophisticated international repertory. Once the change is recognized, the national style should be performed according to its national characteristics. There is really no trick to recognizing the change; the only time it is important is when the composer has made it obvious and therefore has intended that the mixture be heard. In some cases the contrast of styles may be quite strong, and it is then up to the musical tastes of the performer (or director) to decide whether to emphasize the contrast strongly or to modify it. Each case must be decided on its own. The only 'wrong' interpretation would be to attempt to blend it in as if there were no change. If the composer had wanted the composition to be performed in one style, he would have written it that way.

4

Voices and Instruments

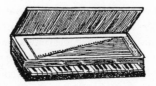

OR THE MUSIC of any era the very sounds of the voices and instruments are important factors for authentic re-creation. Even with the amount of choice in performing medium given to performers in the early centuries, there were traditions and customs that affected all performances, certain limitations to the vocal and instrumental technique and the sounds and combinations of voices and instruments. To perform the music as it was originally intended we should be aware of the kinds and combinations of musical sounds common in the early periods, for it was these sounds that the composer had in mind when he composed. The purpose of this chapter is to present what is known about historical vocal technique, instruments, and instrumentation, so that this knowledge can be applied to the discussions of the repertory in chapters 5 and 6.

The voice

In determining the actual sounds of the early centuries, we are in a far better position with instruments than with voices. Museum instruments can be played and new instruments constructed to approximate those found in paintings and other iconographic sources, which will give at least a general idea of the original sound. But there is really no way to know what kinds of sounds were made by the singers. Sound quality cannot be described clearly in words, and thus we are left with a few vague descriptions of singing and singers, technique instructions in vocal manuals of the late Renaissance, some iconographic evidence, and the music itself.

Much use has been made of the iconographic evidence that sometimes depicts singers with heads raised, mouths wide open, and a look of strain on the faces (see illustrations 1 and 6). This has been interpreted as evidence that strained vocal practice was the norm in early singing, and indeed it may be true. On the other hand the few comments about singing in the writings of the Middle Ages refer to 'sweet' and 'pleasing' sounds; this is of little help, however, for what is considered sweet in one century may not be in the next. It is, of course, difficult to depict a singer in action, and thus the distorted features in the iconography may be only artistic distortion in order to lend a sense of activity to the painting. We can assume that in the early centuries there was as much variety in the voices and styles of delivery as there is today, but we shall probably never know for certain what was considered to be a standard of beautiful vocal sound – or even whether there was a standard.

Instructions for singing begin in the late fifteenth century, and even then they mostly refer to the method of performing rapid ornamental passages (see chapter 7). Nevertheless, they do furnish a beginning, and some information can be gained from them.

FIFTEENTH- AND SIXTEENTH-CENTURY INSTRUCTIONS

The voice is referred to by a number of writers from the late fifteenth, sixteenth, and early seventeenth centuries from France, Germany, and especially Italy. The most detailed instructions come from Hermann Finck (1556, Wittenberg) and Giovanni Maffei (1562, Naples), but their advice is supported by remarks in other writings, from those of Conrad von Zabern (1474, Heidelberg) into the early years of the seventeenth century.[1] Because of the agreement – or lack of disagreement – in the various instructions and their fairly wide geographical distribution, they can probably be taken as a general European view of singing in the late Renaissance. The information in these writings can be summarized as follows:

Advice given by two or more writers
1 Sing with the mouth open only as wide as in casual conversation. Do not open it wide or close the teeth.
2 Place the singing tone in the front of the mouth. Avoid singing from the back of the throat or through the nose.
3 Use a moderate tone. Do not force the voice.
4 Sing with a steady tone that does not change in pitch, volume, or intensity. This appears in the context of a criticism of singers who attempt to convey emotion by unsteady vocal production – by varying the intensity and pitch of a single note or by rapid and frequent change of volume in a short passage. It probably does not intend to advocate colourless and unvarying expression. As early as 1535, Sylvestro Ganassi[2] was urging instrumental-

ists to imitate singers' use of flexible volume for expression, and Giulio Caccini gave a number of expressive vocal examples in his instructions of 1601[3] (discussed in chapter 8).

5 Rapid notes should receive clear articulation. Passages with text should receive clean articulation with the tongue, and untexted passages should be articulated clearly in the throat. However, Finck warned against sounding like a goat!

6 Avoid excessive body motion while singing. Maffei found so distasteful and distracting the custom of expressing emotion with trembling lips and motion of the head, body, hands, and feet, that he forbad any motion at all. He even recommended that singers use a mirror to help limit excessive eye motion. Zacconi (1592)[4] agreed that excessive motion was to be avoided, but he stopped short of Maffei's extreme, and Caccini, writing for the professional, encouraged support of expression by the use of body motion.

Advice from a single writer

From Maffei

7 For melismatic, untexted passages place the tip of the tongue at the root of the lower teeth.

8 Wait four to five hours after eating before doing vocal exercises so that the windpipe will be clean and agile.

9 Select a practice area with a good echo so that you can judge the quality of what you have just sung.

From Finck

10 Lighten the voice as it rises and become more sonorous in the lower range.

11 In four-part singing, ideal qualities for voices are: superius, sweet; middle, modulated; discant, sonorous; bass, rugged and heavy. Do not overextend the voice in order to overpower the others, but balance all the voices as in a well-voiced organ.

From Conrad

12 Do not add 'h' sounds to vowels on melismas, as for example 'ky-ri-he-he-he.' He called this practice 'rustic,' a term he also used to describe singing through the nose.

13 Vowels must be pronounced clearly.

14 Do not sing with vibrato. In context Conrad directed this remark to choral singers.

Vowel sounds

Among the three writers who mention vowels there is virtually no agreement as to which to use and which to avoid for melismatic passages: Finck said that *i* and *e* are the best and *a*, *o* and *u* should be avoided; Maffei that *o* is the most beautiful, *u* and *i* are ugly, and *i* is especially bad for sopranos; and Caccini that the open vowels are more sonorous and allow better control, *u* is better for sopranos, and *i* is better for tenors. They all agreed that some vowels make the voice howl while others are beautiful. Their lack of agreement can only be explained as differences in language or dialect or in individual voices and artistic taste.

As mentioned above, the instructions are mostly for beginners and in reference to rapid ornaments (except for Caccini), and it is therefore not clear to what extent they should be taken to cover vocal production in non-virtuoso singing. There is some comfort in the knowledge that for the most part the late-Renaissance instructions agree with what is still thought to be good vocal production – sing from the front of the mouth, avoid throat and nasal sounds, do not open the mouth too wide – and both Maffei and Finck mentioned that the voice must be quite flexible and express the sentiment of the song, and that to do so the voice must be light. The only real disagreements with modern vocal taste would seem to be in the areas of volume and vibrato; the Renaissance writers advise a fairly medium tone rather than the more forceful opera volume often found today, and vibrato was considered to be an ornament – something to be added from time to time just like a trill or mordent.

THE EARLIER CENTURIES

The amount of agreement gives a bit more weight to the instructions, but we still do not know for how long these principles had been in use prior to the late fifteenth century. For the earlier centuries we can only guess by looking at the music itself and noticing that much of it contains rhythmically complex passages, frequent rapid sections, and fairly simple consonances and dissonances. These demands suggest that the attitude of the sixteenth-century writers towards the voice would be even more appropriate for the early centuries: a good vocal tone is one that is light and agile. This would allow the singer to execute the delicate nuances and rhythms and at the same time accomplish the rapid passages, either written or improvised. Naturally the style of the individual song – sophisticated or peasant-like – and the language of the text would influence vocal delivery to some extent, but if the delicate nuances of much of the vocal material were to be brought out and the rapid *passaggi* articulated (see chapters 7 and 9), the voice would have be clear and light.

The evidence that we have suggests that singing was an activity for everyone, regardless of social level, age, or sex. We know, of course, that only males sang in church, so that church music, especially music for the Mass, is properly presented by men and boys; we also know that professional musicians were usually male, but documents show that at least as early as the fourteenth century some of the minstrels were women. The secular repertory was apparently sung by both males and females, and although women did not sing at liturgical functions (except in convents), they could have sung motets, hymns, and other devotional material when not directly associated with a liturgical service. Much of the vocal repertory, therefore, is available for female as well as male voice, and by transposition most of it can be moved into a convenient vocal range.

The few problems caused by transposition include inversion of lines, such as transposition of a tenor melody for very high voice: either the lines would be inverted, producing intervals not intended by the composer, or else a performance of the accompanying lines would be so high as to sound unmusical. For much of the repertory, transposition of a fourth or fifth up will accommodate most female voices, and transposition down one or two steps will usually put an otherwise high tessitura within the range of a baritone. In works for accompanied solo voice in which the melody is in the highest voice, it is usually possible to transpose only the solo part up an octave, leaving the accompanying lines at the written pitch. In these cases the individual composition must be judged by listening first to the written pitch and then to the detached octave.

Modern pronunciations do not correctly represent the sounds of the early languages. Pronunciation of all languages has changed since the early centuries – in fact, there is even a difference between the pronunciations of the fourteenth and the sixteenth centuries. In some languages many of the vowels are now given completely different sounds, and in others the number of letters actually pronounced has changed. The result is that words that rhymed in the early centuries do not rhyme in today's pronunciation, and the sounds and rhythms of the old languages are very different from those of today.

If modern musicians intend to re-create the sounds of the early compositions then certainly the correct pronunciation is at least as important to a singer as is a historical instrument to an instrumentalist. Unfortunately, whereas a number of good historical instruments are readily available for the instrumentalist, help with early language pronunciation lags far behind. Occasionally a modern edition will include a pronunciation glossary,[5] but otherwise the only guides easily available are those for fourteenth-century English and Renaissance French.[6] There is no easy solution to this problem; unless performers happen to live near a university with early language specialists whom they can consult, they can only be aware of the problem and continue to wait for pronunciation guides in the other languages. Several publications are currently being proposed, and perhaps before too long singers will have the information necessary to produce all early languages with the correct historical sounds.

Instruments

The employment of early instruments is one of the most deceptive aspects of early music performance. Although it may appear to be a simple matter, selecting a historically authentic instrumentation actually requires a fair amount of information and an equal amount of careful thought. The most frequently encountered error stems from an unconscious lumping-together of all early music into a single category and the resultant belief that any early instrument and every instrument combination is therefore appropriate for any composition. The instruments for a particular work are thus chosen according to personal preference without regard for century and with the only limitation being the range of the instrument itself. There is often no thought that instruments popular in the sixteenth century may not have even existed in the fourteenth or that combinations popular in one century may have been avoided in another.

Selecting historically authentic instruments is not the most important aspect of early music performance; the primary efforts of performers should be directed towards producing the most stylistically correct performance of the music. This is often made easier, of course, by the use of the correct historical instrument, but if modern performers treat the musical considerations as most important, in most cases the choice of the right instrument will then become clearer. Performing with historical instruments should be viewed as an aid to the correct stylistic performance of early music, not as an end in itself. To perform on the correct period instrument does nothing more than allow one an opportunity to apply more easily the principles of historical style. The best reason for selecting a historical instrument for a given work is to re-create the kind of sounds the composer and the people of his time would have expected, because in this way we can come one step closer to the composer's intentions. Early music as defined for purposes of this book includes the music in Western Europe before about 1600, which covers five centuries and at least five major geographical locations. Each century, each locality, and often each kind of musical occasion had its own favourite or usual mode of performance, and careful early musicians will take the time to acquaint themselves with those details.

In the current style of early performance it is common for a single ensemble to play the music of several different centuries, cities, and occasions in a short span of time – often within the same program. If one were totally fastidious about instrumentation, a small ensemble would have to perform on as many as fifty to a hundred instruments in a single program, and even if the financial implications of this were not prohibitive, the practical problems of daily practice and tuning-time on stage would be. Nearly everyone will thus have some need to make compromises; this is a common fact of performance life. But to admit to the practical need for compromise is not the same as to say that any instrument that looks and/or sounds early is a good or acceptable choice. The compromises that must be made should be made with a full knowledge of what is historically correct and why. In this way, should the historical instrument not be available, a substitute can be chosen from among some acceptable alternatives, and the performance style of the correct instrument can be approximated.

SOURCES OF INFORMATION ABOUT INSTRUMENTS
AND THEIR COMBINATIONS

The information we have about early instruments comes from several sources. The best of these is, of course, actual instruments that survive in museums and private collections. When no authentic instrument survives there is iconographic evidence – such as paintings, drawings, sculptures, intarsias, contemporary accounts, and descriptions in theoretical writings. We can look to a number of recently published books in which this information is collected and presented in synthetic form as a survey, and also to periodicals which are devoted completely or in part to research into early instruments.[7] However, the state of research on early instruments is far from complete because we simply do not know much about certain instruments. If an instrument does not survive in a collection we often have very sketchy knowledge of its exact size, shape, tone colour, and so on. Perhaps the extent of the problem can be seen by consulting the excellent book by Frederick Crane which lists every known extant medieval instrument.[8] The book is very small and can be used as a type of antidote to the often elaborate descriptions of some instruments to be found in the surveys. When no authentic instrument survives, the compilers of these surveys must make do with extremely vague accounts in contemporary writings together with iconography and some old-fashioned guessing.

Considerable caution must be exercised in assessing the iconographic evidence. Artists, for example, do not always wish to depict reality, and even when they do, they can often be misleading. Illustration 2, the well-known Grünewald painting, is obviously full of errors; the bow simply cannot be held in that position, and there is no sensible reason for construction of a viol in that shape. Thus this picture can easily be rejected as evidence of actual performance practice or instrument shape; the artist wished only to represent angels playing music, and he did not care about the accuracy of the instrumental image. In illustration 3, there are a number of instruments being played. We know from other evidence that this is a highly improbable ensemble; the loud and soft instruments did not play together. Should we reject this also as a symbolic painting without exactness of detail? Perhaps, but the instrument shapes appear to be much like those in many other paintings and are therefore believable as individual instruments even though the actual ensemble may be in question. It is possible that the artist wished to depict a sequential performance – first one group and then the other – a difficult task in a single painting. Iconographic evidence, then, must also be weighed very carefully to avoid misinterpreting the information that is given.

Even at its best the iconographic sources can give us only an approximate idea of external properties. For many of the instruments from before 1500, in the absence of a technical contemporary account (of which there are very few), it is not possible to know with any degree of certainty such details as the internal bracing of bowed and plucked instruments (an important factor in determining tone colour and volume); the material used for strings or their thickness; the dimensions of bore or the exact placement and size of fingerholes for wind instruments; and the thickness and shape of reeds. The number of unanswered questions about certain of the early instruments is multiplied many times over if we add to this our ignorance of tone preferences, bowing techniques, and so on. As we approach the end of the

Renaissance the number of unanswered questions becomes fewer because of the increasingly larger number of surviving instruments and the increased accuracy of the contemporary descriptions, but problems do still exist.

However, we should not dwell overly long on the problems; many scholars are interested in instruments, and the results of their research constantly add to our knowledge.[9] With all the areas of doubt and uncertainty, we are still closer to a historically accurate performance when we use what little we do know than when we disregard the information completely. Let us, then, proceed with the information we already have at our disposal.

POPULARITY AND COMBINATION OF INSTRUMENTS

One of the most useful items for obtaining an overall view of instrument changes through the early centuries is the chart drawn by Herbert Myers after a similar one by Anthony Baines and reproduced here as chart 1.[10] The Myers Chart gives the relative popularity of instruments during the early centuries and is useful in several ways. The first section can be used to select instruments that would be the most likely choices during a given era. To anyone choosing instruments for a composition from about 1350, for example, the chart provides the information that harp and psaltery should be the plucked string instruments first considered since they are the ones most frequently mentioned and painted during that time. The gittern, lute, and citole are also possible choices, although less frequently found, but the vihuela would not be a correct choice until the second half of the fifteenth century.

The second section of the chart is divided into two complementary parts: in 'Standard ensembles' can be found the names of instruments that frequently performed together; and 'Major developments' points out significant changes in the function of some of these ensembles and major changes in instrument construction. This information is amplified beneath the chart.

Table 3 offers a digest of certain kinds of details concerning the most popular instruments and can be used in conjunction with the Myers chart for additional technical information once the instrumentation for a particular composition has been selected. If, for example, a gittern has been selected, table 3 provides information about the type of strings, tuning, performance function, the other instruments usually played with it, and the geographical area where it was most often used. When used together, the Myers chart and table 3 should provide enough information for a fairly accurate choice of historical instrumentation.

INSTRUMENT SELECTION

Selecting a solo instrument for any given situation is fairly simple: all instruments could, and apparently did, serve as solo. The only limitations would be range, the peculiarities of certain instruments (for example, a plucked string might not be an ideal choice for a sustained solo), and the tradition of associating certain instruments with specific occasions (some were used more frequently for sacred music, others for secular; see column 5 in table 3). The problems arise when selecting combinations of instruments that would have been frequently found together during the centuries and locations in question, as follows.

The Middle Ages

Today we tend to classify instruments according to their accoustical properties; woodwinds, percussion, and so on. But in the late Middle Ages the separation was more according to volume – loud and soft (*haut* and *bas*) – as Edmund Bowles has pointed out.[11] The instruments were played in combinations within the groupings of loud and soft, but instruments from one group were never played with instruments from the other for obvious reasons of balance. This does not mean that a particular repertory or specific functions were designated for one kind of ensemble. With a few exceptions, the distinction of loud and soft did not enter into the selection of an ensemble to play for a particular occasion. That kind of choice was made according to other factors.[12] Except for the trumpet repertory and function, which was highly specialized, the loud and soft ensembles shared a common repertory and were called upon for many of the same occasions; both loud and soft ensembles, for example, played dance music and were called upon to entertain at social functions. A description of social functions at the court of Charles v gives us an idea of how the different ensembles were used: heralds (trumpets) announced the beginning and end of the feasts; loud instruments provided the music during the banquets (see illustration 4); and soft instruments and voices were reserved for after dinner in a more intimate (and quiet) setting.[13]

The loud instruments were trumpets, shawms, drums, and bagpipes. In the soft group were all the plucked strings, the bowed strings, portative organ, flute, recorder, cornamuse, and bagpipe; the bagpipe's appearance on both lists suggests that there were two different kinds, loud and soft. (The iconography shows several different kinds: large and small; with one drone, two drones or none; with conical and cylindrical chanters and drones, and even with two chanters.)[14]

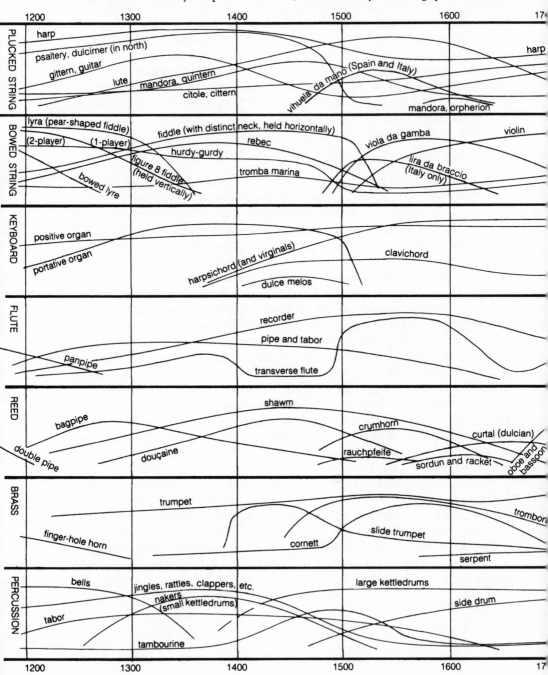

CHART I

Myers chart of instrument popularity in medieval and Renaissance European music

The following curves show the approximate frequency of employment of various instruments and ensembles in courtly and professional music, based on literary and iconographic information.

PLUCKED STRING

harp
psaltery, dulcimer (in north)
gittern, guitar
lute
mandora, quintern
citole, cittern
vihuela da mano (Spain and Italy)
harp
mandora, orpherion

BOWED STRING

lyra (pear-shaped fiddle)
fiddle (with distinct neck, held horizontally)
(2-player)   (1-player)
rebec
viola da gamba
violin
hurdy-gurdy
figure 8 fiddle (held vertically)
tromba marina
lira da braccio (Italy only)
bowed lyre

KEYBOARD

positive organ
portative organ
harpsichord (and virginals)
dulce melos
clavichord

FLUTE

recorder
pipe and tabor
panpipe
transverse flute

REED

shawm
bagpipe
crumhorn
curtal (dulcian)
douçaine
rauchpfeife
double pipe
sordun and racket
oboe and bassoon

BRASS

trumpet
finger-hole horn
cornett
slide trumpet
trombone
serpent

PERCUSSION

bells
jingles, rattles, clappers, etc.
large kettledrums
nakers (small kettledrums)
tabor
side drum
tambourine

1200   1300   1400   1500   1600   17

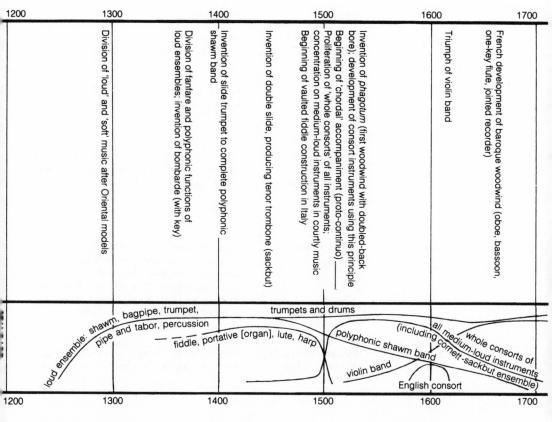

This chart by Herbert W. Myers is an expanded version of a portion of figure 49 of Anthony Baines'
Woodwind Instruments and Their History (London, Faber & Faber 1957), p. 210. Used by permission

Important instrument developments, ca 1500

- Vaulted fiddle construction in Italy, producing violin/viola and *lira da braccio*.
- Invention of viola da gamba.
- Production of complete families ('whole consorts') of all types of instruments; first evidence of bass members of families: bass recorder, bass flute, bass gamba, bass violin ('cello), bass rebec.
- Italian soft-case harpsichord and virginals construction; evidence of string-keyboards at 8' (and lower) pitch.

- Reappearance of transverse flute, first as a military, then as a consort instrument.
- Ascendance of the cornett (and descendance of the shawm); concentration on medium-loud instruments in concerted, courtly music.
- Addition of sixth course to the lute (first mentioned by Tinctoris, ca 1487); conversion from plectrum to finger-plucked technique.

TABLE 3
Early musical instruments

instrument	dates	description
BAGPIPE	continuous from early centuries	many varieties: 0, 1, 2 drones; 1, 2 chanters; cylindrical and conical drones and chanters
*CITOLE	13th and 14th cent., less in 15th	4 metal strings; wooden frets; plucked with a quill
*CITTERN	late 15th to early 16th cent. forward; developed from citole	originally 4 metal strings, brass frets; plucked with plectrum of bone, ivory, or wood, also with fingers in late 16th cent.
CORNAMUSE/ CORNAMUSA	13th cent. forward	often mentioned but there has been much confusion about shape and other details; a woodwind and probably a reed; in mid-17th-cent. France it was a musette (= small bagpipe) with a chanter but without a bag; in Italy it was a capped reed with a cylindrical bore, stopped at the lower end.
CORNETTO/ ZINK	Germany from 14th to 17th cent.; other countries beginning in late 15th cent.	both curved and straight; separate and integral mouthpiece; larger sizes from end of 16th cent.
CURTAL/ DULCIAN/ DOLZANA/ FAGOTTO/	from mid-16th cent.	bass became bassoon in 17th cent.; developed into an entire family of sizes by end of 16th cent., but lowest sizes were the most used
FLUTE	earlier than 12th cent.	always cylindrical with no keys; absent in 15th cent.; light tone but shrill top range

1 Pitches are indicated as follows:

c¹ c⁰ c⁰   c¹ c² c³

* Indicates that pitch is not necessarily a specific sound. The notes given refer to intervals and positions on theoretical scales. Actual sound probably varied.

TABLE 3 (continued)

tuning and range[1]	function	ensemble	location
variable, but range usually no more than a 9th	folk music, dance	usually solo; in Middle Ages with shawm	pan-European
	with troubadour songs; dances in Spain; by 15th cent. a peasant instrument	solo and with vielle	France, Spain, Italy from 13th cent.; Germany, England from 14th cent.
early 17th cent.: French Italian and English	light entertainment; in 17th cent. in barbershops to entertain patrons	solo except for English broken consort	England primarily; also France, Italy
		with soft instruments	France, Italy
from a° (g°) cornettino from e'	virtuoso instrument in 16th and 17th cent.; played superius and doubled top voice in church choir	often found as highest part with set of trombones; also in various soft ensembles	Germany and Austria in Middle Ages; pan-European in 16th and 17th cent.
tenor from G° to f' or g'; bass from c° to d' or g'	doubled bass line; played continuo	large ensembles of voices and soft instruments; small ensembles with viols and keyboards	Italy, Spain by mid-16th cent.; England Germany by end of cent.
soprano in d², alto in g', tenor in d'; late 15th cent. bass in g°	military association in Germany and Switzerland during Middle Ages; art music from late 15th cent.	with tabor in military; with soft instruments in Renaissance	Germany from 12th cent.; France from 13th cent.; England in 14th cent.; pan-European after 1500

	TABLE 3 (continued)	
instrument	dates	description
*GITTERN	from mid-13th cent.	3–5 strings, 4 most popular; gut strings – perhaps just a small lute or guitar
*GUITAR	from 13th cent.	4 or 5 courses
*HARP	from ancient times	one of the most popular instruments in Middle Ages and Renaissance; in 14th-cent. France had 24–26 strings; grew in size through Renaissance; usually gut strings, but some had metal; most had bray pins
*HURDY-GURDY	from before the 12th cent.	12th- and 13th-cent. models required 2 performers; 2 or 3 strings; 1 or 2 drones or parallel melody strings
KEYBOARDS:		
HARPSICHORD	from late 14th cent.	several varieties of sizes and number of strings
*CLAVICHORD/ (EXCHEQUER?)	from mid-14th cent.	fretted clavichord allowed only some notes to be played polyphonically
*PORTATIVE ORGAN	from 12th cent.	sacred and secular use as melody instrument; no polyphony until early 16th-cent. models
POSITIVE ORGAN	from ancient times	by 13th cent. widely used in church; multiple manuals and pedals from late 14th cent.
KRUMMHORN/ CRUMHORN	from late 15th cent.	descended from bladderpipe (13th cent.); known from 1511 in Germany; 4 sizes

	TABLE 3 (continued)		
tuning and range	function	ensemble	location
[musical notation]	accompanied voice	small groups of soft instruments	France and England
common 4-course in 16th cent.: *[musical notation]*	in France light court music; elsewhere folk music	mostly solo, but also as continuo and with soft instruments	pan-European
in Middle Ages from F° to c³; diatonic; extended range in 16th cent.	solo and with small groups in Middle Ages; as continuo in Renaissance	most often with voice and/or lute; also with flute and other soft instruments	France especially, but pan-European
in Middle Ages 9 notes: one octave plus B-flat	2-man instrument in Medieval iconography; 1-man with chanson de geste and other secular music from 13th cent.	solo and with voice	Spain, France in 12th cent.; pan-European after 14th cent.
variable	solo, ensemble, continuo from late 15th cent.	voices and ensembles	pan-European from 15th cent.
G° to f²	solo	none	France, England from 14th cent.; pan-European after 1450
from b° or c'; chromatic for 2½ octaves	sacred and secular including dance	solo, voice, small ensembles, especially with vielle	popular in Italy; pan-European
variable according to size	church music	solo, with choir	pan-European
soprano in c'; alto in g°; tenor in c°; bass in c° (F°)	always ensemble, sacred and secular	often in closed consort and with sackbuts and some ensembles of soft instruments	Germany in late 15th cent.; England in early 16th; Italy and France in mid-16th cent.

TABLE 3 (continued)		
instrument	dates	description
LUTES:		
CHITARRONE, ARCHLUTE, THEORBO	from late 16th cent.	5–8 courses over fingerboard plus variable number of bass strings off-board 3 or 4 strings
LONG-NECK	from early Middle Ages	3 or 4 strings
SHORT-NECK	from 13th cent.	very popular in late Middle Ages and Renaissance; originally unfretted and played with quill; frets and finger-plucked from 15th cent. and 5th and 6th courses added; gut strung; many family members, large and small – see gittern, theorbo, archlute
*LIRA DA BRACCIA	late 14th to 16th cent.	5 strings with 1 or 2 additional off-board; early models were tenor (viola) size; in late 16th cent. larger models
LYRA	from ancient times to late Middle Ages	plucked like harp; some bowed varieties in late Middle Ages
NAKERS	from 12th cent.	began as small military paired drums and grew in size; some as big as modern timpani in 15th cent.
PIPE AND TABOR	from 13th cent.	3- or 4-hole pipe; small drum with snare on upper head; single player
*PSALTERY	from ancient times	many shapes; single, double, triple strung; 8 to 24 or more courses; played with plectrum or fingers; metal strings; much used in Middle Ages
RACKETT	late 16th to 17th cent.	complete family in Germany from early 17th cent.; lowest models were the most used; remodelled in 18th cent.
REBEC	from 13th cent.	2 to 4 gut strings; some with frets; 3 sizes by early 16th cent.; treble used in Middle Ages, tenor and bass from mid-15th cent.

TABLE 3 (continued)

tuning and range	function	ensemble	location
bass-tenor range	continuo, ensemble, solo	with voice and ensembles of all sizes; with keyboards	pan-European
octave, 5th, 4th	dance, vocal accompaniment	solo, soft ensembles	pan-European
major 3rd in middle, all others in 4ths; diatonic low strings added in 16th cent.	in Middle Ages for vocal accompaniment, dance, sacred and secular ensembles; in Renaissance for solo, ensembles, continuo	solo, with voice, often with harp; after 1450 played single lines in ensembles; continuo	pan-European
tenor size in 16th cent. [musical notation]	improvised accompaniment for voice	with voice	Italy
5, 6, 7 strings diatonic; re-tuned in mode of each song	vocal accompaniment	solo and with voice	pan-European
	in 13th cent. military; from 14th cent. forward in secular ensembles	with loud instruments – shawm, trumpets, cymbals; in military with flute	pan-European
	dance music; after 1400 a peasant instrument	solo	pan-European
small models from g°; others variable	sacred and secular, solo and ensemble	with voice and soft ensembles	pan-European
compass of 12th; soprano g°–d'; alto/tenor c°–g°; bass F'–c°; great bass C'–G°	sacred and secular; usually 8 basso doubling for instruments and/or voices	voices and soft ensembles	Germany in mid-16th cent.; pan-European in late 16th cent.
usually 5ths	secular only; dance music	solo, and soft ensembles	popular in Italy, some in France and England

TABLE 3 (continued)		
instrument	dates	description
RECORDER/ FLAUTO DOLCE/ FLUTE À BEC	from 12th cent.	several sizes by 15th cent., full family by end of 15th cent.; wide cylindrical bore until 16th cent.; tone stronger and range more limited than baroque models
SHAWM	from 12th cent.	loud double-reed; by 14th cent. soprano and alto sizes; full family by 16th cent.; modified to become oboe in mid 17th cent.
TABOR	from earliest times	many sizes; usually with snare on upper surface
TROMBONE/ SACKBUT	from early 15th cent.	succeeded slide trumpet; originally tenor size; 3 or 4 sizes by mid-16th cent.
TRUMPET	from ancient times	usually played in pairs for heraldic occasions; both straight and 's' shape; by 16th cent. performers had specialized technique in the higher register
SLIDE TRUMPET	late 14th to early 15th cent.	became the trombone; long mouthpipe was held and remainder of instrument was moved to obtain a full scale
*VIELLE/ FIDDLE	from 11th to 16th cent.	descended from plucked strings; flat bridge and many shapes and sizes in Middle Ages; most were tenor (viola) size, but evidence of larger and smaller models exists in iconography; 4 or 5 gut strings, often 1 off-board; flat bridge suggests multiple drones
*VIHUELA	flourished in 16th cent.	several sizes but alto was most popular; 11 or 12 gut strings in 6 courses

TABLE 3 (continued)

tuning and range	function	ensemble	location
sopranino in g²; soprano in d²(c²); alto in g'; tenor in c'; bass in f°; great bass in b°	sacred and secular; by 16th cent. a virtuoso instrument; doubled instruments and voices	all sizes of soft ensembles; played independent line or doubled; mixed ensembles and consort in Renaissance	Europe from 13th cent.; England from 14th cent.
1½ octave range: soprano in d'; alto in g°; tenor in d°; bass in G° (D°/C°)	military use in Middle Ages; with trumpets as tower watch until 17th cent.; dance from 15th cent.; polyphonic ensemble from 15th cent.	with trumpets and drums in military; slide trumpet and trombone for dance; with trombone for polyphony	Italy from 12th cent.; pan-European from 13th cent.
	military; occasionally dance	with trumpets and flutes	pan-European
alto in d°; tenor in A°; bass in D°	to support church choir, dance music, polyphony	with shawms, trumpets, choirs, mixed ensembles	Burgundy from 1421; pan-European from late 15th cent.
varied with size	military, dance music, to signal from towers, heraldry	with drums, sometimes shawms	pan-European
varied with size	dances and loud music at banquets	with shawms	France, Burgundy, Italy, England, Germany
sacred music: _[musical notation]_ secular music: _[musical notation]_	sacred and secular music in Middle Ages; not much used after 15th cent.	solo and with citole, harp, and lute in soft ensembles; vocal accompaniment	pan-European
[musical notation]	aristocratic instrument; sophisticated solo literature	solo and vocal accompaniment	Spain

	TABLE 3 (continued)	
instrument	dates	description
VIOL	from mid-15th cent.	first appears as tenor vielle with curved top, rounded bridge, and 6 strings; other sizes from early 16th cent.; addition of soundpost in early 17th cent. made tone more robust
VIOLIN	from early 16th cent.	began as alto (viola); family by end of 16th cent.; became favourite virtuoso instrument in Italy by late 16th cent.

Loud instruments

Of the loud instruments, bagpipes were usually found alone, often playing for dancing. Their repertory could be any of the monophonic secular music. Bands of four to six trumpets were employed by the nobles and/or municipalities from as early as the thirteenth century and served for playing fanfares for various state occasions and signalling from the city towers.[15] They added ceremony and excitement to such events as jousts and processions (see illustration 5); descriptions of grand occasions report the presence of as many as a hundred. They were a symbol of rank and should not be considered an important artistic ensemble.[16] The trumpet repertory was never written down and probably consisted of improvisation and set formulae passed on by rote memorization. Very little is known of what was performed by these groups.[17]

From the late fourteenth century forward, two or three shawms, first with a slide trumpet and later with a trombone, made up one of the most popular ensembles for performing dance music (see illustration 6). Iconographic sources such as this show that, although these bands often had four musicians, only three performed at a time; one of the shawm players is usually found resting. The dance repertory for this ensemble in the fifteenth and early sixteenth centuries was apparently made up totally of two-part and three-part improvised counterpoint over a basse dance cantus firmus (a technique discussed in chapter 8). The shawm bands also served on other occasions for which the repertory was selected according to the occasion from the polyphonic sacred and secular music, both texted and untexted.[18]

Soft instruments

Ensembles of soft instruments were more flexible than loud ensembles in that

	TABLE 3 (continued)		
tuning and range	function	ensemble	location
4ths with 3rd in middle; variations for lyra style in 16th cent.	sacred and secular; very popular; virtuoso repertory	closed consort; soft ensembles; vocal accompaniment; solo	pan-European
as now	sacred and secular but played by pro-fessionals (as opposed to aristocratic perfor-mers of viols)	all sacred and secular ensembles; solo from beginning of 16th cent.	Italy in early 16th cent.; pan-European late 16th century

all instruments could be combined freely with one another and soft ensembles could also be combined with solo voices.[19] There were no set ensembles such as the shawm band, but certain instruments were more commonly used in ensembles than others. Most ensembles included at least one plucked instrument; lute and harp are the two most frequently found, and although today we would immediately think of them as polyphonic instruments, there is evidence that until about 1450 both were monophonic, played with a plectrum.[20]

Iconographic and literary evidence indicates that instrumental ensembles of the Middle Ages tended to combine unlike sounds, a choice supported by the music. There is much evidence in all forms of medieval art that tastes favoured contrasts rather than similarity, and if we look at medieval music, this preference will often be evident. In much of the polyphonic repertory each line moves at a separate pace and has its own melodic interest and separate phrase lengths. To support the separate and often melodically independent sounds of much of the medieval repertory, the instruments chosen were those which balanced one another in volume but contrasted in sound colours. An instrumental performance of a three-part composition might have included, for example, one plucked string, one bowed string, and one woodwind. Other frequently used combinations included the contrasting sounds of two quite different sounding bowed strings, for example, rebec and vielle, or different sounding plucked strings, for example, gut and metal strings. All lines of a polyphonic medieval composition often share a common melodic range, and therefore performance on contrasting instruments helps the listener to follow the individual melodic contours which otherwise may be obscured by the crossing and interweaving of the parts. In all cases, however, the choice of different or similar instruments should be made according to the

4.1 Guillaume Dufay 'Helas ma dame,' bars 1–8, contratenor
Guillaume Dufay *Opera Omnia* ed. Heinrich Besseler, vol. 6 © 1964 by Armen Carapetyan,
American Institute of Musicology/Hänssler-Verlag, D-7303 Neuhausen-Stuttgart (West Germany) No. 60.106.
Used by permission

demands of the music. If the lines of the music contrast with one another, so should the instruments. On the other hand, medieval pieces can be found in which two of the lines are similar in melodic curve and rhythms (such as the lower two parts in example 2.1), and in these cases it is often possible and even desirable to use matching instruments, for example, two bowed strings, or two lutes. The Renaissance preference for similar instruments and families of instruments did not come about overnight, and medieval works can be found which seem to indicate an emphasis on the similarity of parts rather than the difference. The important point is to look to the music for clues of this nature and choose your instrumentation to emphasize whatever is emphasized in the music itself.

In matching an instrument with a line of music the abilities and inabilities of the instruments themselves also must be kept in mind. The most versatile are the plucked strings because of their comparatively wide range, their ability to make large skips without undue emphasis, the ease with which they play stop-and-go parts, and their ability to blend. They would be an ideal choice for a line such as example 4.1. Their drawbacks are that they cannot play a sustained line and in some combinations they are not strong enough to provide balance as either superius melody or supporting tenor line. They are ideal for contratenor parts in almost any soft instrument combination, and as long as balance and other factors are kept in mind, they serve well on the other lines as well. A common combination in the fourteenth and fifteenth centuries was a duet of plucked strings, either two lutes or lute and harp. When a harp is used, it should be remembered in assigning parts that it is difficult for a harper to alter occasional notes chromatically, but otherwise the instruments should be equal. In a three-part composition one instrument could be assigned two parts, in any combination (although polyphonic performance on lute and harp is not authentic until the early fifteenth century), or the contratenor line might be omitted (see below, pp. 97–9).[21]

Woodwinds and bowed strings can play sustained lines, can achieve smooth legato, and are generally strong enough to support the lowest lines and bring out the superius. Their drawbacks are difficulties in performing

It is not possible to make a single short list of the five or six 'most useful' early instruments which would be correct for all performing ensembles. Each ensemble must make that choice individually depending on its size, its particular interests in performing mostly medieval or mostly Renaissance music or a combination of both, and the amount of performing to be done with singers. There are, however, several instruments which were extremely popular in the early centuries, as can be seen in the Myers chart and table 3, and every early ensemble should seriously consider acquiring these as the basic and stable instruments to which others can be added in varying numbers depending upon the particular repertory and circumstances:

1 *Lute* The lute is found in various sizes throughout both the Middle Ages and the Renaissance. For a single first purchase, a tenor seven-course instrument is the most versatile. It can be played monophonically with a plectrum for music before about 1450 and polyphonically with fingers for Renaissance music. The seven courses make the single instrument capable of performing most of the repertory, including that of Dowland. For more specialized repertory the lutenist can easily move to other members of the family when needs and finances allow. The lute has a rich solo repertory and is in constant demand as an ensemble instrument and for vocal accompaniment.

2 *Harp* With the lute, the harp is the most frequently pictured instrument up to 1500. A twenty-four to twenty-six-string Gothic harp with bray pins will manage monophonic and some polyphonic music up to about 1550. The Gothic harp cannot change chromatics quickly, but it is useful on a single line in some small ensembles for solo voice accompaniment and as a double for soft instruments (see the discussion of doublings in chapter 6). For later Renaissance music a larger harp without bray pins but with a larger range is usually necessary, and for the early medieval repertory the harper can easily develop technique on a medieval lyre.

3 *Vielle/fiddle* With a range similar to viola ($c^°$–e^2), the vielle or fiddle is a versatile instrument up to about 1500 as a contrast with plucked strings. Useful for medieval tenor lines, for accompaniment for solo voice, and in small to medium ensembles, although the flat bridge seen in most representations suggests that its principal use was the monophonic repertory.

4 *Tenor viol* The tenor viol is a good substitute for the vielle for groups playing more early Renaissance than medieval repertory and in need of a strong voice going to $G^°$. Most viol players adapt easily to treble and bass for music of the later Renaissance.

Other useful instruments such as flute, recorder, and sackbut are usually

TABLE 4
Useful early instruments

PLUCKED STRINGS	BOWED STRINGS	BRASS	DOUBLE REEDS	OTHER WINDS	KEYBOARD	PERCUSSION
most useful instruments						
lute	vielle (M)	slide trumpet (M)	alto shawm	alto flute	portative organ (M)	tabor
harp	tenor viol	tenor sackbut (R)	schalmei	alto recorder	harpsichord (R)	tambourine
psaltery (M)	bass viol (R)	cornetto (R)	bagpipe (M)	tenor flute	positive organ	nakers
gittern (M)	treble viol (R)	bass sackbut (R)	bass curtal (R)	tenor recorder		bells
	rebec (M)		tenor shawm (R)	soprano recorder		
	viola (R)			bass recorder (R)		
	violin (R)					
less useful instruments						
long neck lute (M)	hurdygurdy (M)	alto sackbut (R)	tenor curtal	soprano flute	clavichord	
cittern (R)	crwth (M)		krummhorns	bass flute (R)		
guitar (R)			rackett	pipe and tabor (M)		
vihuela (R)			kortholt			
lyre (M)			rauschpfeiff			
			bass shawm			

M = principally medieval use
R = principally Renaissance use

found in early music ensembles, and their importance need not be elaborated upon here.

The instruments are listed in table 4 according to their relative usefulness in performing medieval and Renaissance repertory, with and without voices. They are ranked beginning at the top of each column according to both their usefulness in performing the repertory and their apparent popularity during the early centuries.

A GUIDE TO SUBSTITUTES

The following list assumes that your ensemble will have some of the most useful early instruments and may have access to some non-period instruments which can be used to approximate the sound of the historically correct instruments when playing with a group of historical instruments. (My opinion on the availability of the early repertory to players of non-historical instruments is expressed in the preface).

When using any of the following substitutes performers should make themselves acquainted with the sound properties and limitations of the authentic instrument (available on recordings) and then adapt their approach to more nearly approximate the historical sound and style.

Historical instrument	Possible substitutes
cittern/citole	several wire-strung folk instruments such as mandolin (restrung)
cornetto	violin or clarinet with 'edgeless' sweet tone (very soft reed)
curtal	modern bassoon with more open reed and less dynamic flexibility
gittern	treble lute, rebec, or vielle plucked with plectrum
medieval lute	baroque lute with plectrum – monophonic
Renaissance flute	baroque wooden flute without dynamic flexibility – medium-soft tone
medieval/Renaissance recorder	baroque recorder without extremes of dynamic flexibility – use more definite articulation and a fairly breathy tone

rebec	violin with gut strings or treble viol with light bow
Renaissance guitar/vihuela	modern guitar with gut strings and fairly dry tone or baritone ukelele with gut strings
Renaissance viol	baroque viol, but with more articulation in place of volume for expression (a Renaissance bow would help)
shawm	English horn with open, loud reed and no dynamic flexibility
slide trumpet/Renaissance sackbut	modern trombone with a small, open-throat mouthpiece and no 'edge' to the tone; should blend easily with voices (learn legato tonguing from cornetto instruction manuals)
vielle	viola with gut strings or tenor viol with light bow

In all cases, when using a substitute in an ensemble of historical instruments, the substitute must adapt tone, volume, and playing style to those of the historical instruments.

PART TWO

The Repertory

Music for Soloists and Ensembles of Soloists

Selection of performance mode

URING THE EARLY CENTURIES the selection of a specific mode of performance for any given work was left to the performers. Although much of the music was originally conceived in order to set a text, performers were free to choose a totally vocal performance or a totally instrumental one, or to combine voices and instruments. Their choice was probably based on practical considerations: availability of performers, the style and ranges of the parts, and the occasion. But it was made within the bounds of current customs, and the objective of this chapter and the next is to discuss those customary modes of performance in the various centres of Europe during the early centuries in order to understand what would probably have been chosen in various circumstances. That is not to say that in special circumstances unusual or bizarre performances would not have taken place. But the focus of this study will be upon the most usual and probable performance practices in centres where a choice of performance mode was possible.

Although the composer rarely prescribed the choice of performing ensemble in the Middle Ages and Renaissance, this does not mean that he composed without an ensemble in mind. In most instances he wrote for a particular occasion and therefore knew the probable performing ensemble, and to some degree he would have taken this into consideration when composing. However, he would no doubt have been content with a good performance by any of a number of combinations of voices and/or instruments in the tradition that was current.

To select an authentic performance ensemble for the repertory we must take into consideration two elements: the probable original intentions of the composer and the ensembles popular at the time he was composing. Information on the latter can be found in a number of historical studies which will be summarized in the following pages, but in narrowing down the selection, the music itself still provides the most help. If we look at the music to ascertain the composer's musical intentions, the selection of probable performance ensembles will usually become quite evident. I have already acknowledged, however, that there is ample documentation that the demands of the musical lines were frequently overlooked by performers in order to achieve other goals, and modern performers are also welcome to choose these solutions as long as the choice of ensembles is probable for that particular era.

Performance with voice

By far the largest share of surviving early music involves the setting of a text. Throughout the period everyone sang: men and women, solo and in groups, formally and informally. The people in religious orders sang sacred music for hours every day; peasants sang while they worked and while they relaxed; professional entertainers sang in the taverns, squares, and courts; and the nobility sang as part of their courtship. They sang alone or accompanied by instruments, and although only a portion of the repertory survives, it is vast and varied. In this chapter we will be concerned with soloist performance, which should be understood as music for one singer to a part, including a single soloist and ensembles of two or more soloists.

The decision as to whether a particular genre of music should be considered for soloists or for a larger ensemble is often somewhat arbitrary. Since the composer rarely specified this and our knowledge of this type of custom is limited, the selection in many cases is made by attempting to determine the intention of the composer. However, many compositions discussed here as best suited for solo performance will work with two or more singers to a part, and most ensemble music can be performed adequately with one singer to a part, regardless of the original intention. The inclusion of any genre of music in either this chapter or the next, therefore, does not rule out the other mode of performance; it means only that to me one method appeared to be preferable, given the information we have and the demands of the music.

THE MEDIEVAL REPERTORY

Monophonic songs

The repertory of monophonic songs extends from the twelfth to the fifteenth centuries and includes chansons from as early as the jongleurs, troubadours, and trouvères, the Latin songs of the goliards, songs of the Minnesingers and Meistersingers, some early Italian laudas, Spanish cantigas, and the monophonic conductus. [1] The extent of this repertory is large, but little is performed in concerts by modern early music groups because of problems both with presenting the text and with the realization of a monophonic composition in concert.

For purposes of discussion these compositions can be divided into two basic types: syllabic, in which for the most part each syllable receives a single note; and melismatic, in which there are far more notes than syllables. There is a variety of forms involved in both types – some with repeated melodic sections and others without internal repeats; some with only a single verse of text and others with many. For the performer, however, there are certain ways to approach a monophonic song which need be adjusted only slightly depending upon the type of setting, form, and number of verses (but see the discussion of multiple verse texts below, pp. 109–10).

All texts were intended to be understood by the audience, and translations or synopses should always be presented for texts in a language foreign to the listeners. In addition the performer must always express the text as much as possible. None of the repertory, however, is so dependent on the textual message as is the syllabic monophonic-repertory with multiple verses. This can be best described as 'heightened poetry'; that is, the music is obviously subservient to the text and was written principally to help the recitation of the text. Some of these relatively short and simple melodies are attractive and can stand on their own as independent musical compositions, but the major objective of the music was apparently to help convey the poetry, and therefore all performances of this material should be aimed at presenting the text as the foremost element. It is difficult to do justice to this repertory because it requires either an audience that comprehends medieval languages or very clever presentation. Since the first solution is improbable, I shall dwell upon the second.

The easiest solution, if it would work, would be to sing a translation of the text. Unfortunately, poetry rarely translates without loss of both meaning and its original beauty as poetry. Further, since many of the musical settings were written to set the sounds of the original language, often they will not serve the flow of another. Depending upon the text, however, it is sometimes possible to translate medieval French into modern French or medieval German into modern, and in rare cases to translate from, for example, Italian into modern English. The degree of success depends entirely on the nature of the original and the ability of the translator not to destroy the poetry or cause distortion in the musical setting.

The more frequently chosen methods of communicating the message of the text to the audience are to present a translation or a synopsis of the text either in program notes or by recitation. These topics are discussed below (pp. 221–2).

Syllabic songs

As with all the monophonic repertory, performing syllabic songs requires considerable effort on the part of the performers. The singer must work at expressing the text with much vocal inflection and some facial and body gestures (but see instruction 6 above, p. 56), especially in order to sustain interest in a poem of many stanzas with repeated music, and must be prepared to embellish the melody from verse to verse and be free with the tempo as an aid to expression.

We do not know how this repertory was usually presented. There are illuminations in the troubadour manuscripts showing some of the poets with musical instruments, but Hendrik van der Werf points out that this may be merely symbolism and does not necessarily mean that the songs were usually accompanied, any more than we should believe that those poets depicted on horseback always recited or sang while mounted.[2] An unaccompanied vocal solo is an acceptable and often quite attractive method of presentation. In fact, unaccompanied solo voice makes a good contrast in a concert of otherwise accompanied or polyphonic material.

It is known that instruments were sometimes played by the people who sang this repertory, and therefore instrumental accompaniment is also a possible mode of performance. The instruments most often depicted with solo singers of the Middle Ages are: harp, lute, portative organ, vielle, and psaltery. The instrument chosen can double the melody line at pitch or octave, play a more simplified version of the melody line as in example 5.1, or play a simple counterpoint[3] or even a drone (the iconography suggests that the medieval singers often accompanied themselves). The instrument can be used to set the scene with a prelude,[4] to space verses of text by repeating the entire melody or just a phrase or two, to play a short melodic section between verses, or to punctuate phrase endings by inserting small flourishes. Possibilities for a typical presentation of monophonic song include:

1 unaccompanied voice;
2 accompaniment by a single instrument (especially plucked string);
3 accompaniment by two or three contrasting instruments which could serve by: doubling the melody, inventing simple counterpoint, playing a drone, or playing prelude, postlude, instrumental verses, and phrase punctuations.

5.1 Anonymous 'Miri it is' with melody simplified

At the beginning of the twentieth century much work was done on the troubadour and trouvère repertory by French scholars. Since the notes of the original settings do not give evidence of a great variety of rhythms, a system was developed whereby the perceived rhythm of the text was adopted for the music. The practice was then applied to much of the rest of the syllabic repertory, and although the end result is musical, the theory has come under severe attack in recent years.[5] In the near future new and different rhythmic transcriptions may be presented to the musical world, but until that time the available transcriptions can serve, and when thought out from the point of view of presenting the meaning of the text clearly, they can add a large variety of music to the early repertory now in performance.

Melismatic songs

The melismatic melodies are not quite so dependent upon their texts – not that the poetry is of any lower quality, but the composer's contribution is of a more sophisticated nature than in a simple syllabic setting. These melodies do not take a subservient position to the poetry, as in the majority of syllabic settings, but are often the artistic equals of the text and therefore are more available for performance without text – either as a totally instrumental performance or as extended instrumental verses within a vocal performance. The melodies contain substantial passages or florid melismas and therefore require an agile voice and highly developed instrumental technique. Many contain ornamental passages that suggest the *passaggi* that would have been inserted extemporaneously by performers of the time (see chapter 7).

Performance possibilities for these compositions are basically the same as for the syllabic songs – voice alone or voice with one or more instruments, although the participation of instruments can be somewhat expanded. A monophonic ballata, for example, either syllabic or melismatic, might be performed as follows:

prelude	instrument(s)
first verse	voice, either accompanied at octave or unaccompanied
refrain	voice, either accompanied at octave or unaccompanied
second verse	voice with drone
refrain	solo instrument, with or without drone
third verse	voice with simple instrumental counterpoint (no drone)
refrain	instrument added to melody at octave, with or without counterpoint or drone
postlude	instrument(s)

The performance suggested above can be accomplished by a single versatile lutenist-singer or by a vocalist with one or more instrumentalists, depending on the ensemble and the program needs. For one of the more sophisticated melismatic settings an instrument could substitute for the voice for an entire verse and refrain as long as the sense of the text is not disturbed (see discussion below, pp. 109–10).

Polyphonic songs

The earliest existing polyphonic repertory for vocal soloists is almost as old as the monophonic. The material ranges from compositions as simple as the syllabic monophonic songs described above to extremely complex works. The performance possibilities for this repertory are many and depend upon a number of factors that will be discussed below, but a correct approach should start with an understanding of the usual methods of polyphonic composition.

Identifying the parts

It must be remembered that for most compositions up to the mid-fifteenth century the tenor line preceded the other parts and was considered the foundation of the composition. The first step in approaching a polyphonic medieval work, therefore, is to determine which line is the tenor. In most editions it is identified, but if you find a composition (such as example 5.14) where this is not so, it is possible to determine which line is the tenor:

1 In a two-part piece it will always be the lower of the two lines.
2 In a three-part piece the highest sounding melody line will be the cantus or superius, leaving the tenor to be separated from the contratenor. (There are a few fourteenth-century French compositions in which the contratenor is written above the cantus, but a contratenor line usually has a distinctive, non-melodic shape.) The two parts have the following characteristics:
   a The tenor is usually the lowest sounding part – especially at cadences; has a relatively smooth-moving melody and rhythm; is obviously the harmonic foundation for both the other parts; can often be performed successfully with the superius as a two-part composition; and often has a text incipit (beginning), if not a whole text.
   b The contratenor is usually the middle voice, although occasionally it crosses beneath the tenor or above the cantus; was written last in order to fill in the harmony and rhythm and therefore is the least independent melodic-rhythmic line (it makes little sense as a solo line); and cannot serve with the superius as a two-part composition.
3 In some three-part music from the thirteenth century the tenor with superius and added contratenor are replaced by a tenor with one added melody called duplum and a later added melody called triplum, as in example 5.3. In these cases both melodies agree with the tenor and can be performed separately with the tenor as well as all together.
4 In a four-part composition the tenor retains the characteristics mentioned above. It can be sorted out from the other parts in that it usually occupies the range second from lowest, having the alto filler written between it and the superius and a bassus written below.

Whether the tenor line should be set off from the other parts or blended depends upon the style of the individual composition, but in all cases the tenor must be presented as the equal of the other parts of the composition because it is the harmonic foundation and in many cases was the composer's method of determining the overall form of the composition. It is not necessary or even desirable to make it stand out; the individual shapes of the lines and performance with contrasting sounds will call attention to each of the lines of a medieval composition. Isorhythmic tenors – tenor lines given a repeating rhythmic pattern, as in example 5.3 – also do not need to be singled out. The isorhythm is an organizational device for the composer, and no special effort should be made to make the pattern more pronounced than any other line in the composition.

Organum

Perhaps the easiest material to discuss is the earliest two-part sacred music with a single text, called organum.[6] Whatever the style of the organum, the evidence we have is that the music called for a pair of solo singers who interpolated these two-part embellishments into what was otherwise a monophonic delivery of the chant by a choir. Performance of the syllabic organum is fairly obvious – two unaccompanied solo voices; there is no evidence and little reason for using instruments in a performance of this material. Melismatic organum, however, presents another problem. This is a slow-moving tenor foundation line over which an extremely florid accompaniment has been written. Although the top line appears to be soloist material, the tenor line seems far too sustained for performance by a single soloist, and the two most popular theories suggest that either a small group sang the tenor line or it was performed on an instrument. At this point in the research the most convincing theory is that when the music was an official part of a church service, it was probably sung in all parts.

Conductus

The conductus repertory offers other possibilities;[7] it was not part of the official liturgy but was sometimes used during a service as processional music, and at other times probably served outside the service for instruction or even entertainment. The conductus, therefore, may not be quite so restricted in its performance mode as a liturgical work and may have been performed with instruments on some of the lines or even doubling voices on all of the lines. Conductus survive for one, two, three, and even four parts, and when sung with clear voices that are well in tune, they are often quite striking for their bold and irregular dissonances. Several different compositional styles can be found in this repertory, and the style must be taken into account when considering a mode of performance.

1 *Voice exchange* Some conductus were written with much of the material shared among the voices; that is, a melodic-rhythmic phrase found in one voice will soon be found in another, as in example 5.2. This integration of material suggests that, if instruments are to be involved in the performance, conductus, unlike other medieval pieces, can be played by like-sounding rather than contrasting instruments in order to support the compositional style.

2 *Lengthy melismas* In some conductus – both those with voice exchange and those without it – the text appears for the most part in a quasi-syllabic setting with long melismatic passages for the first syllable or the last, or for both. In performance these conductus allow for instrumental interludes,

5.2 Anonymous 'Procurans odium,' bars 1–4
Janet Knapp, ed. *Thirty-Five Conductus for Two and Three Voices* Collegium musicum series, vol. 6,
New Haven 1965. Printed by permission of the Department of Music, Yale University

although they can certainly be sung, and the singers may object to giving up
the more virtuoso passages.

3 *Substitute parts* Another group of conductus existed in several independent forms – as a solo tenor, and with one or more of a number of added
parts. This is also true of some of the motet repertory of the twelfth,
thirteenth, and fourteenth centuries discussed below, in which the tenor
existed first as a monophonic song or as a chant to which one or more other
part(s) were later added. These were intended sometimes to be combined
and at other times to be substitutes for one another. Such compositions
allow the tenor to be performed as a monophonic song and to be combined
with a number of different upper parts. Given a bit of creative thought and
some searching, a single tenor could be presented in combination with
several different added lines to form an entire sub-section of a program.

Polytextual motets and chansons

There is a large repertory of polytextual motets and chansons from the
thirteenth, fourteenth, and early fifteenth centuries.[8] The texts involve
sacred, secular, and even profane topics in various combinations. Much of
that repertory is made up of compositions in which the melodies, rhythms,
and phrases of each part are different from the others, as in example 5.3. It is
obvious that in this work the composer was emphasizing difference and
contrast, and thus a performance should support this by helping the lines
maintain their individuality. If all three parts are sung, each singer should treat
his line as a separate melodic entity. Care should be taken, of course, to sing in
tune and in rhythmic synchronization with the other performers, but the
expression of each line should be based on its own demands, and no attempt
should be made to present a single unified expression. This type of
composition should be treated as a combination of three somewhat indepen-

5.3 Anonymous 'Entre copin et bourgeois,' bars 1–5
Hans Tischler, ed. *Montpellier Codex* vol. 3. A-R Editions, Inc. 1978. Used by permission

dent melodies, and although the singers should strive to balance one another, they should not attempt to blend. If instruments are chosen to double or replace some voices, they too should add separate colours and should stand apart from the voices and from one another. In example 5.3 the independence of the individual parts is further emphasized by their separate texts, but even in those compositions in which only a single text exists, lines with separate shapes should be played or sung so as to be heard as separate.

In his recent edition of the thirteenth-century Montpellier Codex,[9] Hans Tischler states that the motets were probably meant to be art music rather than church music, and that performance probably often included instruments. In a typical thirteenth-century three-voice motet such as example 5.3 the two upper voices are texted in full and the tenor is given only in incipit. This suggests an instrumental performance for the tenor, although a vocal performance is certainly possible. But what of the confusion of texts in the ears of the listeners? It is thought that these motets were usually performed privately, without an audience, and therefore the individual singer would have no problem comprehending the text of his own part. But this is of little use for modern performers who may wish to perform before an audience. It is possible, of course, to sing the texts simultaneously, having provided the

5.4 Guillaume de Machaut 'O livoris feritas,' bars 13–30
Leo Schrade, ed. *Polyphonic Music of the Fourteenth Century* vol. 2. Editions de L'Oiseau-Lyre 1956.
Used by permission

audience with translations or synopses, but another possibility is sequential texting in which the motet is performed several times in such a way that each line of text is sung without textual opposition from the other parts. For a motet such as example 5.3, the following suggestions and variations are possible:

1 Perform the tenor on an instrument and sing the other two parts, one at a time, against it, creating two different two-part compositions.
2 Sing the tenor first as a monophonic composition, then perform it on an instrument while the upper parts are presented as in 1 above.
3 Double all parts with instruments and perform the motet three times, each time singing only one line while the other two are performed on instruments.

If any of the above suggestions are followed, it may also be a good idea to sing through the motet one final time with all texts sung simultaneously. In some of the compositions it would appear that there is a relationship among the texts – elaboration, contrast, or irony. When such is the case, a final simultaneous performance would reinforce that aspect.

A later medieval polytextual motet, represented by example 5.4, suggests an intended performance by two voices and an instrument. An entirely vocal performance is always possible, but in this composition a string instrument or

5.5 Thomas (?) Damett 'Credo,' bars 73–83

Andrew Hughes and Margaret Bent, eds. *The Old Hall Manuscript* vol. 2. © 1969 by Armen Carapetyan, American Institute of Musicology/Hänssler-Verlag, D-7303 Neuhausen-Stuttgart (West Germany) No. 64.602. Used by permission

organ could perform the tenor line more easily. It would also be possible to substitute an instrument for the first or second line in many of these later compositions (although this could not be done for the top line in this example because it has a monophonic introductory section for the top voice); however, two voices would make a better balance if there is any alternation, as in bars 27–30 of this example.

Late medieval sacred music

Some of the most rewarding and challenging vocal music of the early centuries can be found in the fourteenth- and early fifteenth-century motets, Mass sections, and full Masses.[10] These compositions obviously grew from the earlier tradition in which the difficult polyphonic material was performed by soloists, but exactly how long polyphony remained the property of soloists, and when the tradition changed to performance by small choir, is not known. Andrew Hughes provides evidence that in England some of the sacred polyphony included sections for choir from as early as the mid-fourteenth century.[11] In the English repertory there is often a difference in the style of the music written for chorus in that it is frequently less rhythmically complex, as can be seen in example 5.5. This would tend to support the view of Manfred Bukofzer that the change from soloist to choir performance occurred at the time when a change can be seen in the actual style of the writing – generally from about 1430.[12] By accepting the information from both scholars we can arrive at general guide-lines for a decision about when this repertory was first sung by chorus: the mid-fourteenth century for England, and the mid-fifteenth century for the rest of Europe. But since the change did not happen all at once or at the same time in every location, most of the sacred music up to the last third of the fifteenth century can probably be thought of as suitable for either soloists or small choir depending on the individual characteristics of the piece; the more intricate the individual line, the more suitable it is for a soloist.

Performance of the soloist portion of this repertory requires skilled singers. The lines are full of complex rhythms and often contain extended rapid passages that tax even the most agile voice. The ranges of the texted parts as written usually place this music best for all-male performance – one or two counter-tenors and tenor, or counter-tenor, tenor, and bass-baritone. A mezzo-soprano can often be substituted for counter-tenor if necessary. Transposition up as much as a third or fourth is possible for much of the repertory without making the entire composition too shrill, but transposition down more than a second usually makes the sound too muddy.

The biggest problem in this repertory is what to do with the untexted lines; there is little historical evidence to support performance by an instrument (see the fuller discussion above, pp. 36–8). If it is decided that an instrument should be used on the untexted lines, however, the most likely choice is bowed strings if the part is somewhat sustained – vielle or tenor viol, whichever balances the voices. For lines that are rhythmically active and melodically angular, a plucked string would be the best choice.

Secular polyphony

For the secular polyphonic repertory up to the last third of the fifteenth century there is a great variety of compositional styles and therefore there are many acceptable ways to present it in performance. The secular literature was apparently almost all soloist repertory and gives the performers a sizeable number of possible combinations of voices and/or instruments for any composition. The fact that text may not have been supplied for all parts in the manuscript source of the edition does not preclude a totally vocal performance. Custom allowed any line to be sung, although some lines are more easily sung than others; the performer need only choose whether to vocalize an untexted line on a neutral syllable or to underlay the text, subdividing the notes when necessary in order to fit in all the syllables.

Example 5.6, a chanson from the early fifteenth century, allows the following possibilities:

1 Voices on all three parts.[13]

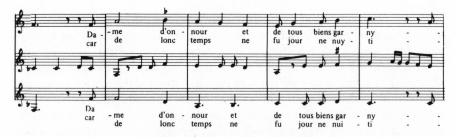

5.6 Anonymous 'Dame d'onnour,' bars 5–9
Gilbert Reaney, ed. *Early Fifteenth-Century Music* vol. 4. © 1969 by Armen Carapetyan,
American Institute of Musicology/Hänssler-Verlag, D-7303 Neuhaussen-Stuttgart (West Germany) No. 61.104.
Used by permission

2 Voices on parts 1 and 3, instrument on 2.

3 Voices on parts 1 and 3, leaving out part 2. There is evidence that until the end of the fifteenth century many compositions were regularly performed with one less than the full number of parts. The part to leave out if you have to (or wish to for variety's sake) in a three-part composition is always the contratenor; in a four-part work it is the alto. This is not possible for all compositions, however, and you should check the sound to see if a significant element of the composition is lost when you reduce the number of parts.

4 Voice on part 1, instruments on both other parts.

5 Voice on part 3, instruments on both other parts.

6 Voice on part 1, instrument on part 3, leave out part 2.

7 Voice on part 3, instrument on part 1, leave out part 2.

We know that all these were acceptable modes of performance for a typical chanson of the late Middle Ages. In this particular composition part 2, the contratenor, would be somewhat uncomfortable for voice, and therefore choice 1 would seem less probable, but theoretically all possibilities should be considered valid and the choice dictated by the nature of the lines in the particular composition, the resources of the performing ensemble, and the needs of the program, in that order.

When choosing instruments to combine with voice(s) the following guidelines should be kept in mind: do not overpower the voice; the tenor line should always be at least as strong as the contratenor; select instruments with contrasting sounds, and select them according to the demands of the parts. These suggestions are discussed in detail above, pp. 62–78.

Selecting instruments for example 5.6 begins with the Myers chart, where a large number of intruments are shown to be historically accurate for the early fifteenth century. The contratenor line, however, contains a large number of

TABLE 5
Performance possibilities for example 5.6, with one part sung

SUPERIUS	voice	bowed string/ recorder/ portative organ	voice	plucked string/ bowed string
CONTRA	plucked string	plucked string	contrasting plucked string	vielle
TENOR	vielle	voice	plucked string	voice

skips and short rests, which suggests that first consideration should go to plucked instruments. A bowed string would also be a possible choice for this line depending on how the other lines are to be performed and how much contrast among the lines is desired. If both the other two lines are to be sung, a plucked string would offer maximum contrast, whereas a bowed string would blend more. A woodwind instrument could also serve but has not been considered because the part lies too low for the known ranges of woodwinds at that time. If the composition is transposed up, a tenor recorder would also be a possible choice for a more blended sound. For performance with one voice and two instruments, the instrument chosen to play either the superius or tenor should probably be one that blends with the voice since those two parts have similar melodic-rhythmic material, while the contratenor should be performed with a contrasting sound because of the contrasting nature of the part. One possibility suggested by the music is to have voices on superius and tenor and an instrument on the contratenor: if the piece is untransposed, the contratenor could be played on harp, lute, psaltery, or vielle; if it is transposed, the same instruments would be suitable, and also cittern, rebec, tenor recorder, and portative organ. If one part is to be sung, possible combinations of voice and instruments are suggested in table 5.

A brief look at two other compositions should help to reinforce the method of determining possible modes of performance. Example 2.1 has only a single texted line, but all modes listed above are theoretically possible. The parts themselves show similarity in melodic-rhythmic material between the contratenor and tenor lines, and therefore the first consideration should probably be given to performing those two lines on similar-sounding instruments to contrast with the texted superius part. Performance on plucked strings is possible, but the rather sustained nature of the lines suggests bowed strings, and range again rules out woodwinds. The most obvious selection would be two vielles or viols (or one of each), but performance with plucked instruments or mixed plucked-string and bowed-string instruments on these two lines would also be historically correct.

Example 3.4 could be performed either with two voices or with a voice on one part and an instrument on the other (also, of course, two instruments alone). Neither part in this composition has musical characteristics that would suggest that one type of instrument would be preferable: there are neither sustained parts eliminating plucked strings nor angular parts recommending plucked instruments over the other groups. In this case, for a mixed vocal-instrumental performance, the choice can be made from any of the instruments popular in the late fourteenth century, as long as the range is sufficient and a balance with the voice is maintained.

The above suggestions for selecting performance modes can apply to all the vocal repertory of the Middle Ages. There are also additional considerations for certain parts of the medieval repertory which require separate discussion.

English carols and German songs

In both English carols[14] and German songs[15] the tenor line is often the bearer of the principal melody and the other line or lines are accompaniment. That does not restrict the possible methods of performance, which are the same as suggested above for any secular composition, but it does suggest that first consideration should go to singing the lower line with the instrument on the top part.

Carols are topical for a variety of occasions, not only Christmas. They can all be performed by soloists, but the burdens of some, especially the three-part burdens, may be for chorus.[16]

Love songs

Love songs are of two general types. They are about either requited or unrequited love; either the poet has achieved his goal and is in ecstasy, or he has been rejected and is in the depths of despair. The two types are quite different from one another, and within the categories there is variety in the manner in which the poet expresses himself and the way in which the composer has chosen to set the text. Beginning in the Renaissance the musical setting usually reflects the general emotion of the text, but in the Middle Ages and early Renaissance that was not necessarily so. Melodies we would judge to be quite cheerful in nature often set the saddest of poems; it was not part of the medieval composers' aesthetic to make the general attitude of the music fit the text. Medieval music is often simply a musical setting for a text, taking into consideration the verbal accents and the poetic form but not usually the content, and many ludicrous performances have been produced from the efforts made to force an emotional quality upon a melodic setting when it is not present in the music. The singer must always attempt to convey the meaning of the text he is singing, but sometimes the musical setting will not be of much help in communicating the emotional content, and no effort should be made to change the music – for example, by slowing it greatly – to make it conform. The meaning of a text can be conveyed by the use of a number of expressive techniques that do not alter the written notes – for example, a passage of quick-moving notes can be made to express happiness by shorter phrases and many accents or sadness by longer phrases, few accents, and a smooth articulation. And a passage of flowing 6/8 rhythm can be changed from a lively sounding two-in-a-bar to a more serious one-in-a-bar or a mournful one-in-two-bars, without changing the tempo. Within the confines of what is written on the page it is up to performers to select the dynamic shape, phrasing, and articulation that best represent the text.

Many of the early texts are quite frank and even vulgar. There are few naïve texts, and any that appear to be simple and naïve are usually neither. The medieval poets were very clever with double meanings, as for example in the bird songs in which each bird has a symbolic meaning. The standard bird symbols (most frequently found in French music, but carrying the same meanings in other languages as well) were: *aigle* (eagle) – royalty, power; *alouette* (lark) – mourning, warning to lovers, springtime, beauty; *corneille* (crow) – craftiness, mockery; *coucou* (cuckoo) – cuckoldry; *faucon* (falcon) – power, royalty, danger; *pao* (peacock) – beauty, vanity; *rossignol* (nightingale) – night, erotic love, passion; and *tourterelle* (turtle dove) – fidelity, loyalty. Performers will wish to think carefully about how much information to provide to a particular audience and on what level to translate a given text.

For suggestions on performance of the secular literature with long untexted melismatic sections, see the discussion above, pp. 38–40.

<h2 style="text-align:center">Caccias[17] (also chasses and rounds)</h2>

Caccias, chasses, and rounds are written as either monophonic or two-part compositions to which another part is to be added in performance by simply making an additional entry on the melody at a specified interval after the first entry has begun. The musical product is always lively and entertaining, and frequently vulgar. To produce the intended results, all texted parts must be sung, for the point of the song is the new meaning caused by singing the text against itself, and there is virtually no textual interest in a performance with only one part sung. The compositions are attractive musically and can be performed by instruments alone, of course, but instruments can also be used either alternating with vocal performance or doubled, which would still preserve the text message while providing variety of sound, for example: first time, entire caccia with only voices on the texted lines; second time, entire caccia with instruments on all parts; third time, final version with voices doubled by instruments.

THE RENAISSANCE REPERTORY

In deciding on the performance of any composition from the Renaissance period the basic principle to be applied is the same one used for medieval music: emphasize whatever is emphasized by the composer. Most Renaissance compositions have lines that are similar to one another, suggesting a performance by all voices, a family of instruments, or mixtures of voices and/or instruments that blend well enough to support the similarity of the parts. But within the general style of Renaissance music there is much variety in the music, and therefore in the possible modes of performance.

Imitative compositions

One of the most characteristic compositional techniques found in Renaissance music is imitation – the integration of some or all of the parts by the use of a single melodic shape which is stated, phrase by phrase, in one part and imitated by the others. Example 5.7 is typical of this technique, which can be found in varying degrees in many motets, Masses, and chansons from France, Spain, and Italy, and to some degree from Germany and England, between 1470 and 1600. The presence of the same melodic material in all parts strongly suggests performance by voices alone or, if instruments are to be mixed with the voices, by ones that are chosen to blend. (As discussed earlier, instruments are probably not a historically accurate choice in the performance of the Mass before the late sixteenth century.) Instruments that generally blend in with voices are viols, recorders, flutes, and trombones, although the particular voices and instruments to be used should be tested for blend and balance.

Of course it is not necessary to perform these works in the manner suggested, but the fact that the various lines are written with similar melodic and rhythmic shapes would recommend matching sounds as being the mode of performance probably uppermost in the mind of the composer, even though we know that they were not always performed that way during the Renaissance. The use of imitation in a composition – no matter to what degree – can generally be considered an indication that similarity of parts is desirable as a mode of performance. Hermann Finck (1556) gave advice for the proper vocal performance of an imitative vocal composition: the beginning voices should be clear and bright, the following voices should all sing in the same

5.7 Josquin des Prez 'Recordare, virgo mater,' bars 1–8
Josquin des Pres *Werken* ed. Albert Smijers, vol. 55, *Supplement* ed. M. Antonowycz and W. Elders, Amsterdam 1969. Used by permission of the Vereniging voor Nederlandse Muziekgeschiedenis, Drift 21, 3512 BR Utrecht, Netherlands

manner as the first, and their text underlay should conform to that of the first voice. All this should be done in order to convey the overall organization of the imitative composition.[18]

In mixing voices and instruments theoretically you may assign the parts in any combination. Experimentation has shown that the most successful combinations usually result from the following assignments: if one part only is to be sung, superius or tenor line; if two parts only, superius and tenor; if three parts, superius, tenor, and bass. The possible choice of instruments is not affected by this, but balance is always a problem when voices and instruments are mixed. Some instruments have limited flexibility of volume, which can detract from an extremely expressive imitative composition.

When choosing to mix voices and instruments in an imitative composition there is another factor that should be taken into consideration: many of these works have a single melody which can be found complete and unchanged in

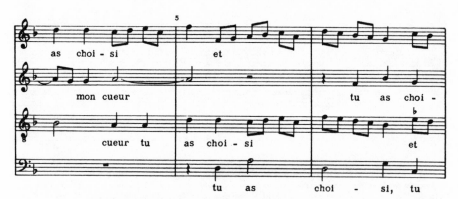

5.8 Clément Janequin 'Puisque mon cueur,' bars 1–6
A. Tillman Merritt and F. Lesure, eds. *Chansons polyphoniques* vol. 4. Editions de L'Oiseau-Lyre 1968.
Used by permission

only one of the lines; although the other lines imitate the melody, their phrases are not complete. It is usually not difficult to find by singing through the parts one by one. In sacred works such as example 5.7, the primary melody line is often a pre-existent liturgical melody which can sometimes be identified in full by consulting the *Liber Usualis*.[19] As a rule of thumb, the compositions closer to the year 1500 have the melody more often in the tenor, and those in the second half of the sixteenth century more often in the superius. In example 5.7 it is in the tenor. Even if there is a primary melody line, it is not essential to sing it, but it does deserve consideration.

In example 5.7 all lines were treated similarly by the composer. Another Renaissance technique involves pairing the lines, as can be seen in example 5.8, in which the composer has paired the soprano voice with the tenor and the alto with the bass. An all-vocal performance is always a good choice, but if you decide to mix voices and instruments, the duet nature of the composition can be emphasized either by assigning the voices to one set of paired parts and instruments to the other or by mixing one voice and one instrument for each paired set. The two pairs will sound different from one another no matter how they are performed because of the compositional technique. Experience has shown that combining voices singing soprano and alto with two instruments on tenor and bass usually results in an unbalanced sound. Attention is invariably drawn to the voices, and a soprano-alto duet distorts the composition (in much the same way that a superius-contratenor duet would unbalance a medieval composition). This is especially true if the lower parts are played by stringed instruments.

Madrigals

A sixteenth-century Italian madrigal is also usually written with similarity and equality in all parts, and because of the particular relationship between text and music in this form, an all-vocal performance appears to be even more definitely recommended. Unlike the compositions discussed above, a madrigal rarely has a complete melody in a single line. It was usually composed phrase by phrase to reflect the text, which explains the lack of the kind of melodic continuity that can be found in other forms from the Renaissance. Since the music of a madrigal is usually so closely related to the individual lines of the text, it is not surprising that some of them make little musical sense when performed without the text, although there is evidence that they were often performed by various combinations of voices and instruments – especially voices and lutes.[20]

Performance of all this polyphonic repertory by mixed ensembles of voices and instruments was apparently quite popular. All types of compositions were frequently performed with voices on some lines and lutes or viols on others, and even by solo voice on the top line and either an ensemble of single-line instruments on the lower parts or the other parts condensed for performance on a polyphonic instrument such as a lute or harpsichord. It was a custom to sing the top line as a vocal solo even when the principal melody was found in the tenor. Some of the repertory does not lend itself well to single voice and instrument(s) regardless of what the various practices may have been in the Renaissance, and modern performers must rely upon their own musical judgment to decide which compositions can be performed in this manner.

If you choose to perform a sixteenth-century imitative composition by combining instruments and voices, the following possibilities should be considered. If the work actually has a full melody in one part, for example in the tenor or superius line, it is a good idea – although not necessary – to assign that part to a voice. If there is definite pairing (see example 5.8), you should think about how you would like the pairs of voices to sound – either similar or contrasting (try it both ways). Once you have decided which parts are to be sung and which to be played you must choose instruments; the general rule is to make the parts blend, which means selecting instruments that match the voices as much as possible. The actual choice depends on the particular voices and instruments involved, but the field of choice is wide: all the following instruments will, in most circumstances, blend with voices and at the same time hold their own on a part: for the soprano line – treble viol, flute, recorder, cornetto, and violin; for the alto line – tenor viol, viola, flute, recorder, and alto sackbut; for the tenor line – tenor sackbut, tenor viol, viola, and curtal; for the bass line – sackbut, viol, and curtal. Of these, experience has shown that the usual best choices for blend with voices are viols on any line and sackbuts on the tenor and bass.

However, blend was not necessarily the only criterion for mixing voices and instruments in the sixteenth century. There is clear proof that in spite of the obvious blended style of the music writing and the theorists' stated preference for that type of performance, one of the most common combinations of instruments with voices during the century was voices and lutes – a combination that offers no blend at all.[21] Amateurs and professionals alike apparently felt comfortable mixing unlike sounds in a typical imitiative late-Renaissance composition. The music suggests certain things, and history records that they were not always observed. You are thus free to choose for yourself, with the knowledge that historical evidence is firmly on both sides of the issue.

Homophonic compositions

Many of the compositions from the Renaissance era can be roughly categorized as having a melody in one part with two or more accompanying lines: such forms as the frottola, the villancico, the lauda, and the Tenorlied can usually be described in this way. Individual compositions vary, of course; some are entirely homophonic with little or no melodic interest in any part other than the melody, such as example 5.9, while in others the accompanying lines have a large amount of independence, as in example 5.10.

An all-vocal performance is usually possible for most of this repertory, but recent research indicates that the frottola was frequently performed with solo voice on the superius melody and instruments on the other parts.[22] (In example 5.9 the text for the lower three lines is editorial.) Several of the other forms such as villancico and lauda also have a superius melody, and a solo voice with

5.9 Alessandro Coppini 'La città bella,' bars 1–6
Frank D'Accone, ed. *Music of the Florentine Renaissance* vol. 2. © 1967 by Armen Carapetyan,
American Institute of Musicology/Hänssler-Verlag, D-7303 Neuhausen-Stuttgart (West Germany) No. 63.202.
Used by permission

5.10 Ludwig Senfl 'Ich weiss nit,' bars 7–13
Ludwig Senfl *Werke* ed. Arnold Geering and Wilhelm Altwegg, vol. 4. Wolfenbüttel and Zürich,
Möseler Verlag 1940. Used by permission

instruments is recommended for much of that repertory as well, especially
when the composition is largely homophonic. The supporting instruments
should be matching sounds that will support but not overpower the solo voice
and should be chosen according to the nature of the lines, as discussed above,
pp. 75–7. It was also common practice in this repertory to reduce the lower
parts for performance on a single lute, harp, or keyboard instrument with the
top line sung. Since many of these compositions have multiple verses, another
possibility is a mixed instrumental and vocal-solo performance in which a solo
instrument replaces the solo voice by performing either a refrain or a full
verse. The solo instrument should contrast with the instrument(s) performing
the lower parts and can usually play an octave higher than written without
damage to the music. If this type of composition is to be given an all-vocal
performance, some of the notes in the lower voices will often have to be
subdivided or otherwise altered in order to fit in all the syllables without
distorting either the text or the music. Advice for underlaying the text is given
above, pp. 26–40.

Many of these suggestions can be used in performing the Tenorlied, except that since the vocal solo is an internal part it cannot be sung or performed an octave higher than written without some distortion of the composition. In example 5.10 the accompanying lines suggest an instrumental performance. They can be performed on families of instruments such as lutes and viols (recorders if transposed up an octave), which would emphasize the similar passages among the lines, but it is also historically correct to perform them on unlike instruments.

Accompanied solo voice

During the Renaissance and after there existed a specific repertory for accompanied solo voice in which the voice was accompanied by lute, keyboard, or viols.[23] The mode of performance for this repertory is specified by the composer (or publisher). Mention of it is made here only to call attention to its existence and as a reminder that the accompanying instruments are by and large interchangeable – that is, lute accompaniment can also be rearranged for harpsichord or harp with a small amount of adjustment. When performing the repertory for single voice the soloist is allowed a wider latitude in matters of tempo adjustment and should feel free to add a relatively large amount of ornamentation.

Text portrayal

Throughout the Renaissance composers increased their efforts to relate the music to the feelings and words of the poetry. This is true of all the secular music and to some extent also of the sacred. In order to interpret the vocal repertory of the Renaissance correctly, therefore, singers must become acquainted with the text and the usual conventions of the text portrayal as well. It would be difficult to give a set of rules for the expression of text content, but a few examples of the various conventions should illustrate the possibilities.

In Renaissance secular vocal music the relationship between text and music was often quite close. This is especially true of the more sophisticated polyphonic music but is also true to some extent in the lesser forms such as the frottola. The individual words (such as *laugh*, *cry*, *high*, *low*) are often given special figures, the phrases are dramatically set off from one another, and even the written pitch occasionally has significance. The musical settings function on several levels, and the relationship requires analysis if justice is to be done to the work in performance.

The most obvious examples of musical portrayal of the text are the onomatopoeic bird sounds which can be found in songs from the late Middle

Ages forward.[24] Clément Janequin made the most of this device in his well-known sixteenth-century chansons where bird calls ('Chanson des oiseaux') and battle sounds ('La guerre') are developed to the extent of virtuosity and allow the singer to interpret them by extremes of vocal techniques.

Some compositions, especially madrigals, go to extremes of melodic 'word painting' – a rather obvious device involving such passages as dotted rhythms for the word *laugh* and rapid, even motion for *run*. The singer should also look for the sudden shift of harmony, the introduction of dissonance, or the absence of harmony as devices to express surprise, anguish, or loneliness. A regular rhythmic accent – especially in triple time – is often intended to evoke the idea of dance, and the performer can help the image by singing in a rhythmic, dance-like manner. Similarly, sections of ponderous chromatic changes or chains of dissonances should be sung with a heavy voice in order to bring out the intended anguish.

In sacred music the devices are usually somewhat more reserved, but one can often find ascending scales for words or phrases referring to the Resurrection or 'ascending into heaven'; descending scales to express motion in the other direction; high notes for the words *highest* and *above*; low notes for *depth* or *lowly*, and a setting of *heaven* with the lower voices suddenly left out to give a more ethereal sound. Since the fourteenth-century Mass by Machaut, some of the essential words have been set with an abrupt change of motion to sustained chordal declamation – a device used in both sacred and secular music to call special attention to particular phrases of text.[25]

The range or tessitura of a composition also could have been planned in association with a text and, although transposition is usually a good idea in order to put a composition in a favourable range, a work such as Josquin's 'Absalom fili mi,' which utilizes only low voices and low ranges, is best left close to written pitch, since the low sounds were probably intended to be part of the text setting.

Once again my advice to the performer is to emphasize what is emphasized by the composer. In a texted composition you should begin with the words and see what musical devices are provided by the composer for their expression and what type of vocal treatment will best express the text.

Multiple-verse texts

The performance of a multiple-verse song is often a problem for early music groups. The questions are, how many verses should be sung, and must a common refrain be sung after each verse? The answers depend on the particular text involved because there are several kinds of multiple-verse poems. Some tell a story and therefore should either be sung in their entirety or be shortened with care so that they make sense. Others contain elaboration or variation on the sentiment of the first verse, so that neither sequence nor number of verses is important and the number of verses presented can be determined by programming factors. As to the performance of common refrains, again the poetry itself must be consulted. In some texts the refrain is needed to complete the thought of each verse, and in others its repetition adds intensity or even irony to the verse. Obviously when the refrain serves such an important function it must be sung each time. There are poems, however, in which the refrain does not contribute significantly to the sense of the poetry but merely fills out an established poetic form. In these works, it is possible to assign some refrains to instruments, thereby lending additional variety to the performance and giving the singer a short break.

Many ensembles avoid performing several verses of a single song for fear of boring the audience with melodic repetition. Certainly, repetition without variation would soon bore even the most dedicated early music devotee, but there are many ways in which performers can make the repeated sections interesting, including changing vocal style to reflect new textual meaning and adding ornaments to vary the melodic line. If the music is worthwhile in the first place, the performance of several verses will be welcomed by the audience. But it is the duty of the performing ensemble to explore the subtleties inherent in the lines in order to make the audience aware of the varieties within the text, melody, rhythms, and harmonies of the work.

In looking for methods of varying a presentation a singer can take the following clues from the text: the overall attitude of seriousness, sadness, or joyfulness; the general tone quality of the language (sophisticated, earthy, and so on); the emphasis of particularly expressive words in the text.

Vocal forms

In all cases, however, whether one or several verses are sung or played, care should be taken to complete the entire sequence of sections, which means paying attention to the form. The problem arises in the secular repertory, both monophonic and polyphonic, up to the end of the fifteenth century, in which different musical forms were chosen in order to reflect the various schemes of the poetry. The music is usually written in two sections which can be repeated separately, depending on the poetic form.[26] An Italian ballata, for example, has two musical sections and a sequence of verses that ends with a final performance of the first musical section. In other words, the end of the composition is not at the end of the page but in the middle. Modern editors usually mark 'Fine' at the appropriate spot, and the text lines are always numbered to show sequence, but performances that end in the wrong place can still be heard much too often.

For vocal performances, the choice of the number of verses sung and decisions to sing the refrain or have it performed by instrument should be determined according to the discussion above. For instrumental performance, all of the repeats of the individual sections need not be taken, but the section played last must be the one that would end a correctly sung performance.

Vocal-instrumental doubling

So far we have discussed performance of the early repertory with one performer to a line of music. It is also possible to add an instrument to some lines – we know that this was done in the early centuries – but doubling should not, of course, be done indiscriminately or without musical purpose. It is valid to add an instrument to a vocal line for purposes of variety, colour, or intensity, but care must be taken that the addition does not injure the composition by destroying its delicate nuances or changing its balance. The decision to double must be made on an individual basis by listening to the composition first without the doubling and then with it to see whether the piece was enhanced by the doubling (if it simply 'does not hurt,' then there is no reason to double). In general, the more complex the individual lines of a composition, the less suitable it is for doubling. For example, the delicate lines of a madrigal such as Gibbons' 'Silver Swan' or Dufay's chanson 'Se la face ay pale' would best be performed without doubling to enable the singers to bring out the subtle nuances of the lines without interference. A fairly robust and straightforward frottola such as Pesenti's 'Dal lecto me levava'[27] might, however, even be improved by certain kinds of doubling.

In the discussion of performance of the monophonic repertory I suggested that doubling either at pitch or octave (up or down) is often effective. When doubling a solo voice it is often preferable to keep the instrument an octave distant for the comfort of the singer. The individual singer may have a preference in this regard, and the particular instrument to be used – not just the type of instrument – also has to be taken into consideration. A plucked instrument at any pitch rarely disturbs the voice because its tone quality is so unlike the voice, but other sustaining instruments, especially recorders, often clash with the voice when doubling at pitch (a recorder sounds an octave higher than written pitch).

To be effective the instrument chosen for doubling should have a tone quality different from that of the singer so that when the doubling occurs a new colour is produced. To double, say, a soprano soloist at pitch with a flute that matches the voice will only reinforce the voice without changing the colour. Intensity will be gained, and some volume (desirable in some circumstances), but the intonation problems and loss of flexibility for the singer will usually not be worth the trade.

We know from Howard M. Brown that sixteenth-century Italian performance practices included doubling all parts of a chanson or madrigal at pitch and/or octave, usually with viols or lutes or a combination of these.[28] It was also the practice to double all parts on a polyphonic instrument such as lute or keyboard. This can be done from beginning to end of a composition, or as one version of several in the performance of a work with more than one verse, or in a repeated performance of a work with only a single text. (Your audience will not object to hearing a text sung twice even if there is no doubling, as long as effort is made during the repetition to express the composition differently in small ways. It is only stagnation that bores.) A simple form of variety in doubling can be achieved in this manner: first time, full madrigal (or chanson) with voices only; second time, instruments only; third time, voices and instruments. In such a performance the repetition of the composition will not be the same each time because the singers can hardly do the same things with the lines when being doubled by instruments. A composition with additional verses would allow for even more variety of presentation, such as performance of one or more verses with solo voice on one part and instruments on the others.

Should the doubling instruments be strings or winds there is occasionally a problem of losing rhythmic precision. This may be corrected by more precise articulation, but if that fails the addition of a polyphonic plucked instrument – such as lute, keyboard, or harp – may lend the needed precision (although it will also thicken the texture).

The selection of instruments for doubling voices must always be done with care to avoid overpowering the singers or clouding the text. As in all performances with voice, the text must be heard distinctly.

Performance with instruments alone

Throughout the early centuries music with a text was considered to be equally the property of instrumentalists and vocalists. The repertory for instrumental performance therefore includes virtually all the music of the early centuries, both sacred and secular, with and without text.

The vast majority of pieces intended principally for all-instrumental performance come from the sixteenth century, when the beginnings of a fairly clear separation between instrumental and vocal writing are discernible. Instrumental performance of the vocal repertory continued on into the seventeenth century, of course, but as the sixteenth century progressed changes came about in the style of music intended for instrumental performance because composers began to take notice of the capabilities of the instruments as distinct from voices, such as idiomatic passages and range. This is not to say that there was little instrumental music before 1500. The problem lies in the fact that only a small portion of the medieval instrumental repertory was written down; the instrumentalists apparently performed much of their repertory from memory and improvised a significant portion of it. The surviving iconography, for example, contains many pictures of dances accompanied variously by bagpipe, pipe and tabor, rebec, vielle, lute, and even solo drum and tambourine, and it is obvious that none of the musicians are reading music. In the later centuries the professionals continued this tradition (although to what degree is not known),[29] but at that time there was also a new written repertory for amateurs. This amateur repertory, together with a more sophisticated repertory for professionals, contributed to the sixteenth-century boom in written instrumental music.

THE MEDIEVAL REPERTORY

The small surviving instrumental repertory of the Middle Ages consists of a few textless works and thirty-seven dances,[30] which is not enough to give us a very clear picture of either the kinds of music performed by instrumentalists or the style of performance. The written accounts are frustrating in that they mention solo and ensemble performances but without giving details. What follows here, therefore, is my attempt to reconstruct a tradition from the small surviving repertory, the vague commentaries, and the iconographic evidence. The early repertory requires a great deal of imagination to bring it to life, and the following suggestions are intended to serve as stimuli for creative ideas on the part of modern performers. Many additional ideas can be found in the recorded performances of a number of fine modern ensembles, and these should be consulted for style and ideas.

Monophonic music

Pictures of instrumentalists from the Middle Ages often show from two to four musicians performing dance music, although we know from other sources that most of the dance music was monophonic. What, then, are they all playing? There are several possible answers, and they are all probably correct, which gives the modern performer a variety of methods for presenting the medieval instrumental repertory. Among the choices open to the medieval performer were the additions of drones and percussion, the invention of preludes, and the obvious possibilities of doubling and alternating performers. All these would have been used to fill out a composition.

Drones

In essence the drone note is a pitch which is compatible with the basic 'tonic' of a given composition. As the various notes and phrases of the melody first agree and then disagree with the drone, tensions are created which are relaxed at the final cadence. There is evidence that drones were a frequent element of medieval performance practice; many medieval instruments such as bagpipes, hurdy-gurdy, and flat-bridge bowed strings include drones as an ever-present element, while other instruments such as the plucked strings allow drones easily. In addition, drones are a major part of a number of surviving folk traditions from Europe to the Near East, where the harmonic tradition is as elementary as that of Western music was from the twelfth to the fourteenth centuries.

A drone can be either stationary or movable depending on the music and tastes of the performers. To find a drone one chooses the basic tonal centre of the piece by surveying the music and noting the initial note and the note most often used at major phrase endings. In all but the most unusual circumstances these notes will be the same as or harmonically compatible with the final note. If this is true, select the final note as the drone for the entire piece. If, however, long sections of the music are incompatible with the final note, a movable drone may be chosen as follows. In the dance 'Belicha', there is a shift of tonal centre. In the opening phrase (example 5.11a) the central note would be D, as it is at the ending (example 5.11b). However, in the fourth of five sections the tonal centre shifts to C for an extended period (example 5.11c). Because of the length of the contrasting tonal centre, you may wish to experiment with a drone that shifts from D to C for the duration of the contrasting section and then returns to D for the close. A single drone on D is, of course, also possible, and you should try both styles before making a choice.

Percussion[31]

Some of the pictures and accounts of the Middle Ages indicate that percussion instruments were used in connection with dance music. The most frequently seen are a small tabor with snare, a tambourine with jingles, a pair of nakers, and small cymbals. Since no drum music survives at all from these early centuries, we are again left to speculate as to what was actually done. It would seem reasonable to assume that the primary service of percussion in dance music would be to keep a regular and steady beat. In addition to this, the drummer can abstract from the rhythms of any dance a simple yet steady rhythm pattern that would assist the beat and blend with the melody.

Preludes

There is evidence that improvised instrumental preludes were often used to

5.11 Anonymous 'Belicha': a/ bars 1–5; b/ ending; c/ Quarta pars, bars 1–4

introduce medieval compositions, both vocal and instrumental. The practical usefulness of this is obvious: the prelude, usually not in strict measure, could serve to allow a string player to check the tuning of his instrument and to adjust any pegs that were not quite accurate for the mode of the piece to follow.[32] It also served to set the modal pattern and tonal centre and gave notice to the listener that the composition was about to begin. The prelude survived for centuries and eventually became the more formalized prelude of the late baroque. Throughout its time it served all these purposes.

How should a prelude be improvised? The ingredients are fairly simple and are discussed in more detail in chapter 8. It need not be long; it can be in irregular measure (alternately slow and fast); it should emphasize the modal centres and the scale of the work to follow. Beyond that, it can either be kept to a simple functional introduction or be used as a fairly dramatic show of technique.

Doubling

Early performers probably often doubled the melody either in octaves or at the unison. This tradition survives in folk music with an interesting twist: no one plays the music exactly as written. There are slight variations in notes, slight rhythmic variations, and differing ornaments applied by each of the performers simultaneously – a style known as heterophony. To accomplish this one should attempt to play in unison (or octaves) most of the time but make separate and different (often clashing) variations. The differences will often be due to idioms peculiar to the particular instruments – a rhythm pattern or quick finger ornament which is especially suited to one instrument and not necessarily to another.

Alternating

All performers need not play all the time, and interesting variations can be made by changing the combinations of instruments on successive verses of the composition. For example, if a flute and harp doubled the melody (in heterophony and at octaves) while the lute played a rhythmic drone for the first several verses, the harp could change to the drone while the lute plays the melody on the following several verses, or the lute (or harp or bowed string) could play some verses unaccompanied, even supplying its own drone accompaniment.

Let us attempt to apply these ideas to an actual medieval dance, for example 'Belicha', a portion of which appears in example 5.11 (the entire dance can be found in several editions).[33] We shall begin by selecting a likely medieval ensemble: lute, vielle, flute, and percussion. The first item of business is the prelude, and we must look to the dance for its important notes. For the opening of 'Belicha' it would seem to be D and secondarily A. A prelude suitable to this would then emphasize the scale of the opening and closing phrases by using the two important structural notes, D and A. To begin with, the prelude might even borrow a little of the melody from the dance, although they need not be melodically similar. Example 5.12 is a fairly simple prelude constructed from the known principles; that is, it is in a free rhythm, sets the scale, and emphasizes the modal structural notes, D and A. This is a fairly straightforward attempt to set the mode. More elaborate preludes can be created without much difficulty as long as the style, scale, and emphasized notes all fit the style of the dance to be introduced.

The end of the prelude can then signal the beginning of the dance, which may either begin immediately after the sounding of the final note of the prelude or be separated by the entrance of percussion or drone. The drone can be of two types: a steady drone (one long tone that continues without interruption, similar to a bagpipe) or a rhythmic drone (one in which the pitch remains the same but with a repeated rhythmic pattern). Either type is effective, and the choice will often be dictated by the instrument itself; for example, a lute or harp cannot sustain. For this dance we shall choose the sustained drone on D whenever it is to be played by the vielle and a rhythmic drone on the same pitch based on rhythms such as ♩ ♪♩ ♩ taken from the dance for lute performance. In addition, the lute can incorporate the secondary tone A in a pattern, as in example 5.13.

In fairly short dances the entire dance can be performed conveniently by a single melody instrument, an adequate choice for all dances. But for a lengthy dance such as 'Belicha', you may wish to change instruments from time to time to provide variety for the audience and avoid performer fatigue. In order to decide where instruments can be changed conveniently we must look at the structure of the dance.

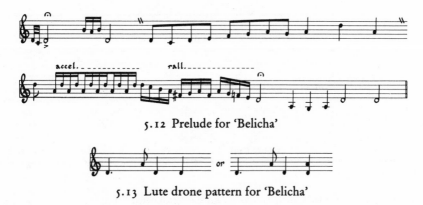

5.12 Prelude for 'Belicha'

5.13 Lute drone pattern for 'Belicha'

'Belicha' is divided into five sections called *partes*, each with the same refrain and endings. Thus the instrumentation can be changed easily at the beginning of each *pars* and also, if you wish, at each repetition of the refrain. This kind of instrumentation stresses the formal structure, a feature frequently found in medieval music. With the above-mentioned ensemble of flute, lute, vielle and percussion, one of many possible presentations could be as shown in table 6.

Many variations on this instrumentation are possible, and a different set of instruments will suggest different variations. The important point is to attempt to emphasize what is already implied in the dance itself – its rhythms, tonal centres, and formal structure. A word of caution might also be called for here in reference to too much change in instrumentation. The proposal above is intentionally rather elaborate in order to point out the opportunities for instrument variation allowed by the formal structure of the dance, and indeed the dance could sound just as attractive without so many changes of instruments. 'Belicha' is a fairly long dance (twelve to fourteen minutes) and therefore can bear that much instrument change without distracting from the music. In short French estampies, however, frequent change would be distracting, and such dances are best performed with a minimum of instrument change or even none at all.

Although the subject of improvisation will be taken up in chapter 8, some thoughts should be introduced here in connection with medieval dances. Since we have so few dances from this era, you may wish to attempt to improvise in the style of what exists. I suggest the following approach.

1 Play over many of the dances often enough to memorize some of them and to become familiar with the style and the idioms, both melodic and rhythmic, that continue to appear.

		dance			
	prelude	pars I	refrain	pars II	refrain
VIELLE		drone	melody	melody	drone
LUTE	solo	drone	drone	drone	rest
FLUTE		melody	melody	rest	melody
PERCUSSION		steady beat	steady beat	steady beat	steady beat

TABLE 6
Performance possibilities for 'Belicha'

2 Attempt to add one more *pars* to an existing short dance.

3 Once you are adept at adding *partes* to existing dances you are ready to improvise an entire dance.

4 Continue to check your ideas with the original dances to make sure you are still using the style and idioms of the original repertory.

In approaching the non-dance monophonic repertory many of the above suggestions can be followed: prelude, drone, performance by one instrument or several. Most compositions are much too short to allow a change of instrument combinations within a single verse, but a change is possible (but not required) if the piece is repeated several times. Usually the addition of percussion is effective only when the composition has a regular rhythm.

Polyphonic music

The medieval polyphonic repertory available for instrumental performance includes several dances,[34] a few scattered compositions intended for instruments,[35] and all the vocal repertory, both sacred and secular. Modern performers are free to choose either loud or soft ensembles for any of these pieces, but the decision to combine like or unlike sounds should be based on considerations discussed above (pp. 63–77 and 90–102).

When a decision has been made to perform a composition with contrasting instruments a number of points must be considered; these can be illustrated in example 5.14.

We shall arbitrarily choose to use soft instruments (although loud ones would also serve) and shall begin with the tenor line. For reasons of balance it is a good idea to consider the lines in their probable order of composition: tenor, superius, contratenor, the ranges of which are shown below.

TABLE 6 (continued)

	pars III	refrain	pars IV	refrain	pars V	refrain
dance (continued)						
VIELLE	rest	melody	drone	drone	melody	melody
LUTE	drone	drone	melody	melody	drone	drone
FLUTE	melody	melody	rest	rest	melody	melody
PERCUSSION	steady beat	steady beat	steady beat	steady beat	steady beat	steady beat

5.14 Anonymous 'Orsus, vous dormés trop,' bars 1–18

Willi Apel, ed. *French Secular Compositions of the Fourteenth Century* vol. 3. © 1972 by Armen Carapetyan, American Institute of Musicology/Hänssler-Verlag, D-7303 Neuhausen-Stuttgart (West Germany) No. 69.010. Used by permission

TABLE 7
Suggested instrumentations for example 5.14

SUPERIUS	recorder	rebec	gittern/citole
CONTRATENOR	gittern	citole	harp
TENOR	harp	lute	vielle

Because the tenor line is fairly sustained we shall assign it to a vielle (although other possibilities exist and will be discussed later). This will bring out the line firmly and supply a strong harmonic foundation line to the piece. Since the upper part carries the principal melodic interest in this piece it should be assigned to an instrument that not only contrasts with the vielle but clearly holds its own in balance against the tenor. For contrast we shall select a recorder. With the two most important lines instrumented we must now select an instrument for the contratenor, the least important line. In this case the part involves stop-and-go sections (see, for example, bars 13–17), a characteristic of many contratenor parts and one that works best on a plucked instrument. Our choice for this part, then, could be either a lute-type instrument or a harp, and the choice should be made depending upon the relative volume of the instruments available. Some harps have a rather loud tone, which in this case would distract from the tenor line and might overbalance it. It is important that the contratenor not overbalance the tenor line, and therefore if a harp is chosen it should be one with a tone lighter than that of the vielle.

If this instrumentation is selected, one additional point to consider is that the superius line calls for the next-to-lowest note on the tenor recorder, which may not sound out clearly. The most logical solution is to play the line up an octave on an alto recorder, although this is not necessarily the best answer in every case. For this piece an octave transposition for the superius line will be acceptable; it is melodically independent of the other two lines and never goes below the other two to become the harmonic bass.

Of course these instruments are not the only possibilities. A treble plucked string or bowed string could just as easily handle the superius line, and the bottom two lines could be assigned to other instruments as well. Depending on the relative volumes of the particular instruments chosen, assignments shown in table 7 are also possible. What is important is that the line fit the instrument, that the instruments assigned to the superius and tenor lines balance one another and that the contratenor remain in the background, and that the instruments selected have contrasting tone colours in order to bring out the individuality of the lines.

The instrumentation does not always work out as easily as this, and we must be ready to adjust to a variety of situations. What could we do if, for example, the tenor part of a fourteenth-century work such as example 5.14 called for several notes lower than exist on the only medieval bowed string instrument available? There are several solutions that might be suitable depending on the composition under consideration.

1 Transpose the piece up far enough that the range of the part falls within the range of the instrument. There was nothing sacred about the written pitch in the Middle Ages (although in the Renaissance it was sometimes a different matter). Much of the evidence we have suggests that the notation was chosen mostly for the convenience of presentation on a staff, but that there was often no specific pitch in mind. The pitch at which any work sounds musical depends to some degree on its instrumentation; change the instrumentation and often the pitch should change (and vice versa). A serious early musician should learn the skill of transposing for this reason. It greatly extends instrumental possibilities – an important factor for ensembles with limited instrumental resources.

2 Choose a light-toned Renaissance or baroque viol that has the needed range. To make a correct choice of a substitute instrument you must have some idea of the sound of the correct instrument and then make every effort to approximate that sound. This means, for example, not using the full potential volume of a baroque viol or a violin when they are chosen to substitute for a medieval vielle, or, if substituting a baroque lute for a medieval one, using a plectrum and avoiding the polyphonic capabilities of the baroque instrument.

3 Change the lute or harp that does have the range from the contratenor to the tenor line. If the plucked string and the bowed string simply exchange parts you may solve the range problem but create the balance problem discussed above; the contratenor must not overbalance the other lines. This can sometimes be solved by simply leaving out the contratenor, as suggested above (pp. 97–8).

Finally, if none of the above suggestions solve your range problem and at the same time allow the work to be performed musically, simply put the work back in the file. There is enough music available that will fit your ensemble well without musical compromise.

THE RENAISSANCE REPERTORY

Dance

After the fourteenth-century dances, the next sizeable collection of dance music appears in the Renaissance beginning in the sixteenth century. A number of dance collections were published for four- and five-part instrumental ensemble, especially in France, which can be approached in a similar way to the vocal music already discussed.[36] Because of the similarity in the lines of the sixteenth-century dance in example 3.3 the best choice for instrumentation is like-sounding instruments – either loud or soft, but not mixed – or blended sounds such as recorders and viols. These dances do not seem to be harmed by transposition, and thus moving the pitch up a fifth, an octave, or even two octaves to fit the available matching instruments creates no problem. (Two precautions: do not transpose only some of the parts without checking to be sure that the harmonies are not inverted; and transposing anything down very far tends to muddy the sonority.) It is also possible to substitute or double a lute or harpsichord in these dances, as was the sixteenth-century custom, and a very attractive instrumentation can result from this. For example, in a set of dances such as example 3.3 the instrumentation could be a family of recorders (up an octave) with a lute doubling at pitch. The lute could play along on just the melody at times or on just the lower part, substitute for all parts or just the lower three parts, and even remain silent through some section repeats (although you would not want to try more than one or two of these variations in any one dance). These same possibilities exist with harpsichord or harp as well.

As with the medieval dances, it is always possible to add percussion. A tabor or tambourine can be used quite effectively to lend a steady, regular beat to the music. Percussionists must remember that their principal job is to present a simple, steady beat; beyond that they may select a few rhythms from those in the dance melody as long as the overall effect is one of percussion *support*.

When the dances were played for dancing, the sections were apparently repeated not once but many times. Variety was obtained by inventing ornamentation which was changed each time the section was repeated. This is still an attractive way to present the music even in concert, with each section repeated four to six times and new ornamentation introduced – perhaps increasing in virtuosity – with each repeat (see chapter 7 on ornamentation). This should be considered an opportunity for instrumentalists to display their invention and technique, as it was by the performers in the early centuries (and as it is by twentieth-century jazz musicians). It helps to keep the music alive and becomes a never-ending challenge to performers at all levels.

The dances were apparently played in variable sets of contrasting metres and dancing styles; for example, a pavan in duple metre followed by a galliard in triple, then perhaps a few other contrasting dances, and finally a very quick dance, although we do not yet know much about which dances were

5.15 Heinrich Isaac 'La Martinella,' bars 44–50

Johannes Wolf, ed. *Denkmäler der Tonkunst in Österreich* vol. 28. Graz, Akademische Druck- u. Verlagsanstalt 1907 (1959). Used by permission

commonly associated with one another or even the number of dances commonly played in a set. When performed in concert they can be played separately or several contrasting dances can be presented as a 'suite,' beginning with a stately dance and ending with a quick one, all assembled as contrasting metres and characters according to a common tonality. They could be introduced by a prelude – either improvised or selected from the existing sixteenth-century repertory – and linked together with hardly a break.

Non-dance repertory

There are several different varieties of instrumental music from the Renaissance other than the dance repertory.[37] A number of works from the fifteenth century come down to us without texts, and at least some of them must have been intended originally as instrumental music. The repertory from the mid-fifteenth century Burgundian court, for example, includes many untexted works.[38]

The basic approach to performing these instrumental compositions is the same as that for an instrumental performance of a vocal work. Examples 5.15 and 5.16 illustrate the approach; both works appear with titles rather than text incipits, and as Brown has observed, this suggests that they may have been conceived originally for instrumental performance.[39]

'La Martinella' (example 5.15), contains a number of sections which are imitative or quasi-imitative in all parts. Since in this way the composer stresses the homogeneity of the lines, the optimum performance ensemble would be either a family of instruments or instruments that blend well. Also to be taken into consideration is the fact that all parts contain passages of relatively long notes sounding against more rapidly moving notes in the other parts. This is an important consideration in choosing instruments because in this piece the

5.16 Alexander Agricola 'Comme femme,' bars 1–3
Alexander Agricola *Opera Omnia* ed. Edward R. Lerner, vol. 5. © 1969 by Armen Carapetyan,
American Institute of Musicology/Hänssler-Verlag, D-7303 Neuhausen-Stuttgart (West Germany) No. 62.205.
Used by permission

long notes are important thematic material and therefore must 'sound out' against the other parts. If they were merely filling a harmonic function while the principle thematic interest was in the moving parts the question of balance would not be quite so important. A combination of, for example, a lute against two sustaining instruments would be a poor choice for this work because the sustained thematic material would be clear when played by the sustaining instruments but covered when played by the lute, thus distorting the imitative balance intended by the composer. Acceptable choices for this composition would include those shown in table 8, or combinations of other bowed strings with flute or recorder, provided care is taken to note the actual sounding pitch of the winds.

The music of example 5.16 suggests that the superius and bassus parts should be performed on matching instruments because of the amount of material shared. The tenor (middle line) of this work, however, is somewhat different from the other two voices, and its material should be brought out by a contrasting instrumental sound. It must be remembered that the tenor is the basis of the composition, and so the instrumentation should allow this line to be heard at least as clearly as the other parts. A lute on the tenor line against two viols, for example, would make a good contrast only if the lute chosen had a robust sound and the viols were light enough to keep the balance. Some suggestions for the instrumentation of this work are shown in table 9.

TABLE 8
Suggested instrumentations for example 5.15

SUPERIUS	tenor viol	soprano recorder*	tenor recorder
TENOR	tenor viol	alto recorder*	tenor viol
CONTRATENOR	bass viol	tenor recorder*	bass viol

*or flutes transposed up an octave or a fifth

TABLE 9
Suggested instrumentations for example 5.16

SUPERIUS	lute	treble viol	flute*
TENOR	harp or viol	lute	portative organ or psaltery*
BASSUS	lute	bass viol	vielle*

*transposed up an octave

Late Renaissance instrumental forms

Throughout the sixteenth century a number of new names for instrumental music came into existence. Some suggest the origin of the melodic content, such as a canzona, which presumably began as an instrumental arrangement of a chanson melody; others suggest function, such as prelude or intonazione, or describe the style of the writing, such as ricercare, which appears to be named after the improvisatory style and perhaps the repeat of thematic material. Performers of early music should be aware of the original function of the instrumental work they intend to play because it may suggest certain performance ideas: toccatas should be regal, preludes should be free and dramatic, for example, although by the mid-sixteenth century many of these names seem to have become interchangeable. The selection of instrumentation should continue to be dictated by the individual musical lines of the composition, that is, similar lines should have similar sounds while contrasting lines must have contrasting sounds.

Instrumental works can also be found in the style of the frottola or Tenorlied (examples 5.9 and 5.10), with all parts supporting a single melody line, or with paired or grouped parts (as in example 5.8). These features of a composition are never difficult to find because they should only be taken into consideration when the composer has made them obvious. When a clear attempt by the composer to blend or contrast is recognized, performers should seriously consider a mode of performance that will emphasize those elements which the composer has emphasized, and a thoughtful choice of instruments can aid in this effort.

You should not feel restricted solely to the suggested method of determining instrumentation if practical considerations demand otherwise. Brown has shown that Renaissance musicians were not always sensitive to the intentions of the composer; there are documents telling of instrumentation, doublings, and ornamentation that all but destroy the finer elements of a composition.[40] It is undeniable, however, that the intentions of the composer are a good place to start, and if after identifying these, other considerations have to enter into instrument choice, then at least you will have begun by considering the requirements of the music and will be aware of the extent of the compromises you intend to make.

Instrumental performance of the vocal repertory

The principles for selecting instruments for the Renaissance vocal repertory are those discussed in chapter 4 (pp. 77–8), and are basically the same as those used for vocal performance: families of instruments or matching sounds to achieve similarity of parts, contrasting sound combinations to support the differences.

An imitative composition such as example 5.7 would suggest performance by a family of instruments such as viols, lutes, or recorders or by matching sounds such as trombones and cornettos, viols and recorders (or flutes), and so on. We do know that imitative compositions were sometimes performed with unmatching sounds, and modern performers are not historically wrong to choose that kind of instrumentation. Certain kinds of combinations, however, can cause serious musical problems especially a mixture of plucked sounds with any other. In these combinations the individual parts are always heard as separate, even in homophonic sections written to sound as a series of chords. The degree to which this distorts the music depends upon the composition and the particular instruments chosen; not all imitative compositions or all contrasting combinations present this problem. Before choosing contrasting instruments for an imitative piece it would be wise to listen to it performed with matching sounds so that the amount of distortion caused by contrasting instruments can be assessed.

Some degree of contrast is sometimes called for, as in the type of voice pairing found in example 5.8. Any number of combinations of instruments are possible, depending upon the amount of separation and blend desired. A combination of plucked strings with either bowed strings or winds will emphasize the separateness of the pairs, whereas a mixture of winds and bowed strings or a combination of different-sounding plucked strings or winds or bowed strings would provide a more blended sound. Once again the amount of separation indicated in the music itself will help you decide how much contrast to use, and experimentation is always a good idea.

For compositions in which the melody stands apart from the other lines, such as examples 5.9 and 5.10, contrast seems to be definitely called for. The melody can best be brought out by assigning it to one type of instrument while the other lines are performed by a family of a different type, such as solo recorder with viols or solo bowed string with lutes. This kind of composition also lends itself easily to reduction of the accompanying lines for performance by lute, harp, or keyboard with the melody sounded on any contrasting instrument.

When the melody is found in an internal line, as in example 5.10, care must be taken that it is not overpowered by the instruments assigned to the accompanying lines. A sackbut on this line against strings or woodwinds would work very well. A krummhorn is also a possibility as a contrasting instrument for a Tenorlied melody line if the range is suitable; there is evidence that this instrument was popular in Germany throughout the sixteenth century. As a general rule, however, krummhorns work best in family; when one is used as part of a broken consort it often calls attention to itself, thus destroying the equality of the parts. In a work such as example 5.10 some emphasis of the tenor line is called for, and thus a krummhorn would be a possible choice.[41] Performance by a family of instruments or by blending combinations is always possible and historically authentic for music of the Renaissance period.

SPECIALIZED REPERTORY

Music designated for certain instruments or with technical requirements best suited for a certain instrument can be found as early as the fourteenth century. As the centuries progressed, the instrumental repertory increased in quantity and in its exploitation of the individual technical idiosyncracies of the different instruments. By the end of the sixteenth century there were substantial printed repertories available in all European countries for lute and keyboard instruments and a modest amount for vihuela, guitar, cittern, and viol.

The purpose of this section is to identify and discuss some of the repertory – especially the earliest examples – which is particularly suitable for certain instruments, and although collections of music are identified here as probably written for a particular instrument, they need not be considered exclusively the property of that instrument. The musicians of the early centuries borrowed freely from one another's repertories, adjusting and rearranging whenever necessary, and some of the music described here can be adapted easily for other instruments. More extensive lists of collections and bibliographies are given in chapter 11.

Keyboard

Keyboard instruments have a repertory dating from the end of the fourteenth century. The music is actually for any instrument capable of sounding more than a single note at a time, which makes much of it suitable for positive organ, harpsichord, and clavichord. Some of this repertory can be played on a harp, and even on a lute, since the change from single-line to polyphonic performance on that instrument began some time in the fifteenth century. Performance of this music by two or more single-line instruments is often possible and as successful musically as when it is performed on a single polyphonic instrument.

The earliest keyboard sources are the Robertsbridge Codex from the late fourteenth century and the Faenza Codex[42] from the early fifteenth. All the music is in two parts – a florid upper line and a less demanding lower line – and, except for the eleven sacred intabulations which suggest performance on an organ, it is not clear that the music was definitely intended for solo keyboard. Both manuscripts include dances and highly ornamented intabulations of vocal works, most of which can be performed successfully on many instruments or pairs of instruments. Because of the nature of the voice-crossing in some of the Faenza compositions, if a keyboard is chosen, a two-manual instrument is sometimes required.

Two- and three-part writing suitable for any of a number of instruments can also be found among the more than 250 works in the so-called Buxheimer Orgelbuch,[43] mixed with compositions displaying a measure of idiomatic keyboard writing, such as chords or lines designated for pedals. The Buxheimer is an excellent source of fifteenth-century preludes, intonations, and dances which are welcome items for fifteenth-century programs because of the almost total absence of this repertory in any other source. The intabulations of vocal works from all three manuscripts can be performed on their own as separate works or incorporated into a performance of the vocal originals. In the last-mentioned function two cautions should be expressed: there is sufficient variation between the intabulations and the vocal versions that they usually cannot be performed simultaneously, although the intabulations can serve well as separate instrumental verses in a performance of the vocal version; and you may have to transpose one of the versions because the intabulations have often been transposed to a range more convenient for the intended instrument. The Robertsbridge repertory contains intabulations of three sacred works from the early fourteenth century, possibly by di Vitry, the Faenza has works by both French and Italian composers of the fourteenth century including Machaut and Landini, and the Buxheimer offers a rich selection of works by fifteenth-century composers including Dunstable, Dufay, and Ciconia.

Early works more idiomatic for keyboard are contained in the collection of ricercare, motetti, and canzoni by Marc Antonio Cavazzoni[44] printed in 1523 and collections of French and Italian dances printed respectively by

Attaingnant in 1530 and Gardano in 1551.[45] From the mid-sixteenth century forward collections of dances and more sophisticated compositions abound for keyboard instruments in general as well as functional works such as preludes, intonations, and toccatas for church organ. As Howard Ferguson points out, keyboard preludes are directly related to the medieval preludes discussed earlier in this chapter.[46] They were originally improvised and generally free in style. Many of them allow a very free approach to arpeggios, scaler flourishes, and the like and are best performed without strict measure. Intonations are similarly constructed and serve to set the mode for whatever is to follow. Toccatas have a dramatic flourish; they were originally intended to serve as processional music and therefore have contrasting sections with frequent cadences to allow the performer to end immediately if the procession has concluded or to go on to another section (or repeat one) if more music is needed. Girolamo Frescobaldi's directions for the performance of toccatas in his publication of 1614[47] suggest that free interpretation is necessary and that the performer is welcome to select or omit sections at will.

Deserving of special mention are the themes and variations found in late sixteenth- and early seventeenth-century collections such as the Fitzwilliam Virginal Book.[48] These are written variations for amateurs which are presumably in the style improvised by the professionals of the day. After becoming acquainted with the variation style in these collections, modern performers should feel free to add new variations to those already found in the collections. It will be noticed that these variations usually retain the phrase lengths of the original theme and the general harmonic sequence. The variations lie mainly in rhythmic, textural, and division-type inventions.[49]

Lute

Although the lute was one of the most popular instruments in the Middle Ages, a separate repertory was not written for it until the sixteenth century. Until the fifteenth century the lute was a single-line instrument and apparently performed the monophonic repertory and one line of the polyphonic (its particular suitability to fourteenth- and fifteenth-century contratenor lines has been noted earlier in this chapter). The change from use of a plectrum to a polyphonic finger technique in the fifteenth century made available some of the repertory in the earliest keyboard manuscripts; indeed, several scholars claim that at least one of the Buxheimer compositions was intended specifically for lute. For those two-part works not easily adaptable for solo lute, lute duet is a possibility and was a common ensemble.

By the beginning of the sixteenth century a specialized lute notation had developed in all countries. From that time forward we have a large repertory of dance music, vocal intabulations, ricercares, canzonas, and so forth written to explore the particular capabilities of the lute and notated in lute tablature. The earliest of the sixteenth-century repertory consists of vocal intabulations, instrumental compositions for one and two lutes, and accompaniment for solo voice by Francisco Spinacino, Joan Ambrosio Dalza, Francisco Bossinensis, Arnolt Schlick, and Vincenzo Capirola,[50] all from the first twenty years of the century. Modern editions of sixteenth-century repertory are published regularly and notices of new releases can be found in the lute journals.[51] In addition, the American Lute Society has a microfilm catalogue of unpublished lute music which is available to members.

Various ensembles

Other than the specialized collections already mentioned, a small amount of music was written for solo viol, and there were several collections of duets that could be played by a variety of instruments[52] and a number of instrumental collections for three or more parts that were designed for ensemble playing by any instrument combinations. We know from other sources that families or matching instruments were the preferred combinations, but the prints do not specify. Instead, they state in various languages that the music is suitable for any combination of instruments. Music of this kind – that is, instrumental ensemble collections containing a variety of forms and of various degrees of difficulty – is available from the early years of the century.[53] The various modern-day recorder societies make much of this music available either in printed editions or in manuscript copy available at low cost upon request. These compositions are often arranged with the parts in several different clefs to accommodate a variety of instrument combinations.[54]

Music for Large Ensembles and Dramatic Productions

 E SHALL COMPLETE our discussion of the early repertory by looking at two separate categories of music; that which was intended for ensembles larger than one-on-a-part, and a variety of music that can involve dramatic production.

Music for chorus

Up until the late Middle Ages polyphonic sacred music was always performed by soloists, but by the mid-fifteenth century the tradition was changing and the choirs in many churches were being assigned the polyphonic Masses and motets. The style of the compositions themselves changed from the rhythmically complex and separated lines of the Middle Ages intended for soloists to smoother, less intricate rhythms and similar lines which allowed for, or was intended for, choral performance (see the discussion of English sacred polyphony above, pp. 96–7).

The repertory of sacred music suitable for chorus includes compositions by practically every prominent composer from the fifteenth century forward. Modern performers need only select a composer and they will find a variety of motets, Masses, and other sacred items such as psalm settings, Magnificats, and Lamentations from which to choose. There are rarely any directions in the music to indicate the size of the performing group, and thus in modern performance of this repertory the decision as to whether any particular sacred composition from the fifteenth century should be considered for soloists or for chorus must be made on an individual basis, according to whether the lines are more medieval or Renaissance. Although soloists can sing either style, a chorus would be quite uncomfortable with the rhythmic figures of the complex medieval style, and many of the subtle nuances would be lost.

Research into the sizes of church choirs reveals that in the fifteenth century they tended to range from ten to twenty singers, and in the sixteenth century from fifteen to forty, generally growing larger as the era progressed.[1] The size varied, of course, depending upon the relative size and importance of the church, but these figures will give some idea of the possibilities. Distribution of the voices appears to have emphasized the outer parts by assigning a larger number of singers to bass and soprano lines. A twelve-voice choir, for example, would apparently have been divided as follows for a four-part composition: five (or four) sopranos, two altos, two tenors, and three (or four) basses. In 1447 the chapel choir at Cambrai was made up of seven sopranos, four contratenors, five tenors, seven contrabasses, and six boys,[2] and in 1448 it consisted of six sopranos, three contratenors, three tenors, seven contrabasses, and six boys.

The boys were a separate ensemble, but on some occasions they apparently performed polyphony with the men. It is not clear what part or parts the boys would sing on those occasions; the addition of six voices to the soprano line would surely have overbalanced that part. Some of the boys could also have sung the contratenor line, which would have allowed a distribution of voices similar to those quoted above. For compositions with five or more parts, the voice distribution would presumably have been in the same proportions, for example, seven sopranos, four altos, four first tenors, five second tenors, and six basses.

In a modern performance the distribution of voices given above should be observed. An all-male chorus is preferable since it was the sound the composer expected to hear. If necessary, women's voices can be used, but they should approximate the pure sound of boys' voices to help reproduce the intended Renaissance sonority.

For some time it was believed that instruments were used with Renaissance church choirs in the performance of polyphony, but I have already cited recent research which suggests that instruments were rarely used in church performance until late in the sixteenth century.[3] The presence of any instrument in church other than the organ would have been highly unusual. The correct historical performance of sacred music, therefore, is with voices alone. It is possible that motets could have been performed occasionally for private, non-liturgical devotional purposes, and on those occasions instruments could have been employed; however, this would not have been true of the Mass, which would have been sung only in church as part of the liturgy, usually by unaccompanied voices.

VOICE AND ORGAN

Many churches had organs which served in a variety of ways, such as playing processionals and recessionals, providing instrumental solos during the service, and occasionally performing in conjunction with voices, although even then the organist usually performed solo. There is evidence, though, that in England during the fourteenth century the organ supported the voices on some occasions during the singing of the liturgy.[4] When performing with voices the organ on rare occasions doubled the vocal lines of motets or hymns, but until the end of the sixteenth century it more often played independently in *alternatim* style. There is evidence that the organ would alternate with the chorus in performing verses of psalms, hymns, and even sections of the Mass Ordinary such as the Kyrie, as described above (p. 33). Only a small amount of the instrumental music survives from organ *alternatim* performances[5] because the organist apparently improvised a polyphonic setting around the notes of the chant for the phrases he performed. For the capable organist who has studied the style of sixteenth-century improvised counterpoint, this would make an interesting and highly authentic mode of performance (see discussion below, pp. 190–4). The other possible *alternatim* performance for this repertory is alternation between polyphonic sections and choral unison of the chant portion in the manner outlined above (p. 33). This could be done by having the chorus as a whole sing both polyphony and chant or by separating the choir into a chant group and a polyphonic group.

CONDUCTING

The Renaissance sacred repertory, although intended for chorus, must be treated by the conductor in a manner different from the choral music of later centuries. The compositions were written to accommodate more than one singer to a part, but they often retain the independence of line associated with music for soloists. In the imitative Renaissance style the lines all share common melodic-rhythmic patterns, but only occasionally do they have the same melodic curve at the same time, and the conductor can often do little for the chorus as a whole other than accurately mark the passage of time. Each line must usually be rehearsed separately before all the parts can be put together. This music cannot be conducted in the same manner as, say, a work by Mozart or Brahms, because at any one point each line often traces a separate expressive pattern. The conductor must be careful to bring out the polyphonic nature of these works and avoid the temptation to force the parts into a unison expressive pattern that would destroy the individuality of the lines. Not all Renaissance sacred music is written in the imitative style, of course, and even those that have a preponderance of imitation often have passages of homophony which allow the choir to express the music as a unified group. But the conductor must be careful to understand the compositional style so that he can help the chorus express the music as it would have been expressed in the Renaissance.

Sacred music, especially the fairly lengthy motets and Mass movements, offers great variety on both the large and the small scale. There are often contrasting sections within a single movement, set apart by noticeably different rates of speed, as well as contrasts on smaller levels from phrase to phrase. The process of interpreting this music – as with all vocal music – begins with determining the overall tone of the text, for example supplication in the Kyrie and exultation in the Gloria. In some cases, especially in large motets, it will be found that the text includes a change of mood. The key words should be sought out to ascertain if the composer has decided to emphasize them with special musical figures. The next step is to look at the musical phrases themselves to see the kinds of contrasts the composer has built in either to support the text or simply to add variety.

THE PROTESTANT REPERTORY

A separate repertory of sacred music developed in the newly formed German Protestant church beginning in the early sixteenth century. The texts are in German rather than Latin, and compositional styles include several new types of chorales and psalm settings in addition to those already discussed. To encourage the congregation to participate in the singing, simple melodies were composed which were then set in one of two basic styles: either a choral style which could be sung in all parts or a chorale-like melody to be sung with contrapuntal accompaniment by instrument(s). The melody in both types can be in either the tenor or the soprano line, and performance possibilities include chorus alone or chorus with instruments. The instrument choices include organ or families of winds or strings functioning either as accompaniment or as doubles for the vocal parts. Repertory can be found in chapter 11 under Germany, fifteenth–sixteenth century.

CEREMONIAL MOTETS, DIVIDED CHOIR

The large ceremonial motets from the end of the sixteenth century provide a sizeable repertory for choral performance both with and without instruments. During this period churches began adding instruments to the choir for performances on special occasions, and composers provided a repertory that would accommodate this. The best known of the large works are by Giovanni Gabrieli – especially his motets for divided choir.

Although all Renaissance music makes use of contrast in various ways, works for divided choir emphasize contrast as an essential part of the compositional technique. This can be seen developed to the extreme in Gabrieli's late works such as the well-known *In Ecclesiis* (example 6.1). This work calls for three different groups of performers: the first four-part group marked 'voce' is for SATB soloists; the second set, also SATB, is marked 'capella,' which means chorus; and the last six parts are marked individually for instruments. The whole is accompanied by organ. The contrasts that can be seen in just the few bars given in example 6.1 include: three contrasting groups (soloists, chorus, instruments); three styles of writing in bars 116 and 117 (extremely ornate, moderately decorated, and sustained); and an abrupt change of rhythmic style from complex and multi-level in bars 116 and 117 to simple and dance-like in bar 119. Other types of contrast found in compositions of this kind consist of the use of the different groups alone or in various combinations such as setting off a single voice from one group against another full group: for example, capella tenor against the instrumental ensemble. Since the groupings produce-contrasting sounds the composer can often make extensive use of a small amount of material by giving a phrase first to one group and then to another. The varieties available in the sonority lessen the need for variety in thematic content.

In a work such as *In Ecclesiis* the performers need only bring out the contrasts built into the piece. In this work it would be possible to double either of the vocal ensembles with instruments, although to double the soloists would tend to compromise their essential contrasting quality of solo sound (and the kinds of expression a soloist can give a line). If the chorus is to be doubled the instruments should be selected to contrast with the instruments called for in the third group. Possible choices would be either a family of viols or even flutes or recorders at the octave. The instruments required for the third group are specified by name, but the 'violino' part would require an instrument with a range similar to that of a modern viola, and a bass trombone would be needed for the lowest line. The organ part furnished by the composer is only a figured bass in the original. According to Denis Arnold[6] the organ accompaniment in this situation was in simple chords, as shown in his editing of this example. The more flamboyant continuo style was not used when accompanying large ensembles.

Not all divided-choir pieces are as specific about personnel as *In Ecclesiis*. The contrast in some is achieved by the composer's distribution of voice parts –

6.1 Giovanni Gabrieli 'In Ecclesiis,' bars 116–20

Giovanni Gabrieli *Opera Omnia* ed. Denis Arnold, vol. 5. © 1969 by Armen Carapetyan,
American Institute of Musicology/Hänssler-Verlag, D-7303 Neuhausen-Stuttgart (West Germany) No. 61.205.
Used by permission

120

for example, mostly high voices in one choir and low voices in the other. For divided-choir compositions with equal voice distribution a contrast can be made by the numbers of singers assigned to a part – for example, one choir with four to six voices to a part and another with one or two voices to a part. If instrumental doubling is desired the choice of instruments should be contrasting families of sounds. The customary doubling favoured the use of trombones with cornetto, families of viols or violins, and sometimes recorders or flutes and curtals. There is no evidence that trumpets were ever used in these compositions.

It is effective, although not necessary, to separate the choirs physically from one another when performing a divided-choir piece, but care must be taken in this regard. Even in the best acoustics separating them by more than 50 metres will cause synchronization problems that could spoil the performance. Separation by as little as two or three metres will give the desired effect of opposing sound forces.

The Gabrieli repertory is not all that is available for divided choir. Motets, psalms, and Magnificats by Willaert, Lasso, Schütz, Praetorius, and others were written for two or more groups with and without instruments. A sizeable repertory also exists for combinations of choir and soloists other than divided choir. The Old Hall and Eton manuscripts[7] have already been mentioned in this regard; it would seem to be a technique frequently found in English music of the late Middle Ages and Renaissance. A number of hymns and motets from the fifteenth century employ *alternatim* between unison chant verses and polyphonic soloist settings, and entire sections of some fifteenth-century Masses appear to call for a change from choir to soloists. This is not always specified in the music, but the change to a more rhythmically complex style would suggest soloists. An example of this can be found in the 'Benedictus' of Dufay's *Missa: Ave Regina Caelorum*, where the rhythms become more complex just at the point where the parts are reduced from four to two, similar to the change seen in example 5.5.

SECULAR MUSIC

Apart from special ceremonial occasions such as the *intermedii* described below (pp. 143–4), ensemble performance of secular music was apparently mostly intended for soloists. This does not mean, however, that a chorus cannot perform at least some of the repertory. The imitative chanson and madrigal repertory with detailed text association and delicate nuance is best left to soloists, but the more homophonic repertory from the Renaissance lends itself to choral performance, and there is quite a large selection in all languages that fits this description: frottolas, villancicos, vilanellas, and non-imitative chanson of several styles. The compositions that work best are those which require the broad expression that one can expect from a chorus as opposed to the tiny nuances best executed by solo voice.

If desired for contrast, the vocal parts can be doubled by instruments according to the principles already discussed: families of instruments as first choice; blended sounds as second choice. For a large choir, doubling by instruments at pitch, for example viols, can be augmented by additional doubling at the octave by recorders or flutes. After the mid-sixteenth century it was also the practice to add chordal accompaniment instruments such as lutes and keyboards.

Large instrumental ensembles

Large instrumental ensembles were rarely used in the early centuries other than for outdoor processions where, one would gather from the descriptions, the colourful pageantry was of more importance than musical values. From as early as the thirteenth century, fanfares performed by four to ten trumpets apparently welcomed visitors and returning nobles and signalled various ceremonial occasions, although we do not know what they played. But apart from that type of occasion, instrumental performance of either vocal or instrumental music was usually by soloists until the end of the sixteenth century. Some of the material can be made to serve for large groups, and the principles of selection are the same as for music for large vocal ensembles: compositions with comparatively broad homophonic phrases lend themselves to larger groups more easily than those which require delicate nuance. In addition to the vocal repertory mentioned above, some of the dances found in the Susato, Gervaise, and Attaingnant collections[8] can serve, although obviously no ornamentation can be applied in group performance.

Intonation – one of the most difficult problems with instruments of any era – is especially a problem with doubled early instruments, more so with woodwinds than with strings and brass. Thus, if a large ensemble performance is unavoidable because of programming needs, the problems can best be minimized by subdividing the ensemble into several smaller ensembles of like instruments, which would preferably be one to a part. In this way the impression of a massive ensemble can be given without encountering all of the intonation problems. For example, a performance of a set of four dances can be given with three different groups of instruments – families of recorders, viols, and sackbuts and cornetto. Each family could be assigned one dance to perform by itself with the entire ensemble heard together only on the last (and shortest) dance. On the perils of combining instruments it is perhaps fitting to quote Bottrigari (1594) here: 'Musicians should abstain from concerti [mixing together keyboards, strings and winds] and not try in the future to make connoiseurs of music laugh at the great confusion of different instruments, by multiplying which they hope to work miracles.'[9]

The best advice concerning massed instrumental ensembles is to avoid them. Early music is chamber music. For those who prefer larger sounds I suggest the extensive repertory from other centuries written with large ensembles in mind.

Dramatic productions

Music is often called upon to assist in dramatic productions, and the early centuries were no exception. For the modern early music ensemble willing to assist in these productions they offer a legitimate opportunity to present music in a setting other than the usual concert format and to reveal to the public yet another view of the art of the early centuries.

We know that music was present at various kinds of plays and dramatic presentations all through history. The development of opera at the very end of the Renaissance was the largest full union of drama and music, but throughout the Middle Ages and Renaissance there were other associations that spanned the extremes from total use of music in liturgical drama to the incidental song or dance in mystery plays and secular court drama.[10]

LITURGICAL DRAMA

Liturgical drama offers an extremely flexible mode of dramatic production. Dramas surviving from the tenth to the sixteenth centuries include subjects such as the Resurrection, the birth of Christ, and the miracles of St Nicholas. Ensembles can choose short dramas such as the simple one-scene Resurrection play which can be performed by four soloists in less than fifteen minutes or large dramas of several scenes lasting nearly an hour which require ten to fifteen soloists, chorus, and instrumentalists. A number of these are currently available in modern editions[11] offering varying amounts of staging detail, but modern performers must still fill out the details of staging and music according to what is known of historical style and using some creative imagination.

The earliest liturgical dramas from the tenth to the twelfth centuries were performed in a church setting under conditions that probably did not include instrumentalists, but they were done within a context that suggests that in a

The Angel at the tomb asks of the three Marys:

Quem que — ri — tis in se — pul — chro Chris — ti — co — le?
(Whom do you seek in the tomb, followers of Christ?)

The Marys reply:

Je — sum Na — za — re — num cru — ci — fi — xum o ce — li — co — le.
(Jesus of Nazarus who was crucified, o heavenly one.)

The Angel says to them:

Non est hic sur — rex — it si — cut pre — di — xe — rat;

I — te nun — ti — a — te qui — a sur — re — xit di — cen — tes:
(He is not here, He has risen as he promised; go and announce that He has risen saying:)

6.2 Resurrection drama from the twelfth century

present-day re-creation the performers can interpolate varying amounts of vocal music. The dramas after 1300 were often used to instruct the local citizens in a context not connected with the liturgy, so the use of instruments was allowed even though the dramas were often performed inside a church.

Most of the surviving manuscripts give only the barest of directions. Example 6.2 is a good example of the small amount of information supplied in an early manuscript. This play is the briefest version of the Resurrection drama and was presented at a short ceremony just before Mass on Easter morning. A modern ensemble wishing to perform this dialogue will need to augment the directions in terms of staging and music. There must be some prop symbolizing the tomb, and the actors must be given directions for entrance and expression. There is reason to believe that some attempt would have been made to dramatize the scene in terms of actions and gestures.[12]

In the original setting the actors would have been part of a fairly large procession approaching the place provided for the reenactment, and a procession offers an excellent way for a modern cast to enter the performance area. All members of the procession should be singing a processional antiphon (found in the *Processionale monasticum*).[13] Those for Easter include 'In die resurrectionis,' 'Sedit angelus,' 'Surrexit enim,' and 'Vidi aquam.' The choir should remain in the performance area for the duration of the play and join with the cast in singing a second processional antiphon as they exit at the end of the drama. In addition, immediately after the third line of the play, it would be appropriate for the choir to join the Marys in singing the antiphon 'Surrexit Christus,' which is sometimes specified in the manuscript. Thus, merely re-creating the scene surrounding the early liturgical drama presentation results in the three short lines growing to a much longer presentation. Historically the cast would have been all male, although there would not seem to be anything preventing a modern performance with women. The pitch of the music can be adjusted to a comfortable range, but all parts must be changed the same distance (although a change of octaves is always permitted).

Modern performers must assume that the creative people of the Middle Ages would have filled out this drama and music as they would have the material we have discussed in earlier chapters. Given the outline of the drama and the music for the specific lines of text, it is then left to the modern director to see what is necessary to bring the drama to life as it might have been performed in the Middle Ages. It goes without saying, of course, that anyone wishing to re-create one of these dramas correctly must become familiar with medieval drama customs as well as those of musical performance. The following general suggestions are offered as possibilities depending upon the needs of the particular drama chosen.

The plays furnish the essential lines of the drama, but in some of them an appropriate motet or hymn could be interpolated in order to augment one or more scenes. For example, a scene involving the Annunciation may suggest that Mary reflect on the event after the announcement by the angel. In this case a motet or hymn from the repertory of that century can be added, even though not specifically mentioned in the script. Care must be taken, of course, that the interpolations are logical and that they do not interrupt the flow of the drama.

A chorus should be added to most liturgical dramas, especially to those obviously enacted as a part of a sacred ceremony, as described in connection with example 6.2. Many of the dramas specify the singing of the hymn 'Te Deum laudamus' after the last line, and this should be sung by the entire cast, including the choir. The 'Te Deum laudamus' offers an opportunity for both divided choir and the use of parallel organum.[14]

Instruments can be interpolated into the larger dramas even when not specifically called for in the manuscripts. The possibilities for instrumental accompaniment in monophonic song have already been discussed above (pp. 88–90), and these suggestions can be followed in the dramas as well. Instrumental music may also be of service as background for dramatic action that has no assigned vocal music and as interludes for changes of scene. Both monophonic and polyphonic conductus and motets can serve in these instances and should be chosen to match the geographical area and century of the play. Some dramas call for scenes of a secular nature in which dances and dance music can be interpolated to bring more life to the play. As long as the additions have dramatic purpose it can be assumed they would have been added by creative directors of the early centuries.

SECULAR DRAMA

Only a few secular dramas survive from the early centuries in which music plays an extended role, although nearly all dramas need music for incidental purposes. The well-known *Jeux de Robin et Marion* by Adam de la Halle[15] has music within a spoken play and allows some creative elaboration on the part of musicians by way of instrumental preludes, postludes, and accompaniment. A comparison of several of the currently available recordings of this play will give some idea of the amount of latitude available to the modern re-creator.

Throughout the early centuries secular dramas and morality plays used music in at least an incidental capacity. Early dramas from most of the European countries are currently enjoying a revival, and most could use music for incidental purposes to lend more ceremony and some new dimensions to the production. For medieval plays, music can be selected from the conductus, motet, and dance repertories as well as the wealth of monophonic and polyphonic secular material. For the fifteenth and sixteenth centuries the possibilities include the secular vocal and instrumental repertory, including Brown's edition of French theatre music[16] and English music from Henry VIII's court.[17]

INTERMEDII

In Italy during the Renaissance there was also a tradition of celebrating important events such as weddings with large dramatic and musical productions. We know that music played an important part in the Poliziano play *Feste d'Orfeo* in 1480, but the music was probably improvised, and none has survived. In the sixteenth century these celebrations included grandiose dramatic productions into which were inserted tableaux with music called *intermedii*. Howard M. Brown has given an accounting of the music performed on these occasions in Florence with both the music and instrumentation for many of the productions.[18] The entire performances from 1539 and

1589, including the music, are available in modern editions.[19] The productions included singers and instrumentalists in increasing numbers. According to Brown the production of 1539 could have been performed by eight singers and eight versatile instrumentalists, whereas that of 1589 would have required sixty singers and from twenty-four to thirty instrumentalists.

The requirements of scenery, stage machinery, and costumes are correspondingly large, but an ambitious producer could re-create one of these productions for a suitably grand occasion by consulting the books cited above. For a less ambitious occasion one or more of the tableaux or even just the musical portion of an *intermedio* could be adapted for performance by a medium-size ensemble of voices and instruments. It should be kept in mind that the ensembles described by Brown were for a very large theatre; all the doublings may not be necessary for a smaller concert hall, although the distribution of parts and the kind of instrumentation should be retained no matter what the size of the ensemble (see above, pp. 139–40). It is interesting to note that in the first half of the sixteenth century the usual instrumentation included unbroken consorts of families of instruments – viols, lutes, flutes, and trombones. Later in the century some consorts were modified by the substitution of stronger instruments on the bass line – for example, a bass viol instead of the lowest member of the krummhorn family – and keyboards and lutes were added to most ensembles. This basic concept of instrumentation trends should be kept in mind for all ensembles, not just those for *intermedii* performances. Although Brown's documentation is only for Italy, there are indications that the trend was pan-European to some degree.

Quasi-dramatic music

The repertory of early music also includes compositions that can be presented in a dramatic manner although there is little evidence that it was originally intended for such presentation. In this category are the various dialogue-chanson one can find in all centuries, including the 'Jeux-partis' of Adam de la Halle.

A dialogue-chanson involves a discussion between two people, usually on the subject of love. A single dialogue-chanson can bring variety to a program because the two singers can address one another, perhaps standing a few feet apart and making hand gestures to one another. Examples of individual compositions include the troubadour song 'Chascuns qui de bien amer'[20] and Dufay's 'Estrines moy.'[21] Some of the Italian caccias, for example 'Dappoi che 'l sole' (about a fire),[22] also allow for the performer to do more than stand and look calmly at the audience.

The sixteen 'Jeux-partis' by Adam de la Halle[23] offer the possibility of an even more substantial presentation. They constitute a charming musical discussion of love between master and student; one knows the subject in theory, the other in practice. Not all the chansons or all the verses need to be chosen, but in any case they will require a bit of imagination in order to communicate with a modern audience since they are so dependent upon the text (see discussion above, pp. 86–8). They could be elaborated with instruments and even the simplest form of staging – two lecterns, simple hand gestures, and perhaps an occasional hand prop.

Madrigal-comedies should also be mentioned here, although they are not dramatic *per se*. They are sets of madrigals on a single subject – both serious and comical – which were meant to be seen 'with the mind and not the eye,' as we are told in the opening madrigal of Orazio Vecchi's 'L'Amfiparnasso.' Composers such as Banchieri, Croce, Striggio, and Vecchi[24] wrote a number of these entertaining cycles of madrigals, some of which include characters from the *commedia dell'arte*. They allow for much exaggeration and imagination in performance. Although intended originally for soloists, some sets can be performed by small chorus.

PART THREE

Techniques

Ornamentation

The tradition

HE TRADITION of improvising entire compositions and ornamenting existing works is as old as music itself. In the past each performer was to some degree a composer, and when he was not inventing whole compositions of his own, he was 'assisting' other composers by filling out their works with graces and divisions. There is evidence that the practice continued unbroken from the earliest times until finally in the nineteenth century it was restricted to folk and dance musicians while so-called 'serious' or 'classical' musicians were constrained to play only what was printed on the page. The complex chromaticism of the Romantic era put an end to the freedom that had been every performer's right and duty until then. As a result, the twentieth-century conservatory-trained musician learns to play only what is written and not to add anything – a training that is unfortunately at odds with the performance of early music and must be overcome if early music is to be performed correctly. The composers of the early centuries expected the performer to add to the written score; it was a fact of performance life and everyone accepted it. To re-create the music of the early centuries correctly, then, present-day performers must learn how to ornament and improvise so that they may present the early repertory as it was actually performed.

The task confronting twentieth-century musicians wishing to learn to ornament and improvise early music is both different and more difficult than that which faced musicians of the early centuries. For musicians living in the Middle Ages and Renaissance era there was a tradition which would have been learned as soon as instruction began and would have continued to develop throughout a career. Best of all, there would have been only a single style which would have evolved slowly but would have been common to all performers living in a given area at the time.

Present-day musicians, on the other hand, must learn the entire technique of inventing music after having received a training which specifically discourages this sort of activity and, to further complicate the problem, must learn all at once a variety of styles from several different centuries and places. Nevertheless, in spite of the difficulties, modern performers are encouraged to attempt ornamentation and improvisation which, when finally mastered, will add greatly to the authentic re-creation of the early repertory.

A method book for ornamentation and improvisation has yet to be written. However, several books and articles on the subject lay out the evidence clearly, and there are encouraging signs that method books will be forthcoming shortly.[1] A full treatment of the subject is easily a study of its own, and the approach in this book does not pretend to be complete. What follows here is merely an introduction, exposing the breadth of the subject and suggesting how interested musicians may proceed to develop a knowledge and technique. For reasons of organization the subjects of ornamentation and improvisation are treated separately, but they are closely related and often identical.

The ornaments

Ornamentation is the technique of embellishing a given melodic line. It can be as simple as adding a mordent or filling in a melodic third, or as elaborate as a running passage of many bars. There are two basic types of ornaments – those which decorate a single note, and the longer passages which fill in between notes. For convenience I shall borrow Brown's terminology[2] and refer to the first kind as graces and the second as *passaggi*. Both types were apparently used and intermixed throughout the early centuries. Most of the surviving evidence, however, is of *passaggi*, both in the examples and in the instructional material. But although the graces are less frequently written into the music and receive a more cursory treatment in the manuals, there is reason to believe that they were just as commonly used. They are mentioned by a number of writers, but few examples are given. From the references we can conclude that graces were considered the easiest type of ornament to use but were difficult to write out, and the advice to beginners was to listen to the way they were performed by accomplished artists. The Spanish composer Juan Bermudo (1555) permits only graces, and Brown believes that graces may have been the most common type of ornament in use.[3] This includes mordents, turns, trills, and vibrato.

As with other subjects treated in this study, the specific instructional material comes mostly from the late Renaissance; we have ever-increasing

7.1 a/ Appoggiatura with trill; b/ appoggiatura with mordent (see p. 153)

7.2 Simple *passaggi* (see p. 153)

amounts of information concerning the style and technique of ornamentation beginning in the early sixteenth century. For the earlier period, where only a few theoretical statements are found, it will be necessary to abstract most of the information from the music itself and to attempt to organize it into what appear to be basic principles. Fortunately, we can learn something of the earlier tradition by comparing variant versions of certain compositions and observing the ornamental passages written occasionally into works by composers. There are also a few examples of actual ornamentation written out for a variety of reasons, and by assembling all this information we can form a picture, albeit a somewhat hazy and uneven one, of the tradition of ornamentation throughout the Middle Ages and Renaissance.

GRACES

Ornaments to a single note can be simply a single quick 'finger-wiggle' or something more complicated such as a delicate turn. The instructional material and examples show a variety of types and suggest that most of them had been in common use for some time. We can conclude that the graces themselves were common to all periods and that the variety used in any given period depended mostly on the imagination of the performer. It was specific placement and frequency that were the elements of local style. Unfortunately there are so few surviving examples of music with graces indicated that our understanding of their stylistic traits is severely limited.

Possible graces are mostly of a type that involve the use of a neighbouring note. They include (in modern terms): mordent (upper or lower neighbour); turn (upper and lower neighbour); appoggiatura (entering on the neighbour-

Involving a half-step from below:

7.3 Cadence ornaments found in the repertory which can be transposed to any pitch: a/ found only in fourteenth- and fifteenth-century music; b/ found only in sixteenth-century music; c/ common to all centuries

Involving a whole step from above:

ing note, either from above or below); trill (including intervals of half-step, whole-step, and third); and vibrato (pitch variation of less than a half-step). Variations to these involve the speed at which the individual grace is executed; whether it is executed beginning at the time of the written note, in anticipation, or slightly delayed, and for a trill, whether it is played at a constant or variable speed (getting faster or slower), and whether the trill or vibrato lasts for the full value of the written note, just the beginning part, or just the end. Further, the graces can be combined – for example, an appoggiatura followed by a trill or a mordent, as in example 7.1a and b.

PASSAGGI

The simplest *passaggi* are those used to connect the notes of a melodic line. They can be a direct filling-in of an interval, as in example 7.2a and b, or something a bit more adventurous, as in example 7.2c, or of a more extended length, as will be seen in many of the examples to follow. Variations of *passaggi* are limitless and involve not only length and note patterns but also a variety of rhythms; examples of this variety abound in the sixteenth-century manuals. The individual style changes for the *passaggi* are better documented than those for the graces, and we will find ourselves on more secure ground when attempting to determine the placement and quantity of *passaggi* in the various styles.

CADENCE FORMULAE

A cadence formula is not an ornament *per se* but a particular set of graces, *passaggi*, and combinations of them that was used almost 'pro forma' at the end of a phrase, section, or composition. Example 7.3 is a compilation of a number of comparatively simple cadence formulae found frequently in the repertory.

The evidence

THE LATE MIDDLE AGES

We can begin with some of the earliest known examples of written-out ornamentation: the Robertsbridge Codex from England, written about 1370,[4] and the Faenza Codex from Italy, written about 1420.[5] In both sources vocal music has been ornamented for instrumental performance, perhaps keyboard. By comparing the instrumental versions with their vocal originals we can arrive at some idea of the nature of instrumental ornamentation in those two countries at that time. An examination of all of the ornamented compositions in these manuscripts yields the following observations, many of which can be seen in examples 7.4b, 7.5b, and 7.6b.

1 The notes of the original are usually included in the ornamental passages, although there are occasional exceptions.
2 Motion is stepwise for the most part.
3 When there is a skip of a third the motion usually turns back on itself; that is, it often appears as a move from upper neighbour to lower neighbour (or the opposite), as in example 7.4b, bars 4 and 5 and 7.5b, bars 3 and 5. But note the exception in 7.4b, bar 3.
4 Ornamental figures commonly used include:
   a decorations revolving around a single note (these are like graces but one commonly thinks of graces as being quicker and specified by sign rather than written out): 1 / upper neighbour; 2 / lower neighbour; 3 / both upper and lower neighbour;

7.4 Philippe de Vitri(?) 'Tribum quem,' bars 1–9: a/ vocal original;
b/ Robertsbridge Codex intabulation

Willi Apel, ed. *Keyboard Music of the Fourteenth and Fifteenth Centuries.* © 1963 by
American Institute of Musicology/Hänssler-Verlag, D-7303 Neuhausen-Stuttgart (West Germany) No. 65.303.
(CEKM vol. 1). Used by permission

7.5 Guillaume de Machaut 'De toutes flours,' bars 1–9: a/ vocal original;
b/ Faenza Codex intabulation

Dragan Plamenac, ed. *Keyboard Music of the Late Middle Ages in Codex Faenza 117* © 1972
by Armen Carapetyan, American Institute of Musicology/Hänssler-Verlag, D-7303 Neuhausen-Stuttgart
(West Germany) No. 65.700. Used by permission

7.6 Jacob da Bologna 'Non al suo amante,' bars 1–3:
a/ vocal original; b/ Faenza Codex intabulation

Dragan Plamenac, ed. *Keyboard Music of the Late Middle Ages in Codex Faenza 117* © 1972
by Armen Carapetyan, American Institute of Musicology/Hänssler-Verlag, D-7303 Neuhausen-Stuttgart
(West Germany) No. 65.700. Used by permission

b decorations filling in the interval: 1 / direct stepwise motion for larger intervals; 2 / running passages involving upper and lower neighbours for short intervals.

5 Ornamental passages vary in length from two notes to running passages three and four bars in length.

6 Rhythms used for ornaments can be in either duple or triple division. Both occur equally, regardless of whether the original has duple or triple division. They are often intermixed within a single short ornament: ♫♫♫.

7 The use of unequal notes of a triplet (*notes inégales?*),[6] as in example 7.4b, bar 3, can be found in both sources.

8 In many of the ornamented works the first note is held before the subdivision is begun, as in all examples here, but in some compositions the subdivisions begin immediately.

9 In the Faenza manuscript the treble part only is given melodic ornamentation. The tenor line receives rare rhythmic variation, as in example 7.5b, bar 1. In Robertsbridge the tenor voice occasionally receives short ornamental graces of the upper/lower neighbour variety, as in example 7.4b, bar 5.

10 Both manuscripts contain ornamental versions of three-part originals. In Robertsbridge the contratenor is included but not ornamented. In Faenza all compositions are two-part, omitting the contratenor of all three-part originals.

11 Motives for the ornamentation are sometimes taken from the original, as in example 7.6, bars 1 and 2. This is especially true if the original is a highly florid Italian model.

12 The ornamentation tends to stop, slow down, or otherwise indicate phrase ends clearly, as in example 7.4b, bar 7, and example 7.5b, bar 8.

13 Ornaments are added throughout the compositions.

This gives us some idea of the application of ornaments in instrumental music in these two countries at the end of the fourteenth century and the beginning of the fifteenth. Unfortunately, there are no surviving manuscripts which so clearly present ornamented versions for singers, but some idea of vocal ornamentation can be extracted from variant versions of the same composition and from passages which suggest that the composer may have written ornaments into the piece. The clearest of the examples are Italian, as seen in examples 7.7 and 7.8.

The variant readings of these two fourteenth-century madrigals demonstrate much the same type of ornamentation seen in the instrumental examples. As a matter of fact, all but three of the observations made in reference to instrumental ornamentation are found to be true of these two

7.7 Johannes de Florentia 'Nascoso el viso,' bars 1–8: a/ from Florence, Bibl. Med.
Laur. MS Pal. 87 (Squarcialupi Codex); b/ from Vatican, MS Rossi 215

madrigals: unequal notes (no. 7) are not found in these examples although
they can be found in other Italian compositions of this era; no. 10 does not
apply; and no. 13 must be modified in that the longer ornaments are usually
reserved for long notes or sparsely texted sections. Example 7.9 is not found
in variant versions but is obviously so highly decorated in this single version
that scarcely anything can be added.

No other information exists about vocal ornamentation of this period, but
we can accept these examples as evidence of the type and placement of
ornaments used in Italian vocal music of the late Middle Ages. The
assumption is lent strength by the amount of agreement seen between the
ornaments added to vocal music and those observed in examples 7.5b and 7.6b

7.8 Maestro Piero 'Quando l'aria comenza,' bars 1–5; a/ from Florence, BN, MS Pan. 26; b/ from Vatican, MS Rossi 215

Nino Pirrotta, ed. *The Music of Fourteenth-Century Italy* vol. 2. © 1960 by Armen Carapetyan, American Institute of Musicology/Hänssler-Verlag, D-7303 Neuhausen-Stuttgart (West Germany) No. 60.8010
Used by permission

7.9 Lorenzo Masii de Florentia 'Come in sul fonte,' bars 1–15

Nino Pirrotta, ed. *The Music of Fourteenth-Century Italy* vol. 3. © 1962 by Armen Carapetyan, American Institute of Musicology/Hänssler-Verlag, D-7303 Neuhausen-Stuttgart (West Germany) No. 60.801.
Used by permission

7.10 Forest 'Ascendit Christus': a/ bars 1–4; b/ bars 27–31
Andrew Hughes and Margaret Bent, eds. *The Old Hall Manuscript* vol. 2. © 1969 by Armen Carapetyan, American Institute of Musicology/Hänssler-Verlag, D-7303 Neuhausen-Stuttgart (West Germany) No. 64.602. Used by permission

for instruments. The more reserved type of ornaments found in example 7.7 and 7.8 correspond to those of 7.5b, and the virtuoso ornaments of 7.9 are similar to those in 7.6b. It would appear that the vocal and instrumental styles of ornamentation in Italy in the late fourteenth and early fifteenth centuries were similar.

For the other countries the surviving evidence is not as strong. Although the Robertsbridge manuscript (example 7.4b) indicates that English instrumental ornaments were similar to those found in the Italian instrumental sources, no examples of English vocal music survive from that period with exactly the same style of ornaments. Example 7.10 is from one of the several ornate compositions found in the Old Hall repertory from about 1400. It is typical of all available examples of the English style of embellishing from that period in that it has occasional short ornamental passages leading into a major cadence, as shown in example 7.10b, but there are no extended ornamental passages as exist in the English instrumental composition shown in example 7.4b. The style more frequently involves passages like the one in example 7.10a, which is rhythmically complex but unornamented. Does this mean that in England ornaments were less frequently used in vocal than in instrumental music? It is not possible to say for sure, since it may well have been the tradition to indicate only certain placements of ornaments. We can only observe that no examples exist of highly ornamented English vocal music and that the compositional style seen in example 7.10 involves rhythmic complexities that would have been lost if the piece were too highly ornamented.

7.11 Anonymous 'Mon povre cuer,' bars 1–6

Gilbert Reaney, ed. *Early Fifteenth-Century Music* vol. 4. © 1969 by Armen Carapetyan,
American Institute of Musicology/Hänssler-Verlag, D-7303 Neuhausen-Stuttgart (West Germany) No. 61.104.
Used by permission

There are no French instrumental examples from this period, but some vocal compositions, such as example 7.11, appear to contain ornamentation. The style of ornamentation is somewhere between those of the English and the Italian vocal examples given above. There are a number of ornaments but rarely more than four quick notes in a group. The French ornaments, like the Italian and the English, include both the filled-in intervals and the upper and lower neighbours, but they also employ thirds, often as a substitute for a neighbouring note, as in example 7.11, bars 4 and 6. The quick-moving ornaments are found throughout the phrases and in all lines, but more frequently in the top voice.

To summarize the style of ornaments found in vocal music between 1350 and 1450, we can see that in the countries where evidence survives ornaments are applied mostly to long notes and to passages without text. Ornaments are found in texted passages, but they are less frequent and of the shorter variety. There are individual style differences. In Italy there are some examples of long rapid passages and a large quantity of ornaments similar to the instrumental style; ornaments are applied only to the top voice. In England and France the use of ornamental passages is much more conservative. All ornaments are comparatively short in duration and are applied nearer the end than the beginning of the phrase, especially (but not exclusively) to the penultimate syllable in a phrase. Some short duration ornaments are applied to the tenor, and occasionally some are applied to the contratenor.

THE END OF THE FIFTEENTH CENTURY

The evidence we have for the period from about 1450 to 1525 is that the practices of ornamentation already noted above continued with few real changes. This can be seen in examples 7.12b, 7.13b, and 7.14, which include two keyboard intabulations, one from the *Buxheimer Orgelbuch* of about

7.12 John Dunstable 'O rosa bella,' bars 1–5: a/ vocal original;
b/ intabulation from Buxheimer MS

1460 and the other from the Kotter keyboard manuscript of about 1530, and
two instrumental elaborations of a chanson melody of about 1500 by
Alexander Agricola. Both keyboard examples are from German sources, and
Agricola was a Flemish composer who spent much of his time in Italy.

Examples 7.12b and 7.13b are typical of the style of intabulations found in
the two German sources. Their repertory includes the vocal music of France
and Italy as well as Germany, and the style of embellishment is approximately
the same for all compositions. There are no examples as fully ornamented as in
the most involved Italian style seen in the Faenza manuscript (example 7.6b),
but the principles for the application of ornaments appear to be much the same
as in the earliest intabulations. The kinds of ornaments used are both graces
(or, rather, decorations to a single note) and *passaggi*, but there are fewer
graces. The passages are smoother and tend to be mostly in duple division. In
addition to the written-out graces, in Buxheimer we have the earliest known
example of graces indicated by symbols: see example 7.12b, bars 1 and 2.[7]
Their absence from Kotter or any other manuscript does not, of course,
necessarily indicate that graces were not used, as has been discussed above.

The music of Alexander Agricola is somewhat unusual in that almost all of
it is highly ornate. Only a handful of composers from that time furnish us
with compositions that appear to be already embellished (another is Antoine

7.13 Heinrich Isaac 'La Martinella,' bars 1–7: a/ instrumental original;
b/ intabulation from Kotter MS

Johannes Wolf, ed. *Denkmäler der Tonkunst in Österreich* vol. 28. Graz, Akademische Druck- u.
Verlagsanstalt 1907 (1959). Used by permission

Brumel). It is possible that these men wrote in a style unlike anyone else in
their age, but it is more likely that they were compulsive artists who chose to
write out their own ornament-like passages in order to limit the number of
additions the performers could make. We will probably never know to what
extent Agricola's passages resemble the extemporized ornaments of his era,
but the degree to which they fit in with the other information we have suggests
that they are probably not extreme or unusual, and his music does offer us at
least one composer's ideas from an era that is otherwise poorly documented.

7.14 Alexander Agricola 'De tous biens plaine': a/ version IV, bars 1–4;
b/ version V, bars 1–4

Alexander Agricola *Opera Omnia* ed. Edward R. Lerner, vol. 5. © 1970 by Armen Carapetyan,
American Institute of Musicology/Hänssler-Verlag, D-7303 Neuhausen-Stuttgart (West Germany) No. 62.205.
Used by permission

All this is by way of a warning that the conclusions drawn from the Agricola examples are open to question. Both the examples of Agricola's writing used here, examples 7.14 and 7.15a, are in the sophisticated style of writing that was pan-European, and I consider them to be representative of the ornamented style applied to the more sophisticated repertory in most of the European countries.

Examples 7.14a and b are for three instruments, in contrast to the probably solo instrument of the two keyboard examples. The ornaments here too are smoother than those of the earlier period and are mainly scalar. Ornaments are applied to both superius and bass lines in almost equal quantities but are omitted from the tenor line because of the type of composition, which is a two-part accompaniment of an established melody carried by the tenor. We must be wary of assuming that everything exhibited in these settings would have been extemporized – for example the parallel thirds in example 7.14b, bar 4 – although the frequent long, smooth scale passages were probably part of the instrumental style during those decades.

The ornaments found in these instrumental compositions vary from the earlier examples in small details. Still present are both the upper and lower neighbours for ornamentation of a single note and the filled-in intervals to connect notes. Changes include the following:

1 the flow of ornaments is smoother, as is the rhythm of the originals; fewer

of the quick, mordent-type ornaments are written out, although they could have been inserted by the performer without specific direction;

2 *passaggi* appear to be in duple division for the most part rather than triple, as was prevalent earlier;

3 the running passages tend to be even more consistently stepwise;

4 especially in the Agricola examples there are extended smooth scales after a skip of a fifth or an octave;

5 ornamentation is still concentrated in the superius part although some is applied to other lines; in terms of frequency and quantity of ornaments the order is: superius, tenor, contratenor;

6 in the accompanied melody style (Agricola examples) all accompanying parts receive an almost equal amount of ornamentation.

In the vocal repertory of this period we can see both a continuation of the elements found in the earlier vocal examples and a relationship to the instrumental style. Examples 7.15a and b are in the imitative international style and the other three in the less sophisticated national styles. We can extract these principles as the general style of vocal ornamentation from about 1450 to 1525:

1 In all examples
   a longer ornamental passages appear on longer-held syllables;
   b short ornaments can appear anywhere;
   c long ornaments have mostly smooth rhythms, but uneven rhythms occur frequently in Spanish compositions, as in all the parts of example 7.15d;
   d no examples were found as elaborate as those in the instrumental repertory.

2 In the imitative style the ornaments are placed mostly toward the ends of the phrases.

3 In the national style ornaments appear throughout the phrase and often increase in speed towards the end of the phrase.

7.15a Alexander Agricola 'Se je vous eslonge,' bars 1–6
Alexander Agricola *Opera Omnia* ed. Edward R. Lerner, vol. 5. © 1970 by Armen Carapetyan, American Institute of Musicology/Hänssler-Verlag, D-7303 Neuhausen-Stuttgart (West Germany) No. 62.205. Used by permission

7.15b Paul Hofhaymer 'Einr junckfraw zart,' bars 1–10

H. J. Moser, ed. *Denkmäler der Tonkunst in Österreich* vol. 72. Graz, Akademischs Druk- u. Verlagsanstalt 1930. Used by permission

7.15c Henry VIII 'The Time of Youth,' bars 1–5

John Stevens, ed. *Musica Britannica* vol. 18, 1969. Used by permission of the Trustees of Musica Britannica and Stainer & Bell Ltd

7.15d Hurtado de Xeres 'No tenga nadie sperança,' bars 1–10
Robert Stevenson *Spanish Music in the Age of Columbus* The Hague, Martinus Nijhoff 1964. Used by permission

7.15e Anonymous 'Ayme sospiri,' bars 1–8, cantus only
After Walter Rubsamen 'The Justiniane or Veniziane of the Fifteenth Century' in *Acta Musicologica* 29 (1957)

There appears to be no agreement as to how many parts receive ornaments or to what degree. The imitative compositions are fairly consistent in assigning ornaments more or less equally to all parts, but non-imitative compositions, both all-vocal and vocal with instrumental accompaniment, can be found with ornaments assigned either to the top line or to all parts.

THE SIXTEENTH CENTURY

It was in the sixteenth century that instruction manuals for ornamentation began to appear, the first written by Silvestro di Ganassi in 1535.[8] Supporting that information were lute and keyboard intabulations of all kinds of vocal music which parallel the instructions in the manuals in their use of *passaggi* and thereby lend some support to the method I have used to derive the ornamentation style of early centuries. The instructions are given by vocalists and instrumentalists alike, and all writers made it clear that at least in Italy, Spain, and parts of Germany the style was basically the same for voices and instruments. The fact that there are more instructions for instrumentalists than for singers and statements by some theorists of the time have led Brown to conclude that ornamentation was probably required of all instrumentalists but not necessarily of all singers.[9] Professional singers apparently could be excused the lack of ability to ornament as long as their voices and other kinds of expression were superior, but probably no such leeway was granted to instrumentalists; they were all expected to adorn the music with ornaments to some degree, and a virtuoso performer was one whose ornaments included those of a highly technical nature.

The didactic literature mostly comes from Italy, Spain, and Germany. England and France furnish only the kinds of hints we have seen from earlier centuries – intabulations and some ornate writing, but no written instructions – and thus will be dealt with later. The sixteenth-century writers tended to catalogue the ornaments and give them names; the graces especially were classified with names such as *trillo*, *tremolo*, *groppo*, and *groppo battuto*. The *passaggi* were separated into intervals, beginning with a variety of ways to decorate and fill in the interval of a second and going on to demonstrate creative passages for all intervals and various combinations of intervals.

Basically all the sixteenth-century ornaments turn out to be hardly different from those we have seen in the preceding two centuries. Ornaments can still be thought of either as decorations to or around a single note or as passages of longer duration which connect the notes of the original. The difference is that the sixteenth-century manuals acknowledge that there are different types of embellishments for a single note and that the different intervals or note patterns allow for various kinds of inventive *passaggi*. The information is more detailed than what we have extracted from earlier music, but not really different, either in essence or in application. The following rules are a distillation of the various instruction books as they apply to voice and to most instruments:

1 *Graces*
   a An upper neighbour used as a trill: may continue to the end of the note value; may occupy only a part of the value of the note, as in example 7.16a; or may be sounded in anticipation, as in example 7.16b.
   b An upper neighbour may be used as a mordent, as in example 7.16c.
   c A lower neighbour may be used only as an inverted mordent.
   d Upper and lower neighbours, similar to a turn, may be used alone or in conjunction with a trill or with upper or lower mordents, as in examples 7.16d and e.
   e There are no clear instructions as to the use of vibrato; Ganassi (1542) says it is to be used to reinforce the sad emotions.[10]
2 *Passaggi*
   a Passages are mostly stepwise.
   b Skips of a third generally turn in the other direction.
   c The original notes are usually included within the ornament.
   d The ornamental passage is often constructed so that the final note of the original is used as the final note of the ornament, although there are many exceptions to this.
   e A variety of rhythms can be used.
   f *Passaggi* are of varying lengths from four notes to several bars; they can be all of a single rhythmic and melodic style or can be combinations, as in example 7.17.

By about 1580 there seems to have been a change from the more evenly paced ornaments of the earlier years of the century to bursts of ornaments separated by sections with no ornaments at all.

Although I have separated the different types of ornaments for discussion, in practice they were combined as the needs of the line and the opportunities and skills of the ornamentor allowed.

Many of the writers also furnished a few full examples of their ornaments applied to actual compositions (the source of the last example), and these for the most part tend to be virtuoso displays.[11] The men writing the manuals were known as outstanding virtuosi of their day, and we can probably accept their extremely complex and technically demanding ornamentations as the ultimate – a goal for modern early musicians. We must realize that this type of virtuosity was probably rare and that the majority of performers probably

7.16 Graces by: a/ and b/ Girolamo Diruta; c/ Tomás de Sancta Maria;
d/ and e/ Giovanni Conforto
After Howard M. Brown *Embellishing Sixteenth-Century Music* London,
Oxford University Press 1976, pp. 3, 4, 8

performed fewer and less rapid ornaments. For technically proficient modern musicians who are capable of performing the difficult passages in these treatises, it should be somewhat humbling to remember that the musicians of the time could apparently invent them extemporaneously.

For those countries from which we do not have formal instruction manuals we must again turn to examples from the repertory. Examples 7.18a and b can be accepted as typical of the kinds of ornamented instrumental music in the repertories of all countries. A large number of them were published especially for lute and keyboard and were intended to furnish fully embellished intabulations for serious amateurs. Example 7.18a shows the evenly paced rapid *passaggi* style and example 7.18b the stop-and-go type of embellishments including graces and *passaggi*. Both styles can be found in the repertory of all European countries in the sixteenth century and on into the seventeenth. The embellished repertory therefore supports the supposition that at least in instrumental music the practice of ornamentation described in the manuals was pan-European in its basic concept. The difference in style from one country to the other during the late Renaissance was for the most part one of degree and of preference for one type over the other.

Although there exists an abundance of instrumental music with written-out

7.17 Cipriano de Rore 'Anchor che co'l partire,' bars 1–7: a/ original superius line;
b/ ornaments by Girolamo Dalla Casa; c/ ornaments by Giovanni Bovicelli
After Howard M. Brown *Embellishing Sixteenth-Century Music* London,
Oxford University Press 1976, pp. 43–5

embellishments, the same is not true of vocal music. Whereas the tendency was to furnish amateur instrumentalists with fully embellished music, vocalists received no such help. The accounts in all countries still speak of vocal ornamentations by the professionals, so we know that it existed outside Italy. However, Brown may be right to assume, as mentioned above, that although all instrumentalists, both amateur and professional, were expected to embellish, amateur singers were not. Professionals, of course, would do their own ornamentation, and this would perhaps explain the absence of written-out examples. The information we have for vocal ornamentation is that it was identical to that for instrumentalists in style except that: the most extreme examples were not as rapid or as long as those for instruments; there were not so many sections of long ornaments; and in each phrase the long ornaments were interrupted by sections with no ornaments for the purpose of singing the text.

Near the year 1600 changes in the concept of music gained momentum, eventually bringing about the era we call baroque. The style of embellishing

7.18a Anonymous 'Languir me fais,' bars 1–3
Daniel Heartz, ed. *Preludes, Chansons and Dances for Lute Published by Pierre Attaignant, Paris 1529–1530*
Neuilly-sur-Seine, Société de Musique d'Autrefois 1964

7.18b Anonymous galliard, bars 1–8
Denis Stevens, ed. *Musica Britannica* vol. 1, 1954. Used by permission of the Trustees of Musica Britannica
and Stainer & Bell Ltd

the music was also somewhat new, and although the baroque era is beyond the scope of this study, I will consider the broad general differences in the new style as a method of delineating the style of the Renaissance and to show the direction of the performance practices towards the end of the sixteenth century. What follows is an intentional over-simplification of the complex relationships between the two styles.

THE END OF THE RENAISSANCE

The differences in the new style of ornamentation around 1600 are mainly in connection with the new vocal aesthetic and differ from the earlier practices both in intention and in style, the former causing the latter. Whereas in the earlier eras the reason for embellishing a composition had been principally in order to fill it out with graceful ornaments that also allowed for virtuosic display of technique, the new baroque aesthetic called for the embellishments to support and enhance the emotional and dramatic content of the composition. The two sets of objectives are not incompatable; indeed there is evidence

7.19 Ornaments by Girolamo Diruta
After Howard M. Brown *Embellishing Sixteenth-Century Music* London, Oxford University Press 1976, p. 4

that they existed side by side in both styles. The difference was more in the weight assigned to them: before 1600 grace and display were uppermost, and after 1600 emotion and dramatic effect were dominant. This is especially true in Italy. But the early sixteenth-century writers were already encouraging performers to take into account the expression of the sentiment of the composition, and in spite of Caccini's insistence that all ornaments be dramatically relevant, examples of the early baroque style show virtuoso *passaggi* in the older style which have little connection with the text, as in example 7.20. Elements of the new style are:

1 dramatic figures such as those in example 7.19a and b;
2 entering on dissonances or holding a non-harmonic note;
3 extremes of dynamics on a single note: crescendo, diminuendo, and their combinations;
4 entering a third or fourth below the pitch of the initial note and moving upwards either rapidly or slowly depending on the desired dramatic effect;
5 speeding up and slowing down of trills;
6 speeding up and slowing down of vibrato;
7 extremes of motion caused by holding some notes without ornaments and rapid embellishments of others, depending on the text, as in example 7.20.

The embellishments themselves are really little changed from those used in earlier years; it is their combination and application to the text that has changed. Only nos 2 and 7 can be considered really new techniques; the others we have seen before:

No. 1 contains nothing more than filled-in intervals and upper neighbours, respectively.

No. 3 is an excess of the expression required of every singer at all times, when dealing with musical lines. It is mentioned by Maffei in 1562 and implied by Ganassi in 1535.

No. 4 is an embellishment seen as early as 1400 in example 7.6 and again in the mid-fifteenth century, as in example 7.12b, but instead of merely a preparatory melodic slide, in the new style it has dramatic purpose.

7.20 Giulio Caccini 'Vedrò'l mio sol,' bars 1–8
Giulio Caccini *Le nuove musiche* ed. H. Wiley Hitchcock A-R Editions, Inc. 1970. Used by permission

No. 5 is used at least as early as the *Buxheimer Orgelbuch* and may have been added without comment by earlier performers.

No. 6 is mentioned in Caccini's publication of 1601, but statements by Ganassi in 1542 and medieval theorists (see below) suggest that vibrato itself was not new, and perhaps not even the variation of its speed for dramatic purposes. There are also warnings in the writings not to use it frequently to the exclusion of other ornaments. In other words, vibrato was one ornament among many and should not be used more frequently than any other.

In example 7.20 from Caccini's *Le nuove musiche*, therefore, we see not new material but new uses of old material according to the new concept.

For instrumentalists the evidence suggests that the virtuoso type of rapid, florid embellishment of the sixteenth century was carried on into the seventeenth with as much added of the new dramatic vocal style as it was possible to borrow for instruments. This was especially true in Italy and also in Southern Germany, which was much influenced by the Italian style, and to a lesser extent in the other countries, which were developing independent national styles.

THE EARLIER CENTURIES

For the years before 1350 there is very little concrete evidence for the kinds of ornaments that were added to music. We know from the writings of this period that embellishment was practised, and indeed we would come to that conclusion from what is known of the later centuries.

The earliest theoretical statement on this subject comes at the end of the thirteenth century from Jerome of Moravia, who discussed both graces and *passaggi*.[12] He referred to ornaments as 'harmonic flowers' and said that they must be used to grace music. The descriptions are not clear, but he seems to be referring to short *passaggi* for the purpose of filling in intervals, a 'swift and stormlike' vibration that is probably a vocal flutter, and trills that can be fast or slow, long or short, steady or increasing in speed towards the end. He illustrated only an upper-neighbour trill, explaining that on an organ it is executed in a special way, by holding the principal note and striking the note above it. Ornaments were to be placed on the longer notes of a phrase rather than on the subdivisions.

Additional help in establishing early ornamentation practices can be obtained by comparing variant readings of compositions.[13] This evidence shows the freedom taken in the transmission of melodies, a concept that is the basis of ornamentation. By noticing the type and placement of subdivisions in different readings of compositions we can form some ideas about what melodic figures were used in subdivisions and where they were placed.

Example 7.21 shows three different readings of a twelfth-century trouba-dour song. The rhythms are not known for this example, but the kinds of melodic subdivisions can be seen clearly. Many more examples such as this could be brought forward from the sacred and secular repertory of the time to provide evidence of the attitude towards subdivision and ornamentation of an existing melodic line. When this is put together with Jerome's description of *passaggi* and graces, we can see that ornamentation was an ever-present element in performance throughout the early centuries.

Fewer facts are available on practice before 1350, but the following principles on ornamentation can be established:
Passaggi
Short, mostly used to fill in intervals.
Graces
1 Mordents may be formed with upper and/or lower neighbours.
2 Jerome's 'swift and stormlike' ornament suggests the kind of quick waver of pitch used in traditional music of the Eastern Mediterranean countries; it can be as narrow as a tight vibrato or as wide as a half-step or step.

7.21 Audefroy le Bastard 'Fine amours en esperance'
Hendrik van der Werf *The Chansons of the Troubadours and Trouvères* Utrecht, A. Oosthoek 1972.
Used by permission

3 Trills may be either half-step or whole step and long or short and may be played at a steady speed or increasing in speed; Jerome described only upper-neighbour trills; on an organ the principal note was sustained throughout the trill.

We cannot determine for certain the extent or placement of ornaments in any given repertory from this period, but the following principles are true in the repertory for which we have facts, and until further information is available they can be accepted as a method of approaching the music before 1350:

1 Most ornaments are stepwise.
2 Lines that have complex rhythms are given short-duration ornaments, mostly graces.
3 Lines that are rhythmically simple receive ornaments of longer duration, *passaggi*.
4 Syllabic text settings receive few ornaments. More melismatic settings allow more and longer ornaments.
5 Ornaments support the formal organization of the compositions; that is, they do not blur cadences or phrase endings.
6 Most cadences receive ornaments on the penultimate note.

We can only hope that by applying the principles above we are re-creating the music correctly. Perhaps soon information of a practical stylistic nature will be brought to light that will give details and allow us a bit more security in the style of ornamenting the music from these early centuries. The only thing

TABLE 10
Ornamentation styles: general practice

	before 1300*	1350–1450	1450–1525	1525–1600
GRACES	mordents, quick wavers, vibrato, trills of half and whole step, with steady or variable speed	same	same	same, used in combinations
PASSAGGI	fairly short, filling in intervals and turning around a single note	mostly stepwise motion in limited range; variety of rhythms; duple and triple subdivision	mostly duple division; wider range	most elaborate ornaments still on top or bottom line; extreme national differences

*N.B. Before 1300 ornaments were applied only to the top line; from about 1400 short ornaments were added to the lower (tenor or bass) line; and from about 1500 ornaments were applied to all lines.

that is certain is that not to ornament at all is wrong. To bring early music back to life requires the live and inventive participation of the performer for all repertories. It is unfortunate that for the earliest repertory, where the evidence suggests that the performers were given the most freedom with the written notes, the information about exactly what they did is so lacking in detail.

Tables 10 and 11 summarize the changes in both the general practice of ornamentation and the national differences. When coupled with table 1 they should serve as a reminder of those details found above and in the repertory.

ORNAMENTATION IN ENSEMBLE

So far we have concentrated on solo ornamentation, but sometimes all musicians in an ensemble ornamented, at least in the sixteenth century. (I refer, of course, to ensembles of soloists for the most part, although according to Vicentino, in 1555, on some occasions after the mid-sixteenth century ornaments were applied when parts were doubled. In those cases only one person on each part added the ornaments while the others performed the part as written. [14] This would obviously limit the kinds of ornaments applied since the correct note would be sounded throughout the time value. An occasional

TABLE II
Ornamentation styles: national differences

	1300–1400	1400–1525	1525–1625
ITALIAN	some graces, mostly *passaggi* of one beat to several bars in length; much variety in range of subdivision and rhythmic combinations	some graces; wide ranges of *passaggi* with much rhythmic variety	few graces; long bursts of *passaggi* with rhythmic variety tending towards the dramatic
FRANCO-NETHERLANDISH	graces and *passaggi*; less elaborate subdivision; more varied rhythms; shorter *passaggi*; use of unequal rhythms	less rhythmic complexity; preference for short groups; more graces	mostly graces; *passaggi* short with even motion; long, even *passaggi* in instrumental music
ENGLISH	graces and *passaggi* rather short; some rhythmic variation in lower lines; *passaggi* less rhythmically varied	some graces and *passaggi*; short and smooth; duple subdivision	some graces; short and long *passaggi* with even motion; in instrumental music long *passaggi* on repeat
SPANISH	some unequal subdivision; quick graces; short and rhythmically varied *passaggi*	many graces and *passaggi*; wide mix of quick, medium, and long groups, both even and rhythmically varied	same
GERMAN	few graces; mostly short *passaggi* for interval fill-in or turning around one note; even and regular	some graces; medium-length *passaggi*; subdivision; little rhythmic variety	conservative use of graces and *passaggi*; some long groups; even rhythm

dissonance would be undetected, but extended use of upper and lower neighbours, for example, would cause sustained dissonance.) The chief differences between ensemble and solo ornamentation seem to be in quantity; the style is the same. We can begin with Maffei's rules for ensemble ornamentation: limit each performer to three or four *passaggi* per composition; ornament principally at cadences; and have regard for other performers, taking care that only one person ornaments at a time.

Maffei's own example supports his rules exactly, but Dalla Casa, writing in

7.22 Cipriano de Rore 'A la dolc' ombra,' bars 1–7:
a/ ornamentation by Girolamo Dalla Casa; b/ original

After Gertrude Parker Smith, ed. *The Madrigals of Cipriano de Rore for Three and Four Voices*
Smith College Music Archives, vol. 6, 1943. Ornamentation from Girolamo Dalla Casa *Il Vero Modo* 1964

1584, is a bit more generous, as can be seen in his embellishments for all four parts of Rore's madrigal 'A la dolc' ombra' (example 7.22). Although Dalla Casa allows ornaments in a few more spots than just cadences, there is some degree of restraint, and he illustrates a rule given earlier by Zacconi: delay embellishments until after the first notes at the beginning of the composition. There is no reference to the use of graces, but we can suspect that they could be added in moderation without causing problems.

Francisco Guerrero, writing in 1586, provides us with a clear statement of duties and cautions for ensemble ornamentation by instrumentalists:

First, Rojas and Lopéz shall always play the treble parts: ordinarily on shawms. They must carefully observe some order when they improvise glosses, both as to places and to times. When the one player adds glosses to his part, the other must yield to him and play simply the written notes; for when both together gloss at the same time, they produce absurdities that stop one's ears. Second, the same Rojas and Lopéz when they at appropriate moments play on cornetts must again each observe the same moderation in glossing: the one deferring to the other; because, as has been previously said, for both simultaneously to add improvised glosses creates insufferable dissonance. As for Juan de Medina, he shall ordinarily play the contralto part, not obscuring the trebles nor disturbing them by exceeding the glosses that belong to a contralto. When on the other hand his part becomes the top above the sackbuts, then he is left an open field in which to glory and is free to add all the glosses that he desires and knows so well how to execute on his instrument.[15]

This statement pertains to performance in Spain from the end of the sixteenth century and agrees with the contemporary example by Dalla Casa in Italy (example 7.22). We have seen that Maffei's statements in the mid-sixteenth century were more conservative and that in the mid-fifteenth century ornaments were usually concentrated in the top voice. The small amount of evidence we have, therefore, suggests that ornamentation of parts other than the superius probably began near the end of the fifteenth century, coincident with the new compositional techniques of the Renaissance period. The tradition of ensemble ornamentation apparently carried on throughout the sixteenth century, at least in Italy and Spain, becoming somewhat more elaborate as the century progressed.

We can now proceed to the practical application of what we have learned.

Ornamentation instructions for modern performers

HOW TO ORNAMENT IN SOLOS

We have seen that there is some difference in style, quantity, and placement of ornaments in the various centuries. But graces and *passaggi* are common to most, and thus we shall begin by concentrating on the ornaments themselves, leaving the consideration of style until after the basic techniques have been grasped.

Start by selecting a composition from the repertory with simple rhythms and melodic phrases, such as example 7.23, and proceed as follows:

1 Play or sing through only the first phrase (bars 1–8) as written several times at the correct performance tempo (approximately ♩ = 120) until you feel comfortable with it. You should be almost to the point of memorizing it.

2 Select a simple cadential formula from example 7.3 and play through the phrase adding the cadence ornament at the point marked c until you feel comfortable doing so.

3 Select two places within the phrase, such as those marked a and b for the addition of a simple grace, upper- or lower-neighbour, as described above (p. 151).

7.23 Anonymous 'Fontaine a vous dire le voir,' superius
After Jeanne Marix, ed. *Les musiciens de la cours de Bourgogne au xve siècle, 1420–1467*
Editions de L'Oiseau-Lyre 1937. Used by permission

4 Play or sing through the phrase several times adding the same cadence formula and the same graces until you can do it with ease and the additions sound graceful. Do not write them down. Ornaments are meant to be spontaneous, and one of the things you are trying to overcome is your reliance on the written page.

5 Play through the same phrase many more times, adding the same kind of grace in a number of other places.

6 When you have enough facility with the single grace to be able to add it virtually anywhere without disturbing the tempo, try another kind of grace and start again.

7 When you have facility with several kinds of graces, try mixing them.

8 Start again, and this time add simple *passaggi*, filling in the interval at d and e, for example.

9 Add back two different graces and perform the passage with graces, *passaggi*, and the cadence formula.

10 Go to the next phrase in the same composition and start again from no. 1 above. The entire composition should be worked in this fashion, phrase by phrase. When you have finished and can ornament in this way with ease you have accomplished a kind of neutral ornament facility that can be adapted to particular styles with only a bit of change.

11 At this point you must consider points of style such as what to add and where to add it. Go to the discussion above and determine the style characteristics of the country and century of your composition (this one is mid-fifteenth-century French). Study the discussion, check with actual examples from the literature, and decide how you must adjust your ornaments to become stylistically correct.

Among the items for singers to consider in addition to those indicated in the discussion are vowels, some of which should not be used for an extended *passaggio* (see above, p. 56), there are two possible solutions:

– change the word underlay (an interesting example of this can be seen in example 7.15e, where the text in the ornamented line was simply not repeated in order to give more flexibility to the underlay);
– use a short ornament instead, if the unfavourable vowel cannot be avoided.

For an instrumentalist the choice of ornaments is occasionally dictated by the technical problems of the instrument – extremely difficult fingering, for example. Each instrumentalist should seek out those ornaments and variations of ornaments that are not only stylistically correct but also lie well on the instrument.

12 Make the additions, deletions, and corrections, and you have completed one ornamentation.

13 Select additional compositions from the same country and era until you finally have a grasp of a single style and can apply the correct ornaments to a good portion of that repertory. As you expand your repertory begin each time with no. 1 above and methodically follow each step, laborious though it may be. As you gain more confidence in your ability and become more familiar with the variety of possible ornaments it will be possible to eliminate the steps one by one until finally, probably after several months of constant practice, you will be able to add a small mixture of graces, *passaggi*, and cadence formulae to an entire composition after first becoming acquainted with the unornamented version.

This approach can be applied to each of the various ornamental styles described here. You should probably limit yourself to one style at a time until you have mastered it in order to eliminate any confusion. Since all styles have the same basic elements, you must keep in mind their differences as to quantity, placement, and proportions. Even the flowing *passaggi* of the late sixteenth-century Italian style are little more than a series of the graces and filled-in intervals, all connected together, although once the number of notes in a *passaggio* reaches a certain point it takes on its own shape, as in the more extensive examples from the manuals. At that time the ornament is far more free. In a rapid *passaggio* such as example 7.17b above, for example, all the notes of the scale are included, and therefore the notes of the original, no matter which they might be, are included in the ornament. This is much closer to improvisation than it is to the more reserved style of adding graces and fill-ins to an existing melodic line, but it can be approached, at least in part, in the manner outlined above.

Most of the early writers emphasized that each musician must eventually establish an individual style – a point made clear by the vast differences in the examples given in the manuals. For modern musicians, however, there is the added problem of first learning to be stylistically correct in the various eras and countries. A personal style is the last step in the learning process and will appear of its own accord once the many examples from the repertory have been studied to the point where they can be imitated with facility.

The following points of caution should be remembered when learning to embellish:

1 Never write down your ornaments.
2 It is a good idea to have the original line from memory when applying ornaments.
3 Always rehearse the embellishments at the correct tempo.
4 Learn one style at a time. Continue to work with a variety of compositions from a single era until you feel comfortable with your ability to stay within the bounds of that particular style.
5 Continually check what you have done with examples from the repertory.
6 When you have enough confidence to ornament in public:
   a Try your ideas out in an ensemble piece rather than in a solo composition; this is Zacconi's advice for the beginner because errors are less likely to stand out in ensemble.
   b Select a set of embellishments ahead of time and stick to them, but do not write them down. When you have more confidence and experience you can be more spontaneous in public.
   c Just add a few short embellishments at first to build your confidence.

REPERTORY FOR SOLO ORNAMENTATION

Virtually every composition, sacred or secular, is a candidate for ornamentation, although there is some evidence that ornaments added to sacred music were a bit more conservative than those for the secular repertory of the same period. Any composition can be considered a soloist piece, including those with melody line plus accompaniment and those performed by an ensemble of instruments, whether they be homophonic, imitative, or of the various medieval styles. A melody line with accompaniment allows the soloist more freedom (for example, a lute song or a frottola with lower parts reduced for lute or keyboard), but it is also possible to have solo ornamentation performed by only one of an ensemble of voices or instruments – usually the top voice but occasionally the bottom.

HOW TO ORNAMENT IN ENSEMBLE

The application of ornaments in ensembles is essentially the same as for solo performance. The only difference is that each member ornaments in fewer places, and the style is more subdued: one does not indulge in the lengthy, flamboyant solo style seen in example 7.17.

It follows that each member of the ensemble must first learn the solo technique described above. After that, proceed as follows:

1 Select a sixteenth-century imitative composition. (There is little evidence that ensembles embellished in earlier centuries.)
2 Learn the composition well without ornaments as if it were to be performed in that manner, that is, work out tempo, expression, and so forth.
3 When the composition is learned, first ornament at the cadences in as many of the parts as possible, bearing in mind that only one performer should be ornamenting at a time. This is most easily done in imitative situations where the voices all cadence separately, but it can be applied in other situations by general agreement of the members of the ensemble. (If the cadencing is paired, for example, you will have to decide which performer will ornament, but look at the parts first; not all parts will lend themselves conveniently to ornamentation at that point.) The ornament is applied to the longer notes in the passage just preceding the cadence note, but not to the cadencing note itself (note the position in example 7.22).
4 If the same line is embellished by several singers in rapid succession, they should attempt to make the ornaments resemble those of the first person to ornament that passage, although they need not be exact – a rather difficult thing to accomplish extemporaneously.
5 A few other ornaments can be added throughout the composition, notably on a new imitative entry, but avoid the first note or two in order to not confuse the pace of the composition and throw the others off the beat.

REPERTORY FOR ENSEMBLE ORNAMENTATION

For ensemble ornamentation the most convenient repertory is the imitative material, both sacred and secular, from the sixteenth century because of the relative ease of avoiding simultaneous ornamentation. But other types of compositions from that century will allow for a modest amount of ornamentation by all members, and occasional short graces can be used without fear of confusing the harmonies or causing great dissonances.

SUMMARY

The evidence that has survived tells us that ornamentation was regularly added in performances of early music. Certain figures peculiar to each century and location were the particular elements of local style, but the basic ideas of graces, *passaggi*, and cadential figures were common to all. In a modern re-creation of this music performers should be prepared to add some of these according to the proper styles, as discussed above, and to decide how much to add within any particular style. It is not necessary for all embellishments of, say, a sixteenth-century Italian composition to take on the florid extremes found in some of the manuals, nor is it wise for many even to attempt this. The performers must decide how much they feel capable of adding. The fact that a sixteenth-century virtuoso wished to display his technical prowess does not indicate either that it was considered in good taste or that everyone in his era strove to emulate him; that some performers in the early centuries displayed their technique at the expense of the music is well documented.[16] What is suggested here is that some ornaments should be added to most early music, and that the quantity and type should be decided according to the evidence of style, the ability of the performer to execute them gracefully, and the effect the ornaments have on the composition. It is up to modern performers to decide for themselves the degree to which they will decorate the music and/or display their technique. The two elements are not incompatible, and each case must be decided on its own.

Improvisation

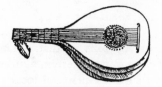

The role of improvisation

MPROVISATION played a large role in the musical life of the Middle Ages and Renaissance. Much of the sacred and secular music, both vocal and instrumental, included improvisation of some or all parts by either a soloist or an ensemble of soloists. The church organist improvised settings of the chant, complete preludes, intonations, and toccatas, and church choirs were expected to improvise polyphonic settings over a cantus firmus and even to improvise freely an entire polyphonic composition. Wandering minstrels and troubadours improvised the melodic settings of poetry, and it is thought that much of Orfeo's part in Poliziano's *Feste d'Orfeo* (1480) was performed as an improvised melody to the improvised accompaniment of a lyra da braccia.[1] Instrumentalists invented entire dances, new verses to existing dances, preludes, and vocal accompaniments, both solo and in ensemble. The fifteenth-century basse dance existed only as a set of long notes which were played by one instrumentalist while one or two others improvised counterpoint around it; and every good instrumentalist was expected to be able to invent a series of variations over one of the standard ostinato bass lines. Improvised performance was a part of every type of music during the early centuries, and some of the techniques will be discussed here.[2] Instrumental improvisation continued to be popular in all countries throughout the Middle Ages and Renaissance and well into the nineteenth century. Vocal improvisation was also popular during the early centuries, but it was less so after the seventeenth, and apparently after the Reformation polyphonic improvisation of sacred vocal music was discouraged in Protestant Germany, although it continued to be practised widely in all other European countries.[3]

The improvisation of imitative vocal polyphony and instrumental fantasias, ricercares, and so on in the sixteenth century requires an extensive knowledge of counterpoint and is therefore beyond the scope of this study. Discussion here is restricted to monophonic and simple chordal preludes and the addition of one and two parts to an existing melody, forms that do not require such a detailed background on the part of the performer.[4]

Improvising a prelude

Instrumental preludes were apparently a fairly common musical form through the Middle Ages and the Renaissance. They were used to introduce sacred and secular music, both vocal and instrumental. A prelude has several practical uses: to set the mode of the composition that is to follow, to check the tuning of the instrument (especially a plucked string), to relax the performer, and to gain the attention of the listeners. They were usually improvised by the professional musicians, but some examples of composed preludes can be found in the keyboard and lute repertories after the mid-fifteenth century.[5]

Preludes were generally monophonic during the Middle Ages (although always with the possibility of a drone) and were usually performed on a lute, harp, or vielle, and in the Renaissance they could be either monophonic or polyphonic and were usually performed on lute or keyboard, although theoretically any instrument could perform one. The use of a prelude in connection with secular music has been mentioned in chapters 5 and 6. In sacred music they were performed on organ and could serve as an introduction to an instrumental work or vocal compositions, either monphonic or polyphonic.

The structure of a prelude is quite free. Its only real musical requirement is to introduce the mode of the composition that is to follow, and thus it can be short, as in example 5.12, although some are longer, as in example 8.1. In most cases it can be expanded to nearly any length depending upon the ability of the performer and the needs of the program. If the performer is capable it is an excellent opportunity to display technical proficiency.

To decide on the notes to emphasize in a prelude you must first examine the composition that is to be introduced in order to determine:

1 the modal final – almost always the final note of the composition;
2 the dominant – the next most frequently used note, usually a fifth above the final (you can determine this by simply observing which note besides the final is most used as a cadence and in positions of melodic importance);
3 the other notes used frequently in the composition.

8.1 Adam Ileborgh 'Praeambulum in D,' which can be transposed to A, F, and G.
Tablature of Adam Ileborgh, 1448. Willi Apel, ed. *Keyboard Music of the Fourteenth and Fifteenth Centuries*
© 1963 by American Institute of Musicology/Hänssler-Verlag, D-7303 Neuhausen-Stuttgart (West Germany)
(CEKM vol. 1) No. 69.010. Used by permission

These are the items you must emphasize in your prelude, and in that order of importance. There are literally no other requirements. The problem faced by the improvisor then, is not that of complying with a rigid set of rules but the opposite: what to do with all of the freedom.

The two notes you must emphasize the most – the final and the dominant – can be brought out by repetition, and therefore the goal is to find interesting ways to vary your presentation of the essential two notes, using the other notes of the mode to do this. The following possibilities are available:

1 *Variable tempo* Preludes usually contain a mixture of fast and sustained passages in a free tempo, presented in a dramatic manner.

2 *Variety of rhythm* You are not constrained to choose rhythms from the composition to follow, although you may do so as a source of raw material. These rhythm patterns should be developed in a far more dramatic way than they are in the composition.

3 *Melodic line* There is usually no real melody to a prelude, although you may choose a characteristic melodic figure from the composition to follow, as in the case of the rhythm. You are also free to develop your own melodic and rhythmic figures as long as the prelude continues to emphasize the mode.

4 *Scale* One method of bringing out the notes of a scale with emphasis on its final and dominant is to single out each note individually and invent a melodic-rhythmic passage around it showing its relationship to the final. Example 8.2 shows this technique in a portion of a prelude centred around

8.2 Section of a prelude

the final G with dominant D. The section in the example emphasizes the notes A, B, and C and their relationship to G and D. The rhythmic and melodic variations possible in this technique should provide material for preludes of any length. The only caution is that you should return to the final and dominant more frequently and more elaborately than to any other note in order to keep the emphasis balanced in their favour.

5 *Contrasting sections* Many compositions involve at least one section in which there is a change of mood, tonal area, or note emphasis. These contrasts can also be emphasized in the prelude in various ways, for example, the employment of the technique described in no. 4.

The above comments refer to both the monophonic preludes and those of the chordally accompanied type from the fifteenth century. The chordal additions were merely simple consonances – open fifths and thirds in the mode – to which was added a free-flowing treble line, as in example 8.1. The selection of chords was made in accordance with the notes emphasized in the composition to follow. The rules of counterpoint given below (pp. 190–7) were followed for the selection of consonances and voice leading.

Improvising to a cantus firmus

The other type of improvisation to be discussed here involves the addition of a line or lines to an already existing melody referred to as a cantus firmus. This type of improvisation took on several forms from parallel lines to counterpoint, and apparently both styles were used beginning in the Middle Ages and lasting well into the seventeenth century.

ORGANUM

The custom of singing a melody in parallel intervals is quite old; we know of its existence from as early as the ninth century. In its simplest form it involves selecting an interval and merely imitating the melody exactly at that interval from beginning to end. The intervals of an octave, a fourth, and a fifth

8.3a Combinations of octave and fifths in parallel organum: o = cantus firmus;
• = added voice

8.3b Modified parallel organum

were all accepted throughout the late Middle Ages and are authentic ways to perform a monophonic melody. The medieval treatises refer only to the application of organum to liturgical music, but we can suspect that it would also have been applied to secular music; the tradition survives in several European folk cultures. The octave, fourth, or fifth can be added either above or below the cantus firmus, and the two intervals can be combined, as in example 8.3a.

Several refinements of the idea of parallel organum grew for short periods of time in the tenth through the thirteenth centuries. One involved beginning and ending each phrase in unison, with the added voice remaining on the first pitch until the interval of a fourth or fifth had been reached, at which point the voices would proceed in parallel motion until the penultimate note of the phrase, as in example 8.3b. A version of this idea continued in England until the late fifteenth century, involving the addition of a voice above the cantus firmus in parallel fourths and a third voice below the cantus firmus in thirds and fifths (faburden). A similar technique was used on the continent (fauxbourdon) in which the cantus firmus is placed in the top voice, the middle voice remains in parallel fourths below it, and the lowest voice provides sixths and octaves with the cantus firmus. Both techniques produced more or less parallel $^6_3$ sonorities. The compositions to which this technique can be applied are fully notated in modern editions.

COUNTERPOINT

The other style of composing to a given melody (cantus firmus) is based on a series of rules that became the foundation of Western harmonic practice for the next several centuries. Students of counterpoint will recognize the rules which, in a more detailed form, constitute the method of polyphonic composition known as 'species counterpoint.' The basis of improvised polyphony is the same as that of written polyphony, but the standards were somewhat less rigid because of the problems involved in extemporized performance. Instrumentalists and singers were apparently capable of improvising in many parts, but only the most common types, two-part and three-part, will be discussed here.[6]

Rules of two-part counterpoint

To construct a single line of counterpoint either above or below an existing melody the following rules were observed:

1 Only perfect intervals can be used at the beginning and end of a phrase: unison, fifth, octave. (Intervals larger than the octave were considered to be the same as those within the octave: for example, a tenth = a third.)
2 Stepwise motion should be used wherever possible.
3 Contrary motion (moving in the direction opposite to that of the cantus firmus) is preferred.
4 Parallel motion is not permitted for the perfect intervals: for example, there should not be two or more fifths in a row.
5 Consecutive perfect intervals of different sizes can be used: for example, an octave followed by a fifth.
6 Several imperfect consonances – thirds, sixths – of either the same or different sizes may follow one another.
7 If the cantus firmus leaps, the counterpoint can move by step in similar (rather than contrary) motion to a perfect consonance.

There were more rules given by the theorists in the various centuries, but these were the essential ones needed to be able to construct a second part to an existing melody. Whether the second voice is written completely above the cantus firmus, completely below it, or crossing it, the rules remain the same concerning the kinds of motion, intervals, and sequences of consonances.

Of the two imperfect consonances it would appear that the sixth was less used and has less freedom of motion than the third. The sixth could be used between perfect intervals and within a passage of thirds, but two or more parallel sixths were used only to signal that the next note was to be the cadence. Parallel thirds did not necessarily have to become a cadence.

The rules given all refer to one note of counterpoint against a single note of the cantus firmus, but the rules can be applied to the composition of a second voice at a variety of ratios to the cantus firmus, as can be seen in the following examples.

Example 8.4 is a two-part composition which illustrates the rules we have seen above. In constructing the simple counterpoint above the melody, the composer has followed the rules for the most part and has occasionally

Make we joy now in this fest, in quo Christus na tus est; E - - - ya.

8.4 Anonymous 'Make We Joy,' burden

John Stevens, ed. *Musica Britannica* vol. 4, 1958. Used by permission of the Trustees of Musica Britannica and Stainer & Bell Ltd

Ky - ri -

e

8.5 Kyrie 'Cunctipotens Genitor Deus,' bars 1–9. Original chant melody is on the lowest staff.

Dragan Plamenac, ed. *Keyboard Music of the Late Middle Ages in Codex Faenza 117* © 1972 by Armen Carapetyan, American Institute of Musicology/Hänssler-Verlag, D-7303 Neuhausen-Stuttgart (West Germany) No. 65.700. Used by permission

dressed up his accompanying line by filling in an interval (bar 2), embellishing an interval with an upper neighbour (bar 3), varying the rhythm (bars 6 and 7), and anticipating the consonance (bars 2–3). Example 8.5 is similar but is carried to the extreme. The example is from the Faenza Codex, already examined in chapter 7 as a source of virtuoso ornamentation. Again here the composer (arranger?) has followed the rules stated above. If we look at it closely we will see that at the beginning and end of each note of the cantus firmus – here coincident with the bar line – he has carefully chosen notes in accordance with the rules. With so many notes in the invented part he is free to

8.6 Guillaume de Machaut 'Je vivroie liement' bars 1–8, with lower accompanying line added

choose any notes in the course of the bar, as long as the first and last are consonant with the cantus note and follow the rules. Further, he has also obeyed the rules of consonance for the first note of every beat subdivision, often – but not always – using as the first note on counts two and three either the same note as on the first count or an octave with the cantus firmus. Exceptions can be seen on count three of bars 1, 4, and 5 where a ninth, a fourth, and a seventh are used. It is significant that this freedom only takes place at the end of the bar, similar to the position of the fourth used in example 8.4, bar 2. The one rule that is disregarded frequently is the one forbidding parallel perfect motion, as in the motion from bar 3 to bar 4 – parallel octaves G♯ to A. However, in this elaborate style it would be difficult to avoid that problem altogether.

Example 8.5 is a fairly elaborate embellishment of a chant, and from the accounts we learn that the general idea is typical of how organists treated chant when performing either independently or on their sections of *alternatim* performances, with either chant or polyphony performed for the other sections. The raw material was simply the appropriate chant melody, which was accepted as a basic cantus firmus to which the upper line(s) would be improvised according to the rules of counterpoint. Further examples in a less flamboyant style can be found in the Buxheimer manuscript.

The rules we have discussed can be applied to invent a second line for any melody. This can be in an elaborate style, as in example 8.5, in which the quantity of the new line overwhelms the original, or in a fairly simple note-for-note style, as in example 8.4, or even in a simplified style such as

8.7 Common cantus firmus cadence patterns

example 8.6, in which a modest accompanying part has been invented to dress up the melody but not compete with it. As long as the rules of counterpoint are obeyed the new line can be added either above or below the original and at any ratio of notes to the original. The details of era and national style, as outlined in tables 1 and 10, must also be taken into consideration.

Cadences

A basic first step in improvising to a cantus firmus is to establish phrase lengths by locating cadence points. Cadences were determined by the melodic shape of the cantus firmus; generally they occurred on the last note of a passage in which the cantus firmus descended stepwise. Common cadence points were on the final note of such patterns, as indicated in example 8.7: for example the whole-step descent in 8.7a, b, and c, or the ascending pattern in 8.7d. Less frequent was the half-step descent in 8.7e (also see below, pp. 198–9). Cadences were not frequent, and if possible notes important to the mode of the cantus firmus were chosen for the cadence, that is, the final, the dominant, or the note below the final.

Improvising two-part counterpoint

The musicians of the early centuries were apparently able to invent these improvisations extempore by merely looking at the original with the rules in mind. There is nothing to stop modern musicians from writing down either simple or elaborate contrapuntal lines, but it is more challenging and more authentic to learn to do them by sight. We shall approach this in much the same way that we approached ornamentation, that is, by learning a neutral, basic technique which can be expanded later and adapted to a variety of styles. It would be helpful if you were able to hear the original line while playing your counterpoint. The best solution is a tape recorder to play back the cantus firmus as you invent your new line.

First you will need to build a small repertory of stock phrases which you should commit to memory. Certain note patterns are common to all melodic lines, and if you memorize their harmonic solutions it will greatly speed up learning to improvise. This does not mean that the invention of a second line is to be reduced solely to set formulae, but you should have a ready solution to

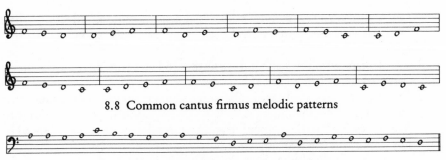

8.8 Common cantus firmus melodic patterns

8.9 Kyrie 'Cunctipotens Genitor Deus'

most situations which can be used by habit if nothing more original occurs to you – a technique used by most twentieth-century jazz musicians.

1 Write out and play or sing into your tape recorder dozens of three- and four-note common melodic patterns such as those in example 8.8. Play or sing each one at various pitch levels and in various modes. Then transpose them to the point of involving scales of up to two flats and two sharps.

2 Learn the rules of counterpoint above and work out one or more solutions for each pattern. At first you can write out the solution for a few of the patterns until you are familiar with the technique according to the rules. But, just as with ornamentation, you should be learning this without reading the solution. As soon as possible commit the counterpoint to memory so that you can add a correct second line by looking only at the cantus firmus. You should learn to improvise both above and below the cantus firmus, and you will therefore need to memorize two different sets of solutions for each melodic pattern. You can either learn both at once or concentrate on either the upper or the lower line until you have acquired facility, then go back and learn the other.

3 When you have memorized a number of solutions to common melodic patterns, apply your technique to larger phrases. Select a simple melodic line such as the Kyrie from example 8.5, given above as example 8.9; the line should be mostly stepwise and have a limited range.

  a Write out the cantus firmus as whole notes.

  b Mentally apply the counterpoint rules for the first eight to ten notes of your example, looking for places to apply the patterns you have memorized. Consider this much of the cantus firmus to be a complete phrase and play your second line in such a way that you form a cadence at the end. Exactly where the cadence should occur must be determined in accordance with the discussion of cadences, above.

c Once you have successfully completed a short phrase, reflect on what intervals you used and check the intervals and progressions against the rules.

d Try it again with the same phrase until you feel confident that you have invented according to the rules.

e Proceed to the next phrase in the same manner, thinking it through first and then playing or singing it. When you have finished the entire cantus firmus, go back to the beginning and attempt the entire melody. Speed is not important but a steady pace is.

4 Select many more melodies from the repertory and write them out as whole notes, gradually increasing their difficulty as you gain facility, that is, more skips and larger ranges. Proceed as above for each until you have acquired facility in inventing note-against-note counterpoint to a variety of melodic shapes. Gradually increase the tempo until you can add your part at approximately $o = 90$.

5 This would be a good point to change sides if you have worked with only an upper or lower voice. Go back to step 1 and learn to improvise the other line.

6 Next, choose melodies with simple rhythms and, beginning in rhythm but slowly, work on your ability to add your line to a part that has rhythm. The complexities of the rhythm should increase as you develop facility.

At this point you have learned a neutral kind of two-part improvisation of the one-to-one type seen in example 8.4. You may wish to adapt your technique to the types seen in examples 8.5 and 8.6 as follows, and of course, considerations of style must be added to all types before you are finished. (See tables 1, 2, 10, and 11 and the discussion on pp. 49–53.)

Simple accompaniment

Your one-to-one technique can now be adapted to the simple style of accompaniment in which the added part moves more slowly than the original melody, as shown in example 8.6:

1 Look for the structural notes of the melody – those of longer duration and in important rhythmic positions – according to the instructions for determining melodic-rhythmic flow on pp. 20–6.

2 Add your part according to the rules of counterpoint considering only the structural notes. You may also add an occasional passing note between your own accompanying notes. These should be added in contrary motion to the cantus firmus, but if they move quickly they need not be considered harmonically.

Florid improvisation

Inventing a florid line requires a combination of the rules of counterpoint and the technique of ornamentation discussed in chapter 7, as can be seen in the following instructions:

1 The first and last notes of your florid pattern should be harmonically compatible with the notes of the original according to the rules of counterpoint.

2 The other notes can be fairly free provided that they do not dwell on notes dissonant with the original and notes harmonically compatible with the original are used at points of major subdivision. For example, in a passage of three beats' duration the first note of beats 2 and 3 should be consonant with the note in the cantus firmus, as seen in example 8.5.

3 The rule forbidding parallel motion of perfect intervals should be observed as far as possible.

Rules of three-part counterpoint

Adding two improvised lines to a cantus firmus is more difficult because each of the two improvisors has to be able to predict what the other will do. From the earliest theoretical writings on the subject of polyphony on through the early Renaissance we are told that all added parts need only be concerned about consonance with the tenor and not with one another. In a small portion of the thirteenth- and fourteenth-century repertory we can find evidence that this rule was taken literally, but in the majority of the polyphonic compositions from that time, and in all works from the fifteenth century forward, we can see that great care was taken to control the amount of dissonance among the parts. One can imagine that more freedom in this matter would have been allowed in improvisations, but even there most of the problems can be eliminated by careful planning and frequent rehearsal.

The placement of the third voice changed at the end of the Middle Ages. As a general rule both parts were above the cantus firmus before 1400 whereas after about 1450 one was above and one below. For the first half of the fifteenth century both could be above or the third part could either be below or weave back and forth. The rules of two-part counterpoint were adjusted in the following ways:

1 Unison, an octave, and a third with the cantus firmus could be added more or less freely in either part, whether above or below.

2 The fourth was allowed in very special cases where there was no possibility of dissonance. It is best avoided in improvisation.

3 The fifth was severely restricted. The problem, like that of the fourth,

8.10 Cadence formula
After Keith Polk 'The Foundations of Ensemble Improvisation in the Late Fifteenth Century'
(unpublished article)

concerned the possibility of the third voice choosing a note that would cause a harmonic clash. For this reason it was seldom used above the cantus firmus except on opening consonances of a phrase where the third voice took the unison or octave, or in cadences as described below. The fifth was allowed below the cantus firmus:

a in the common formula (example 8.10), in which the cantus firmus descends stepwise to the cadence note, the upper part plays a chain of sixths, and the lower line then plays a fifth, a third, a fifth, and an octave;
b at any point where a sixth would be sounded in the upper part (this would require prior agreement between the improvisors concerning the type of cantus firmus patterns in which the interval would be employed, such as on the second sounding of a repeated note in the cantus firmus, as Polk suggests).[7]

4 A sixth was forbidden below the cantus firmus. Above the cantus firmus it was usually associated with a cadence or used as described in no. 3b above.

Cadences

The performers must agree ahead of time where the cadences will occur. This will allow them to align the consonances and to add the chromatics that emphasize a cadence. The position of the cadence was dictated by the stepwise descent of the cantus firmus, as described above (p. 194). Before 1450 the third part commonly cadenced above the cantus firmus, and the most common formula for this was as in example 8.11. Later in the century the lower voice could choose to sound the fifth above the cantus firmus – usually resulting in an octave leap, as in example 8.12a – or could choose unison with the cantus firmus or an octave below. For cadences in which the cantus firmus descends a half step, the common formula was as in example 8.12b. There was also the possibility of a deceptive cadence, which resulted when the lower voice chose to ascend one step on the final note (example 8.12c) to form a third with the cantus firmus rather than jump to a perfect interval. This should be used to avoid what would otherwise be too frequent cadences, but of course it could not be used at the end of the composition.

8.11 Cadence formula with two parts above the cantus firmus
After Keith Polk 'The Foundations of Ensemble Improvisation in the Late Fifteenth Century'
(unpublished article)

8.12 Cadences: a/ octave leap; b/ half-step; c/ deceptive
After Keith Polk 'The Foundations of Ensemble Improvisation in the Late Fifteenth Century'
(unpublished article)

Improvising three-part counterpoint

To learn how to improvise two parts against a cantus firmus it would be best to find another musician who also wishes to learn the technique; both performers should first be able to improvise in two parts. The procedure is virtually the same:

1 Compose and record common cantus firmus patterns.
2 Move slowly and in short phrases at first, attempting both parts above the cantus firmus, one above and one below, and one above with the second weaving above and below.
3 Gradually increase the difficulty of the cantus firmus line and the tempo.
4 Change to a rhythmic cantus firmus.

The possible types of three-part counterpoint are either one-to-one against the cantus firmus or a more florid improvised part in either or both improvised lines. To learn the more florid style begin with simple passing notes and gradually expand according to the method described above for florid two-part improvisation. The earliest examples of music with two florid parts against a cantus firmus do not appear until near the end of the fifteenth century. Prior to that only the highest voice is florid while the other stays at a one-to-one relationship with the cantus firmus, occasionally adding a few passing notes. As with two-part improvisation, the repertory should be studied for details of melodic and rhythmic style.

The technique discussed above can be applied to any of the monophonic repertory of the early centuries, both sacred and secular. Singers and instrumentalists should attempt to add parts to monophonic chant or secular song melodies. Simply choose a monophonic melody or extract the tenor of a polyphonic composition and add your own improvised polyphony to it – a common practice in the early centuries. A combination of instrument(s) and singer(s) is as acceptable as all instruments or all voices. Singers can adopt the text of the original monophonic line or, if more adventurous, can use other poetry from the appropriate era; during the Middle Ages polyphonic compositions often had a different text on each line.

Besides the challenge and general air of authenticity improvisation brings to a program, for instrumentalists there exists an entire repertory of basse dance tenors from the fifteenth century that cannot be performed unless a second (and usually third) part is improvised. The tenors are available[8] and also a few examples of added parts[9] from which some stylistic ideas can be taken.

Articulation

The problem

THE TOTAL ABSENCE of articulation marks in early music is often taken as a sign that each note is to receive equal articulation. This results, of course, from twentieth-century training in which performers are taught to reproduce exactly what is on the printed page as faithfully as possible, but a moment's reflection will reveal how unmusical that would be. It is just as wrong, however, to conclude that the absence of articulation indicates that the composer did not care and that one can therefore articulate as one pleases.

There must have been a basic convention concerning articulation during the early centuries, but composers did not indicate it in the music, just as they did not indicate instrumentation, text underlay, and so on. It was a part of the freedom allowed the individual performer within the confines of the general tradition. The particulars of articulation must have been as much a matter of style as the other refinements we have investigated so far, and we must attempt to recover the general conventions that governed articulation as one more facet of a faithful performance.

The instructions and evidence

SIXTEENTH-CENTURY INSTRUCTIONS

The instructions that have come down to us begin in the early sixteenth century, and so our discussion will begin there. For information concerning articulation during the earlier centuries we shall again turn to the music itself.

Wind instruments

The largest quantity of early articulation instructions refer to tonguing wind instruments.[1] Although some of the instruction books are directed primarily towards players of the recorder, cornetto, or flute, it is clear that the instructions are intended to fit all winds. The writers use a number of different syllables to indicate the placement of the tongue and its motion as well as the strength of the separation. At first it would seem that the syllables they advocate are not the same in the various manuals, but once the differences in pronunciation of consonants and vowels in the European languages are taken into consideration it becomes clear that they actually do agree. The syllables suggested for a medium articulation, for example, are *tere* (several Italian writers), *diri* (Martin Agricola, Germany), and *tara* (Mersenne, France). The syllables are different, but when pronounced in their respective languages they result in approximately the same articulation. The sounds, lengths of separation, and strengths of accent are the same, but the syllables pronounced to achieve them depend on the sounds of the different languages. Rather than complicate the issue here, I shall present only the Italian syllables.[2] The pronunciation of the letters is:

Italian	English
d	*d*
l	*l* (but close to the teeth)
r	*d* (very light)
t	*t*
ch	*k*
a	*ah*
e	*ay* (without the final *i* glide)
i	*ee*
o	*oh*
u	*oo* (as in *choose*)

The writers agree that single notes are articulated by a direct stroke of the tongue to the palate near the teeth. This syllable can be a strong one, as in the letter *t*, or softer as in *d*. This form of single tonguing is to be applied to the relatively slower moving notes of the phrase. We can think of them as 'individual' notes, a distinction that will become clearer below.

For moving passages the writers subdivide the notes into groups of twos, which are to be articulated according to three categories: hard, medium, light, as shown at the top of p. 203.

1 *Hard* (teche) This is equal to the modern 'double tongue' in which the first

hard	te-che	te-che
medium	te-re	te-re
light	le-re	le-re

sound, *te*, is made by a hard and direct stroke of the tongue, as in the discussion of single articulation above, and the second sound, *che*, is made in the throat. This articulation is considered to be too extreme for most purposes, but it apparently did have some application since many of the writers suggested that performers should practice it.

2 *Medium* (tere) This is probably the most frequently used type of tonguing in moving phrases. The first sound *te*, is begun by a direct stroke of the tongue, although not quite as hard as in the first type, in order to allow it to curl back for the *re* sound.

3 *Light* (lere) This was advocated especially for the fastest level of notes. The first syllable, *le*, is sounded by moving the tongue in a manner similar to the *te* sounds of all other articulations but less percussively, and then it is flipped back, as in the *re* of type 2. (Several accomplished North American performers state that the closest English syllables would be *lid'll, lid'll,*[3] although this may produce an incorrect emphasis on the second note.) The writers describe this type as 'sweet' and liken it to the articulation of the *gorgia* (elaborate and rapid vocal embellishments of the Italian singing virtuosos) in vocal music. Ganassi wrote in 1535 that at the fastest speed the second syllable was hardly heard. By assembling the various comments about this type of articulation we can see that it was a very gentle form of separation, and if we note the extreme forms of rapid divisions in example 7.17, it is obvious that in order to keep up the speed only an extremely light tonguing stroke can be applied.

In addition, another kind of articulation without the tongue, called head-breath, is mentioned by several writers. It is not described beyond a mention that the air is released into the instrument without the aid of the tongue.

Although the manuals described four separate types of tonguing (excluding head-breath they are individual, hard, medium, and light), the writers did not mean that only four variations of articulation were possible for wind instrumentalists; Ganassi, for example, mentioned that syllable variables for the two-note types included: for type 1 – *tacha, tichi, tocho, dacha, deche,* etc.; for type 2 – *tara, tiri, toro, tutu,* etc.; and for type 3 – *lara, liri, loro, luru,* etc. Performers are instructed to choose several variations for each type depending upon which are more natural for them. Each variation of consonant and vowel will produce a slightly different degree of separation, and thus what is actually advocated is that each performer develop facility with a large range of articulation strengths from extremely crude (*teche*) to the very gentle (*lere*). The four categories aid in the description, but the desired result was actually an infinite gradation of articulation sounds.

It is interesting to note that all the articulations except individual ones will yield a paired articulation – a strong sound followed by a weak one. 'Strong' is to be understood as a relative term, but it is obvious from the syllables advocated and from the descriptions in the manuals that the first of every pair of sounds was definitely intended to be stronger than the second. This is not to suggest that all the music of the Renaissance was to be performed in groups of two notes, one strong and one weak. The double strokes described above were all intended for use in the relatively fast-moving passages which needed a special kind of tongue motion in order to make articulation possible. Type 1 was extreme and for special effect only. Girolomo Dalla Casa suggested in 1584 that it could be used to cause dread ('far terribilta'). Perhaps he had in mind the sound Monteverdi later referred to as 'stile concitato' – a rough-sounding repeated note symbolizing clash and war. Type 2 was the normal approach to moderately fast passages, and type 3 was for extreme smoothness. Only type 3 could be used in the fastest divisions. Slow-moving notes which were not in motion as subdivisions of the basic unit of measure – in other words, notes that were individually important to the melody – were tongued individually. Since subdivided notes at a fast pace were tongued in a strong-weak fashion, we can probably conclude that all subdivisions of the basic unit of measure should be phrased as strong-weak to some degree, even when they can be tongued individually. As to the strength of the articulation, we shall delay that point until later.

Very little is said about slurs in the early manuals. Dalla Casa was critical of those who slur fast passages just because they have not mastered the type 3 tonguing technique, but by 1636 Mersenne actually indicated slurs in twos. Perhaps the head-breath mentioned by Ganassi a hundred years earlier refers to slur as well. We can suspect that slurring existed and was used in phrases to some extent because it is easy to do, it is the next obvious step after the type 3 tonguing, and it was used by bowed instruments. The extent to which it was used was perhaps similar to that described below.

Bowed instruments

The instructions given for bowed instruments are the same for the overhand bow group (violin type) and the underhand grip (viol type).[4] But because the two different bowing styles have their naturally strong and weak strokes reversed, I shall refrain here from using the phrases 'down-bow' and 'up-bow.' Instead 'strong-weak' will be used and must be adapted to the correct bow motion.

Instructions for bowing are much simpler than those for tonguing. The writers agree that performers must use a strong bow on the odd-numbered notes and a weak bow on the even-numbered, producing exactly the same effect as the tonguing patterns for wind instruments. The extremely long notes are to be broken into two separate strokes, and performers are advised to practise their strokes so that they can deliver separate strokes of equal strength in either direction when required. It is apparent that this last direction refers both to the slow-moving 'individual' notes and to the faster values. The individual notes are to be given their relative strength depending less upon their position as odd or even than on other requirements of the phrase, as discussed below. In fast phrases the notes in duple subdivision would easily fall into the natural strong-weak emphasis of the bow strokes, but not all fast-moving phrases are divided in twos. Performers must be prepared to give the proper strong emphasis to the first note of a subdivision even when it is played in the normally weak bow stroke. Most of the instructions again refer to an even number of notes, but we do have some suggestions for an uneven number. In 1592 Rogniono spoke of two separate notes played in the same direction, and some of the examples indicate that for the group ♩♫ either strong-weak-weak or strong-strong-weak is possible, regardless of the direction of the bow. In 1542 Ganassi advocated arm motion for the relatively slower moving notes and wrist motion for the faster notes.

Most of the instructions for bowing permit slurs within groups having an uneven number of notes in order to recover the bow for the correct strong stroke on the next major subdivision. Ortiz (1553), Rogniono, and Cerreto (1601) actually suggested slurs of groups of fast-moving notes up to four, and small group slurs would seem to be a generally acceptable articulation for fast passages by the end of the sixteenth century.

Keyboard instruments

The instructions for keyboard players[5] make a distinction between good and bad fingers and good and bad notes. The good fingers were usually two and four, the index and ring fingers; the good notes were those at the beginning of a group of two or three, in other words, the notes that fall on the beat or half-beat. We can therefore equate good fingers with strong bows and tonguing syllables, and bad fingers with weak bows and tonguing syllables. The good notes are those in rhythmically strong positions which would receive strong tonguing syllables or bows.

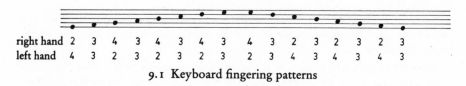

right hand	2	3	4	3	4	3	4	3	4	3	2	3	2	3	2	3
left hand	4	3	2	3	2	3	2	3	2	3	4	3	4	3	4	3

9.1 Keyboard fingering patterns

The thumb (1) and little finger (5) were rarely used except to aid in getting a good finger back on a good note. According to Diruta (1593), a scale passage of an even number of notes, beginning on a strong/good rhythmic position, was fingered as in example 9.1. In scale passages the elbow is swung left or right in order to slant the hand in the direction of the scale to enable the third finger to cross over its neighbour with as much ease as possible. For passages that begin with a short rest, that is, an up-beat pattern, a weak finger was to be used first in order to enable the good finger to be used on the beat or its even subdivision. A right-hand ascending pattern would be fingered thus:

$$\text{♪ ♫♩} \atop 3 \quad 3 \quad \text{etc.}$$

Once again we see that the articulation most easily attained is strong-weak in groups of two. The movement of the third finger over its neighbour in scale patterns renders an articulation of twos just as naturally as the tonguing syllables and the push-pull bowing technique, although in order to achieve that effect a different method is used. Both winds and strings can make their groupings of twos by emphasis on the first note and a lighter sounding of the second. Since that is not possible in the same way on a keyboard instrument, the solution was to leave a tiny space after the strong note, caused by the necessity of lifting the good finger out of the way as the bad finger crossed over it. Emphasis on the good notes could be further exaggerated by even the slightest inequality in the actual execution of the passage (*notes inégales*), an articulation suggested by the fingering (see discussion below, pp. 211–12).

Lute

Lute articulation depends for its basic technique on the alternation of thumb and index finger. The thumb makes a stronger sound than the finger and therefore was assigned to the first notes of phrases beginning on the beat. The finger plays off the beat, either the second note of a duple division or the first note of an up-beat pattern. In triple division the thumb strikes on the beat and two fingers are used for the notes off the beat, and in chordal passages where thumb and fingers are used simultaneously, the single-note subdivisions are

T = thumb   F = finger

plucked according to the principle of placing the accent on the beat or its even subdivision. Some of the more elementary lute articulation patterns are shown above.

It is clear that the common lute articulation will also produce the strong-weak sounds present in the other articulations we have observed. As with the bow, the finger stroke can be made to equal the strength of the naturally stronger thumb for use in slower passages of individual notes, but in faster passages the natural unequal sound will be heard.

Voice

Some aspects of vocal articulation have already been discussed in chapter 4. All writers advocate clear articulation of all notes, although much of the technique cannot be explained with as much clarity as for instruments. In the case of texted passages the advice is to articulate the text clearly, but the situation is less clear in the advice to articulate untexted passages with the throat. The problem concerns how much articulation was expected, since there are no syllables to suggest relative weight, as in wind articulation.

We can assume that for slow-moving passages the amount of separation, accent, and so on would be determined by the musical phrase, just as it would be for instrumentalists. For the approximate sound of the most rapid phrases (*gorgia*) we can use the information in the wind instrument manuals. The softest kind of wind instrument articulation (*lere*) was described by Dalla Casa as being similar to the *gorgia* of singers, and we have already seen that it was described by Ganassi as being so gentle that it was 'hardly articulated at all.' Even allowing for some variation since the two statements are nearly fifty years apart, we can conclude that rapid vocal passages were given the very lightest form of articulation. Further, Zacconi wrote in 1592 that the basis of singing rapid passages is a trill – an ornament that is very lightly articulated with the throat. The rapid vocal passages are therefore articulated as lightly as possible. When these statements are coupled with Finck's advice of 1556 that throat articulation should not sound like a goat, we can find little historical justification for the twentieth-century practice of hard and accented articulation of every note in a rapid passage.[6]

Summary of sixteenth-century articulation

By assembling the advice for singers and various kinds of instrumentalists we can construct a fair idea of the articulation tradition in the sixteenth century. Several of the writers towards the end of the century supported Ganassi's 1535 statement that instrumentalists should look to the voice as their model in all matters of expression. By their own accounts the instrumentalists of the sixteenth century attempted to be as flexible, colourful, and versatile as singers, and thus we can assume a large amount of agreement in their articulation as well as in most other expressive techniques. We can therefore assume not only that the instrumentalists would attempt to imitate the many colours and flexibilities of the voice, as Ganassi clearly spells out, but also that the instructions concerning articulation given by all the writers are an attempt to imitate the technique of the vocalists of the day. In other words, we can probably consider the descriptions of articulations, regardless of where we find them, to be generally applicable to all instruments and to voice. The following summary of the sixteenth-century articulation assumes that to be true, and it is proposed that the following points should be accepted as the characteristic style of the late Renaissance, to be adjusted and adapted depending upon the performance medium.

Single notes

The articulation of the single slow-moving notes in a composition depends mostly upon the musical phrase. The expression of the phrase as a whole must be taken into consideration, and each of the individual notes should be articulated to assist in achieving the desired expression – exactly the same basic principle used in articulating any phrase from any era of music. The difference is that in the sixteenth century all slow-moving notes were given at least some articulation, the amount depending upon the expression desired. There were apparently no slurs in a slow-moving line, but all possible gradations of articulation from detached to extremely gentle were known and practised.

Subdivisions

The basic subdivision in articulation was the alternation of strong-weak in duple groups. For all variants of this the principle was to place the strong articulation on the strong note of the subdivision, that is, on the beat or its even subdivision. Thus in up-beat situations a weak articulation was given to the first note. The strength of the articulation of subdivisions, like that of single notes, encompassed all possible gradations from abrupt and detached to very smooth, and was chosen to best assist with the expression of the phrase.

For the fastest level of divisions – *passaggi* or *gorgia* – the very lightest form was used.

Slur

It would seem that for the most part a slur was used only for graces. The fact that it was so rarely mentioned and given such little space in the manuals suggests that it was not an important part of sixteenth-century style. For the most part all notes (except graces) received some degree of articulation. When used, the slur never extended past four notes in a group; this was undoubtedly organized according to the beat, with a new articulation coinciding with the correct placement of a strong articulation.

Articulation was just one way to achieve expression. Along with this, Ganassi tells us, the instrumental musician must be prepared to vary the expression to imitate the vocalist's range from tender to most lively.[7] Expression should be full of extremes of contrast. If the expression calls for lively playing, all the ingredients – tone, ornaments, and articulation – should reflect this, and to express grace and elegance the ornaments and articulation must be gentle and tender. The standards of artistic expression were obviously much the same then as they are today. The differences between early and modern practices are small stylistic traditions, and a much greater freedom for the performer in the early periods to choose from the available techniques in order to express each phrase according to the demands of the music and in accordance with the style of the era.

THE EARLIER CENTURIES

For the years before the sixteenth century we have no instructions at all and must therefore turn to the instruments and to the music for suggestions on the tradition of articulation.

The bowed and plucked strings from the earlier centuries were different in some ways from those of the sixteenth, but in the matter of sounding technique they were the same: bows always give a stronger sound in one direction than in the other, and although before about 1450 the plucked strings employed a pick, the hand grip of the pick favoured a stronger down-stroke, yielding the same strong-weak pattern as the later thumb and finger. According to what can be seen of the relatively un-curved hand position in the iconography we can also assume that keyboard technique excluded the thumb in the earlier centuries. This also causes a natural strong-weak articulation in moving passages. We cannot know how the tongue was employed in wind instrument performance, but given the strong-weak natural articulation of all other instruments, it is probable that wind players would have developed a technique to match the prevailing articulation – perhaps even the tongue strokes first described in the sixteenth century.

Summary of early articulation

For the early centuries, therefore, a strong-weak articulation pattern can be assumed for notes at the level of subdivision in the same manner as in the late Renaissance. For the articulation of individual notes and the application of the other elements of expression – such as tone, ornaments, and colour – we must examine the intentions of the composer as presented in the music.

We know that in the late Renaissance the expression of the emotional content of the text governed the elements of expression, and the instrument instruction manuals inform us that the instrumentalists were to use the same guide. Thus we can be confident of the basis for assigning the elements of expression in the Renaissance from at least 1500 forward: express the text. This principle was not true of all music in all centuries. In the Middle Ages the music was rarely composed to express the emotional content of the text. (There are some exceptions which will become apparent to the performer once the music is played: for example, the love songs of Francesco Landini.)

For music in which no emotional text relationship is evident, the expression must be derived according to the more abstract principles of motion and rest. There are a number of possible methods of developing motion and relaxation in a line of music: melodic contour, rhythm, and harmony. A composer can select one or a combination of these elements. Simply stated, to increase motion he can add more active rhythmic groups, create a more directly ascending or descending line, or include an increasing number of non-perfect harmonies. Relaxation can be created by reversing these elements: less active rhythms, more wandering melodic line, more frequent perfect harmonies. These elements should suggest to the performer the techniques to be chosen in order to express what the composer has written. Tension can be emphasized by more activity, an increase of volume, and more strident articulation; relaxation by decrease of activity, lessening of volume, and more gentle articulation. A rhythmic line can be emphasized by more obvious articulation and a melodic line by more gentle articulation.

To repeat the key phrase once more: the performer must search the music for the intentions of the composer and, using historical techniques, emphasize what is in the music itself. Articulation, like every other element of performance, is indicated in the music, and the music is ready and willing to

9.2 Tomás de Sancta Maria: two graceful ways to play an even-note passage
After Diana Poulton ' "How to Play with Good Style" by Thomas De Sancta Maria' *LSJ* 12 (1970)

give this information if only the questions are asked of it. It is up to the performer to seek out the inherent requirement of the music, study the basic outlines of historical style, and develop the technical facility necessary to bring the music to life.

NOTES INÉGALES

One final point of articulation should be brought up here. The existence of the performance practice known as *notes inégales* is well documented for the baroque era and after.[8] Less well known is its existence in earlier centuries. The practice involves performing in unequal rhythms passages that are written in equal values. Diana Poulton has documented the instructions for this interpretation from the keyboard and vihuela instruction manual of Tomás de Sancta Maria in 1565.[9] Sancta Maria recommends that passages of equal subdivisions can be performed either as written or, more stylishly, as unequal notes, either long-short or short-long, as indicated in example 9.2. (He further suggests a version of short-term tempo rubato in which the first three notes of a group of four evenly subdivided notes are played more quickly and the fourth is held until the correct metrical time to move forward to the next count.) The *notes inégales* treatment has been seen in the Robertsbridge Codex from England (example 7.4) and can be found in the fourteenth-century Italian dances from Manuscript 29987[10] and in the early fifteenth-century Faenza Codex from Italy.[11] The point is not thoroughly researched yet, but we can suspect that using unequal notes was from earliest times an accepted variation for performing a passage of equal subdivisions. The technique is applied only to subdivisions and never at the level of the counting unit, which means that the shifting of the notes occurs only beneath the level of the count so that the notes on the beat remain there. The amount of inequality used in the baroque period varied from slightly unequal to doubly dotted (♩. ♪), depending on the music itself. The musical examples we have from the early repertory show the ratio of 3:1 (♩. ♪) or 2:1 (♩ ♪) caused by using a triple subdivision.

PART FOUR

Practical Considerations

Presentation

Forming the ensemble

THE SELECTION and presentation of a successful program of early music requires a great deal of thought and experimentation. A number of things must be considered: the repertory, the ensemble, and especially the audience. A program is part of the individual stamp of a particular ensemble, and as such it is partially a personal thing, having to do with individual taste and overall concept; it is therefore not something that can be prescribed. Each group should have a separate and identifiable personality, and what follows here is in no way an attempt to homogenize early music presentations. It should be seen instead as a fund of possible approaches and a source of ideas which can be selected, adapted, and made to serve in a number of ways as the abilities and interests of the individual groups allow.[1]

The size of the ensemble and the abilities of the members will determine to some extent the repertory that can best be presented. If the ensemble is already fully formed there are certain limitations on the kinds of music that can be performed successfully. If the group does not already have a fixed size, decisions should be made concerning what kind of repertory is of interest before the selection of members is completed. The differences have to do with the number of musicians and their abilities. If the ensemble contains a small number – three or four musicians – the medieval repertory may be the most viable, depending on the voices and instruments. Larger groups may wish to perform mostly the Renaissance repertory so that more musicians can participate more often, but again the number and ranges of voices and the types of instruments will help to determine that.

It is tempting to form an ensemble with a large number of people in order to enlarge the possible repertory. In fact, the opposite often occurs. Since a good share of the repertory from both the medieval and Renaissance eras requires four or fewer performers, either the ensemble is restricted to the small repertory of music for many parts or else many performers sit idle while a few rehearse. It should be kept in mind that the choice between a small and large ensemble need not be a definitive choice. For most of the repertory four to six performers work best, and if a good portion of the repertory can be performed with this relatively small number it is always possible to augment the ensemble from time to time as specific repertory requires. In this way the core ensemble can develop a rapport and experiment with advancing its ability to handle various early techniques such as ensemble ornamentation and improvisation and yet have access to instrumental or vocal combinations that are not regularly required. The smaller the group the more easily it will work and the faster the techniques will develop.

The core of a small ensemble should ideally be made up of a good singer and a lutenist, a string player (viol for Renaissance music, vielle for medieval), and a woodwind player. With these performers a great deal of the secular repertory and some of the sacred can be performed. In many cases it will be necessary to substitute instruments for parts originally intended for voice, but that is one of the many flexibilities of early performance practice. If several members can both sing and play, the ensemble is even more flexible. Many small ensembles are more versatile than they realize: an instrumentalist possessing an accurate sense of pitch but not a soloist voice can be used occasionally in a vocal ensemble if given an unexposed line. Vocalists can be given keyboard, psaltery, or percussion assignments if the demands are simple.

Building a collection of authentic instruments is always a good idea, but this can get out of hand and sidetrack you from your main goal, which should be the best possible performance of early music. It is helpful to have versatile members in a small ensemble, but versatility is not an unmixed blessing. Given the practical problem of a limited number of daily practice hours, even the most gifted performer will have trouble keeping up with more than a couple of instruments. If a choice must be made, it is far better to perform the music well on an instrument that is not the ideal first choice than to play it badly on the correct instrument.

Careful and thoughtful search of the repertory will allow a choice of material that uses the musicians to best advantage. Perhaps a good rule of thumb can be borrowed from the commercial world: 'Sell what you have.' Translated into musical terms this means selecting material that shows off the talents of your musicians and either hides or avoids areas in which they are weak.

Perhaps the first thing that should be considered is whether the ensemble should perform in public or should remain, at least temporarily, a reading-learning group. The factors that should help determine this are: the ability of the individual performers, the ability of the ensemble, and the need in your community for an(other) early music ensemble. In other words, ask yourself what you can offer that is worthwhile and not already available. Many of the groups currently performing in public would serve the art and themselves better by performing for their own enjoyment or for an audience of sympathetic close friends. It is a mistake to confuse personal performing enjoyment with those elements that make a good listening experience. The fun element is almost exclusively a performer's criterion; to enjoy a performance a listener needs far more accuracy and communication than many amateur ensembles are willing or able to achieve.

Choosing a program

In choosing material for a program there is no one right way, although there are a few general principles that have proved to be successful and some approaches that can lend interest and appeal. The most frequently encountered program may be referred to as a 'smorgasbord,' that is, 'all the early music we would like to play for you this evening.' The other common type of program is focussed around a theme, and several approaches to this are listed here. Both types can be successful as long as the music is performed well and the program is assembled with the audience in mind.

Possible themes for focussing a program are:
1 *A historical figure*
  The court of Lorenzo de' Medici
  Music for Philip the Good
  The musicians of Maximilian I
2 *A composer*
3 *An era*
  Fifteenth-century music from many nations
  The Spanish Golden Age
  Ars antiqua
  The Reformation
4 *An occasion*
  Christmas
  An *intermedio* from sixteenth-century Italy
  Dedicatory music (motets, chanson, deplorations, and so on, all intended for a specific event or person)

5 *Manuscript/print assembly*
   Petrucci prints
   The Trent manuscripts
   The Mellon Chansonnier
6 *Other varied themes*
   Regrets (a number of chansons with the word 'regrets' in the title)
   Music from France in the fourteenth to sixteenth centuries
   Music of the Meistersingers
   A tour of Spain (music from various Spanish cities)
   Love songs (almost any variety of centuries and countries)
7 *Special shows*
   Liturgical drama
   Music of the French theatre
   Music in Chaucer's time (English music from the fourteenth century, possibly mixed with readings)
   The advantages of programs focussed around a theme are several: they help the director choose from the otherwise overwhelming repertory, give a kind of organization that helps the audience get into the spirit of the occasion, and can be used to help limit the choice of instrumental possibilities.

Good programming

It is not enough simply to choose a number of compositions and play them in alphabetical or chronological order. The audience and the performers need variety, and this can be achieved in a number of ways. Within any group of compositions there are a number of variable aspects already built in:
1 *Length of the compositions* Even if the program contains many similar compositions the lengths can be varied by performing a different number of verses.
2 *Mode of performance* Besides the obvious change from a vocal presentation to an instrumental one, there is also the possibility of inserting an instrumental verse in an otherwise vocal performance and vice versa. Further variations in a group of polyphonic compositions include changing from all voices to solo voice with instrumental accompaniment.
3 *Mixture of settings* Even love songs come in many varieties: dramatic, joyful, melancholy, and so on. A change from a predominantly melismatic composition to a syllabic one or from a work organized in triple metre to one in duple metre also provides variety.
   Variety can even be achieved in performing a series of compositions that

would appear initially to be too similar, such as, say, four late fifteenth-century Tenorlieder:

Lied 1	dramatic	four verses, all with solo tenor voice and three stringed instruments
Lied 2	sad	two verses with tenor voice alone or with lute
Lied 3	joyous	three verses with instruments only, adding more ornaments and percussion on the third verse
Lied 4	melancholy	first verse with instruments only, second verse with tenor voice, third verse with instruments only, fourth verse with tenor voice

Further variety can be achieved by changing the solo voices and/or the instruments in the different lieder, and instrumental compositions, including dances, can be used as separate works, to relieve the vocal material or even as short transitions between songs.

For some compositions several versions are available. A number of the texts and melodies were quite popular in the early centuries, and more than one composer tried his hand at the theme. The chanson text 'Mille regrets,' for example, or the instrumental melody 'La Spagna' can be found in several versions which can be presented either in medley or juxtaposed to lengthen a particular presentation in a program which is otherwise full of short works. In this connection do not overlook lute or keyboard intabulations, which can often be linked to one or more versions of the sung version; Dufay wrote both a three- and a four-part setting of 'Se la face ay Pale,' and a keyboard version can be found in the Buxheimer manuscript. One of the many possible ways of performing this melody would be:
1 three-part with two voices and one instrument
2 keyboard intabulation
3 four-part with various combinations of voices and instruments

It is a good idea to change the size of the performing group during a concert. If there are five members of the ensemble, select some music for one, two, or three performers in order to provide variety for the audience and an opportunity for the other performers to recover and prepare mentally for what is to follow.

Another potential type of variety involves the style of music. Sheer melodic beauty should share the program with technical show and rhythmic interest, the one offering welcome relief from the others. Your audience would like to be treated to all these approaches. The technical show can usually come in the form of a dazzling ornamented version of almost anything on the program.

LITURGICAL MUSIC

The movements of the Mass Ordinary (Kyrie, Gloria, and so on) offer some of the most beautiful and challenging music in the early repertory. But whether it is performed by soloists or chorus, it is difficult for many audiences to appreciate in one sitting an entire Mass that may involve as much as forty-five minutes of detailed listening. In fact the early Mass was not designed for this kind of performance. All movements of the Ordinary except the Kyrie and Gloria were separated by other musical items and prayers. A modern audience may also better appreciate the music if exposed to only parts of the Mass at a time. A program might contain just one or two movements of a Mass, or another possiblity is to spread the movements out over a program, as in the following arrangement:

> Kyrie
> Gloria
> other compositions
> Credo
> INTERMISSION
> Sanctus
> other compositions
> Agnus Dei

If you have chosen a Renaissance Mass performed by a chorus, some or all of the other compositions chosen for the program could be performed by a small ensemble, providing additional variety.

FINALE

Good 'show business' suggests that you attempt to program as a last number a work which involves the entire ensemble. Your audience wants to applaud to show their approval, and you can help them by giving them something flashy at the end. Having the entire ensemble involved in the final composition also helps them to show appreciation for the group as a whole. This is no place for a 'down' composition because it is difficult for the audience to adjust from a sombre mood to express the enthusiastic appreciation they wish to show. This may seem rather too commercial for some, but if you wish to play for an audience you must consider them and their needs.

THINGS TO AVOID

Experience suggests that it is wise to avoid an entire concert of sixteenth-century dance music. Unless you have an unusual audience and extremely gifted ornamentors, this results in sheer boredom for all but the performers because it is nearly impossible to provide enough variety to keep the listeners interested. On the other hand, this repertory makes a good addition to a program of other material, and if your area is fortunate to have a competent teacher of historical dance, a few historical dances (with graceful dancers) are a very appealing addition to a program.

Another thing to avoid is changing instruments for effect; although this has been recommended as a source of variety, it does involve a real danger. It is difficult for performers to keep their concentration on the approximately twenty different compositions that constitute the usual early music program, and this problem is exacerbated each time the change of composition involves a change of instrument. (There is no historical justification for a single performer to change instruments in mid-piece.) In addition, instruments often go out of tune if they have not been played for a few minutes, and this causes tuning delay between numbers, which makes the audience restless. Once you change instrumentation it is wise to retain it for several compositions before changing again, and even then to change only as the music demands. At first frequent change will dazzle the audience, but they soon grow tired of new sounds and look to the musical product, and the performance will be unattractive if the musical interpretation suffers because of the number of instrument changes. In other words, instrument variety should not be looked upon as a major source of interest.

Programs and program notes

It is important to let your audience know what they are listening to. The minimum information to provide would be the titles and composers, and it is also a good idea to include composers' dates (for anonymous works, the period can be given). Your audience would also like to know what you are singing about, and you can inform them by either telling them from the stage or including a full translation, a synopsis, or a description in the program. (For a discussion of singing a translation, see above, p. 87). Before you choose, several factors should be considered.

Giving the information from the stage sets a friendly and informal tone for the concert and warms the audience up quickly, but if this is done by one of the performers it may cause problems for that performer in concentrating on the composition to follow. It also interrupts the flow of a concert and should not be done often. However, it can often be quite successful to have a non-performing narrator recite the translation or a synopsis of the text before a song. The narrator and the soloist should spend time co-ordinating their gestures so that the audience can associate the emotions of the sung version as closely as possible with that of the narration. It is important to keep in mind, however, that trained actors can read a script and sound natural, whereas most others sound stilted when reading, and that will produce an effect opposite to the friendly, relaxed tone you are seeking. Amateurs should speak informally and not read from a script, although notes may be acceptable. Public speaking is not necessarily part of a musician's talents, so unless the delivery is clear, pleasing, and warm the practice is best avoided.

Providing a full translation of a text, which can take up many pages, may result in noise as the audience follows the text, and the loss of eye contact between performer and audience will detract from the presentation. In many cases this may also give the audience more information than it needs. Certain things do not need translation in some places: the Mass, for example, would not need translation for a church group. And a text that is a clever play on words may best be presented as a description rather than as a translation. For a narrative text either a full translation or a stanza by stanza synopsis is usually necessary, but for love songs in which successive verses are only an elaboration of a single idea, often one or two short sentences will be sufficient: 'The poet longs for his fair Anna but she prefers another. He begs for an early death to end his misery.' If this really is the entire message, the expression of the details and nuances of the text can be taken care of by the singer.

Program notes can also be of interest to the audience; information about the court or chapel from which the music originated and vignettes about some of the composers or occasions are of interest and help the audience empathize with the era.

Opinions are divided about including the instrumentation of each work on the program. By all means include a list of the performers, their voices, and their instruments so that the audience can identify the unfamiliar instruments which will no doubt attract their curiosity. However, it is not necessary to list the specific scoring of every composition because this distracts attention from the translation, notes, and music and locks the performers into scoring they may wish to change after the program has gone for printing.

Other kinds of information occasionally found on programs may not be of interest to the audience. Notes that list the manuscript or print sources of each composition are directed more towards musicologists and other early music group directors. This type of fact tends to baffle an audience because they are not familiar with the secret musical information implicit in the fact that a particular composition is from Trent MS 87 or Petrucci's Canti B. This kind of detail and arguments for or against various points of transcription, edition, and so forth are best left to trade journals, academic meetings, and workshops. To sum up, when composing program notes the approach should be to give the audience the information that will best enable it to enjoy the music. Anything else should be omitted.

Sources of Literature and Editions

Finding editions

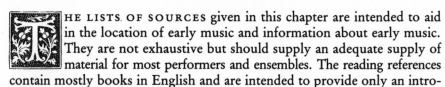

HE LISTS OF SOURCES given in this chapter are intended to aid in the location of early music and information about early music. They are not exhaustive but should supply an adequate supply of material for most performers and ensembles. The reading references contain mostly books in English and are intended to provide only an introduction to the subjects.

Attention is drawn to two of the reference books especially, which are of enormous help in locating music: Heyer *Sets* and Charles *Handbook*. Both list the contents of collections of music and also locate individual compositions by various composers that are 'hidden' in collections and anthologies. Thus, if you wish to find a particular motet by Palestrina, for example, it is possible to locate it in Heyer *Sets* instead of searching through the more than thirty volumes in the collected works of Palestrina. Or if you wish to find some music by Heinrich Isaac, the composer index in both reference books will list a number of collections in which it can be found.

The following lists and the bibliography include only those editions you would not find by looking up the composers' names in the library card catalogue. The *Collected Works/Opera Omnia/Werken* of single composers are omitted if they are collected under the composer's name; thus, the *Opera Omnia* of Alexander Agricola are omitted because they are found under the composer's name, while those of Guillaume de Machaut are included because they are found in *PMF* 2, 3, and in *PAM* 1¹, 3¹, and 4², collections that do not contain the composer's name in the title. Heyer *Sets* and Charles *Handbook* will tell you if the collected works have been published. There is not yet a standard way of listing the names of early composers, and therefore when searching for material in either a book index or library catalogue, you may have to look in several places. Josquin des Prez, for example, may be listed under *J*, *D*, or *P*, or under all three.

KEY TO THE LISTS

All citations in this chapter are given in a shortened form for quick reference. The full reference is given with annotations in the bibliography. Single-volume collections and books are listed by the author's or editor's last name and a word taken from the title: e.g., Apel *Notation* refers to W. Apel *The Notation of Polyphonic Music, 900–1600*. Anthologies and periodicals are listed only in code reference: e.g., GMB refers to A. Schering, ed. *Geschichte der Musik in Beispielen*. Multiple-volume collections are listed in code reference with volume numbers in Arabic numerals: e.g., EDM 5 refers to *Das Erbe deutscher Musik*, volume 5.

In the repertory lists the following abbreviations are used: mono = monophonic; poly = polyphonic. (These abbreviations are used only for music before ca 1400. Music after that date is assumed to be polyphonic unless indicated otherwise.)

SOURCES

1.1 Bibliography

Brown *Printed*, Charles *Handbook*, Coover *Records*, Grove *Dictionary*, Hagopian *Italian*, Heyer *Sets*, Hilton *Index*, Hughes *Sixth*, Lyons *Lute*, Smet *Viola*, Zaslaw *Performance*

1.2 Music history

Brown *Renaissance*, Hoppin *Medieval*, NOHM 2, 3, 4, Reese *Middle*, Reese *Renaissance*, Seay *Medieval*, Wangermée *Flemish*

1.3 Notation and tempo

Apel *Notation*, Bank *Tactus*, Gullo *Tempo*, Jacobs *Tempo*, Mendel *Triple*, Parrish *Notation*, Rastall *Notation*, Sachs *Rhythm*, Waite *Rhythm*

1.4 Instruments and iconography

AMIS *J*, Bachmann *Bowing*, Baines *Instruments*, Baines *Tinctoris*, Baines *Woodwind*, Bessaraboff *Ancient*, Blades *Early*, Blades *Percussion*, Bowles

Haut, Bowles *Hiérarchie*, Bowles *Iconography*, Bowles *Instruments*, Bowles *Musikleben*, Bowles *Processions*, Boydell *Crumhorn*, Boyden *Violin*, Brown *Iconography*, Brown *Instrumentation*, Brown *Voices*, Crane *Extant*, Gill *Plucked*, GSJ, Hunt *Recorder*, JLS, JVG, LSJ, McKinnon *Instruments*, McKinnon *Representations*, Marcuse *Dictionary*, Marcuse *Survey*, Mersenne *Harmonie*, Meyer *Crumhorn*, Montagu *Instruments*, Munrow *Instruments*, Panum *Stringed*, Polk *Bands*, Polk *Dufay*, Polk *Ensemble*, Rastall *Consort*, Remnant *Rebec*, RIDIM, Sachs *Instruments*, Whitwell *Wind*, Winternitz *Instruments*, Winternitz *Symbolism*

1.5 Performance practice

Dart *Interpretation*, Dolmetsch *Interpretation*, Donington *Interpretation*, EM, Frotscher *Aufführungspraxis*, Kottick *Collegium*, MacClintock *Readings*, Strunk *Sources*, Warner *Performance*, Whitwell *Wind*, Zaslaw *Performance*

1.6 Articulation, Improvisation, Ornamentation

a *Primary sources*

Agricola *Musica*, Bassano *Motetti*, Bassano *Ricercare*, Bermudo *Libro*, Bovicelli *Regole*, Brunelli *Esercitii*, Cardanus *Musica*, Cerreto *Prattica*, Coclico *Compendium*, Conforto *Breve*, Conrad *Modo*, Dalla Casa *Modo*, Diruta *Transilvano*, Finck *Practica*, Ganassi *Fontegara*, Ganassi *Rubertina*, Jerome *Musica*, Maffei *Lettere*, Mersenne *Harmonie*, Ortiz *Tratado*, Ramis *Musica*, Rognioni *Selve*, Rogniono *Passaggi*, Sancta *Libro*, Vicentino *Musica*, Virgiliano *Dolcimelo*, Zacconi *Prattica*, Zarlino *Istitutioni*

b *Secondary sources*

Aarset *Improvisation*, Aarset *Polyphony*, AOM 12, Brown *Embellishing*, Erig *Diminutions*, Ferand *Improvisation*, Ferand *Vocal*, Ferand *Sodaine*, Ferguson *Keyboard*, Horsley *Diminutions*, Horsley *Improvised*, Horsley *Techniques*, Houle *Tonguing*, Polk *Flemish*, Polk *Foundations*, Poulton *Graces*, Poulton *Style*, Speck *Relationships*, Woodfield *Viol*

1.7 Periodicals

Periodicals that frequently contain information concerning the performance of early music are: AMIS J, AR, BQ, BWQ, CO, EM, GSJ, JVG, JLS, LSJ

1.8 Instrument makers, dealers, shops, workshops, seminars

Consult the above periodicals

1.9 Language Pronunciation

Alton *Buche*, Apel *French*, Dobson *Pronunciation*, Kökeritz *Chaucer*

1.10 Recordings

Coover *Records*

REPERTORY

Publications that contain instrumental music or vocal music in more than one national style are listed in section 2.2. Compositions are assigned to country according to the national style of form of the music, not necessarily the nationality of the composer. All frottole, for example, are listed under Italy, and all chansons under Franco-Netherlandish, no matter who wrote them. The lists are in approximate chronological order.

2.1 Anthologies

These collections contain compositions in the national styles listed below but are not cited again (Hilton *Index* contains an index to most of them):

a *Medieval and Renaissance*

FM, GMB, HAM, MBA, MM, NAWM, NS, SS, SSA, SSM, TEM

b *Medieval*

AMM, EMB, OMM

c *Renaissance*

AER

2.2 Mixed collection and instrumental music (excluding dance, keyboard, and lute)

SOURCE	CONTENTS
ARS	various
AOM 2, 9	medieval mono and poly
AMP 8, 14	medieval poly
Taylor *Melodien*	medieval secular mono
Bédier *Chansons*	medieval secular mono
Tischler *Motets*	medieval poly
Dronke *Medieval*	medieval secular mono

CW	various poly
Pope *Manuscript*	fifteenth-century sacred and secular
Reaney *Fifteenth*	fifteenth-century sacred and secular
Chominski *Polish*	sixteenth-century sacred, secular, and instrumental
AOM 3, 47	fifteenth- and sixteenth-century sacred and secular
LPM	instrumental
Marx *Tabulaturen*	fifteenth- and sixteenth-century secular, vocal, and instrumental
DTO 77, 90	sixteenth-century sacred and secular
Slim *Nova*	sixteenth-century instrumental
Romano *Duorum*	sixteenth-century instrumental duets
MB 9, 40	sixteenth- and seventeenth-century viols
DDT 16	sixteenth-century instrumental
LP 27	sixteenth-century instrumental
RRR various	sixteenth-century instrumental

2.3 Collections by national style

a *England*

READING

Harrison *Britain*, LeHuray *Reformation*, Stevens *Court*, Stevens *Tudor*, Wilkins *Chaucer*

REPERTORY

Thirteenth and fourteenth centuries

Dittmer *Worcester*	sacred poly
Harrison *Songs*	secular: mono and poly
PMF	sacred and secular poly

Fourteenth and fifteenth centuries

Hughes *Old Hall*	sacred poly
Charles *Pepys*	sacred poly
MB 4	carols
MB 8	Dunstable: complete
McPeek *Egerton*	sacred poly

Fifteenth and sixteenth centuries

MB various	sacred and secular instrumental
EECM all	sacred
Fellows *Lutenist*	secular
Fellows *Madrigalists*	madrigals

TCM	sacred
TECM 1, 2	sacred
RRR various	sacred and secular instrumental

b *Franco-Netherlandish*

READING

Brown *French*, Cazeaux *French*, Wangermée *Flemish*, Werf *Troubadours*

REPERTORY

Twelfth and thirteenth centuries

Anderson *Bamberg*	motets poly
Anderson *Clayette*	motets poly
Anderson *Conductus*	mono and poly
Anderson *Latin*	sacred poly
Aubry *Motets*	motets poly
Bédier *Chansons*	secular mono
CMY 6	secular poly
Gennrich *Lyrik*	secular mono
Gennrich *Nachlass*	sacred and secular mono and poly
Gennrich *Robin*	secular mono
Gennrich *Saber*	secular mono
Maillard *Trouvères*	secular mono
Newcombe *Erart*	secular mono
PAM 11	sacred poly
Rokseth *Polyphonies*	motets poly
RRM various	sacred and secular poly
Thurston *Perotin*	Perotin: complete; poly
Tischler *Motets*	secular poly
Werf *Troubadours*	secular mono
Wilkins *Adam*	secular mono

Thirteenth and fourteenth centuries

AOM 2	secular mono
AOM 9	sacred and secular poly
Apel *French*	secular poly
Günther *Chantilly*	motets poly
PAM 1^1, 3^1, 4^2	Machaut: complete
PMF various	sacred and secular poly
Stäblein *Mass*	sacred poly
Wilkins *Reina*	secular poly

Fifteenth century

Reaney *Fifteenth*	sacred and secular
Marix *Bourgogne*	sacred and secular
Wilkins *Repertory*	secular
CMY 5	masses
Loyan *Trent*	sacred and secular
Pope *Manuscript*	sacred and secular
Atlas *Giulia*	chansons
Brown *Florentine*	chansons
Droz *Chansonniers*	chansons
Hewitt *Canti* B	chansons
Hewitt *Odhecaton*	sacred and secular
Hoppin *Cypriot*	sacred and secular
Jeppesen *Copenhagen*	secular vocal and instrumental
Kemp *Escorial*	secular
Southern *Escorial*	secular
Kottick *Cordeform*	chansons
Perkins *Mellon*	chansons
Picker *Chanson*	chansons
RRM various	sacred and secular

Fifteenth and sixteenth centuries

AOM 3, 22	sacred and secular
Brown *Theatrical*	secular
CMY 2	chansons
DTO various	sacred and secular
Lowinsky *Medici*	sacred
PAM 1	Ockeghem
PAM 9	Willaert: motets
PAP 6	Josquin
Smijers *Ockeghem*	sacred and secular

Sixteenth century

Cauchie *Janequin*	chansons
Cauchie *Quinze*	chansons
DTO various	sacred and secular
Lesure *Parisienne*	chansons
LP various	sacred and secular
Mairy *Chansons*	chansons
Merritt *Motets*	motets
MMF all	sacred and secular

MMR all	sacred and secular
PAP various	secular
RRR various	sacred and secular
SCA 5	chansons
Smijers *Motets*	motets

c *Germany*

REPERTORY

Thirteen and fourteenth centuries

AOM 2	secular mono
DTO 41, 71	secular mono
Hatto *Neidhart*	secular mono
Jammers *Minnesangs*	secular mono
Maurer *Lieder*	secular mono
Taylor *Melodien*	secular mono
Taylor *Minnesinger*	secular mono

Fifteenth and sixteenth centuries

AOM 10	sacred and secular
DDT various	sacred and secular
DTO various	sacred and secular
EDM various	sacred and secular
PAP various	sacred and secular
RRR various	sacred and secular
Schlick *Tabulaturen*	secular

d *Italy*

READING

Brown *Instrumentation*, Chater *Marenzio*, Einstein *Madrigal*, Prizer *Courtly*

REPERTORY

Thirteenth and fourteenth centuries

AOM 9	sacred and secular poly
Liuzzi *Lauda*	sacred mono
Marrocco *Cacce*	secular poly
Pirrotta *Fourteenth*	sacred and secular mono and poly
PMF various	sacred and secular mono and poly
Wolf *Squarcialupi*	secular mono and poly

Fifteenth and sixteenth centuries

Reaney *Fifteenth*	sacred and secular
Pope *Manuscript*	sacred and secular
D'Accone *Florentine*	sacred and secular
Cattin *Laude*	laude
Jeppesen *Laude*	laude
Einstein *Madrigals*	secular
Ghisi *Feste*	secular
Jeppesen *Frottole*	frottole
Monterosso *Frottole*	frottole
PAM 8	frottole
Schwartz *Petrucci*	frottole
Southern *Escorial*	frottole
Einstein *Golden*	madrigals
Slim *Madrigals*	madrigals and motets
Masson *Carnival*	carnival songs
Minor *Renaissance*	secular
AOM 3	secular
Newcomb *Ferrara*	madrigals
Newman *Dances*	dances
Chater *Marenzio*	madrigals
PAM 4^1, 6	Marenzio: madrigals
PAP 26	Vecchi *L'amfiparnasso*
DTO various	sacred and secular
RRR various	sacred, secular and instrumental
SCA 4, 6, 8	secular vocal and instrumental
Torchi *L'Arte* 1, 2	sacred and secular
LP 10, 27	instrumental
Caccini *Nuove*	secular monody
CPS all	secular

e *Spain*

READING

Stevenson *Cathedral*, Stevenson *Columbus*

REPERTORY

Twelfth and thirteenth centuries

Anderson *Huelgas*	sacred poly and mono
Anglès *Cantigas*	secular mono

Anglès *Catalunya*	secular mono
Anglès *Huelgas*	secular poly and mono
Cuesta *Trobadors*	secular mono
Whitehill *Calixtinus*	secular poly and mono

Fifteenth and sixteenth centuries

AOM 3	secular
MME 1	sacred
MME 2, 3, 7, 22, 23, 27, 28, 29	instrumental
MME 4, 5, 8, 9, 10, 33	secular
MME 11, 13, 15, 17, 20, 21, 24, 34	Morales: complete
MME 16, 19, 36	Guerrero: complete
MME 25, 26, 30, 31	Victoria: complete
Ortiz *Tratado*	instrumental
PAM 2	instrumental
Pope *Manuscript*	sacred and secular
RRR various	sacred and secular
Stevenson *Antologia*	sacred and secular

2.4 Dance

READING

Arbeau *Orchésographie*, Aubry *Estampies*, Brainard *Art*, Brainard *Court*, Bukofzer *Studies*, Crane *Materials*, Dolmetsch *England*, Dolmetsch *Spain*, Kinkeldey *Dance*, McGee *Medieval*, WE 6

REPERTORY

AOM 27, Aubry *Estampies*, Bokum *Dansen*, Bukofzer *Studies*, Crane *Materials*, Keruzoré *Estampies*, Kinkeldey *Dance*, LP 9, 10, McGee *Medieval*, MMR 23, Monkmeyer *Antwerpener*, Monkmeyer *Löwener*, Newman *Dances*, Susato *Danserye*, WE 6, Wolf *Tänze*

2.5 Dramatic music

LITURGICAL DRAMA

Collins *Medieval*, Collins *Production*, Greenberg *Daniel*, Greenberg *Herod*, Hollman *Maastricht*, Smoldon *Music*, Smoldon *Pastorum*, Smoldon *Peregrinus*, Smoldon *Planctus*, Smoldon *Visitatio*, Sterne *Getron*, Tintori *Rappresentazioni*, Young *Drama*

INTERMEDII

Brown *Instrumentation*, Gabrieli *Edipo*, Ghisi *Feste*, Minor *Renaissance*, Walker *Pellegrina*

MISCELLANEOUS

Brown *Theatrical*, CPS all, Dutka *Mystery*, Gennrich *Robin*, MacClintock *Balet*, PAM 30, Torchi *L'Arte* 2, Wilkins *Adam*

2.6 Special repertory

KEYBOARD READING

Apel *Keyboard*, Bedbrook *Keyboard*, Brown *Printed*, Ferguson *Keyboard*

KEYBOARD REPERTORY

AOM 1, AMP 15, CEKM all, EDM 37, 38, 39, MB 1, 27, 28, LP 5, WE 3, DDT 1, Bedbrook *Italian*, Benvenuti *Cavazzoni*, Curtis *Keyboard*, Dart *Inviolata*, Dart *Parthenia*, Disertori *Bossinensis*, Froidebise *Orgue*, Fuller *Fitzwilliam*, Henestrosa *Libro*, Jeppesen *Orgelmusik*, Merian *Tanz*, Oxenbury *Intabolatura*, Plamenac *Faenza*, Rokseth *Motets*, Rokseth *Orgue*, Schlick *Tabulaturen*, Seay *Chansons*, Torchi *L'Arte* 3, WE 3

LUTE, GUITAR, AND VIHUELA READING

Brown *Printed*, Gill *Plucked*, Lyons *Lute*, Tyler *Guitar*, Vaccaro *Luth*

LUTE, GUITAR, AND VIHUELA REPERTORY

DTO 37, CMY 4, MME 3, 7, 22, 23, 27, 28, 29, WE 8, Dissertori *Bossinensis*, Fellows *Lutenist*, Gombosi *Capirola*, Heartz *Attaingnant*, Mairy *Chansons*, Marx *Tabulaturen*, Milán *Maestro*, Schlick *Tabulaturen*, WE 8

NOTES

Citations in the notes are given in the form of author's last name followed by a short title; full references may be found in the bibliography. (See also p. 225.)

CHAPTER 2

1 See a detailed discussion in Lockwood *Dispute.*
2 The following discussions are recommended as a place to begin: Hughes *Accidentals*, Bent *Ficta*, Berger *Chromatic*, Lockwood *Ficta*, and E. Lowinsky's introduction to Slim *Nova*. The most recent proposal by Margaret Bent (Bent *Diatonic*) is a very interesting solution in that it could be applied at sight without score.
3 Summarized from Lockwood *Ficta*

CHAPTER 3

1 Lanfranco *Scintille*, Vicentino *Musica*, Zarlino *Istitutioni*, Lowinsky *Text*. A recently discovered additional source, described in Atlas *Luchini*, draws on the work of Zarlino, Vicentino, and Lanfranco, with a few refinements.
2 Lowinsky *Text*, Harrán *Light*. For another summary of the principles of text underlay see Brown *Florentine*, text volume, ch. 15.
3 Not all editions transcribe the old notation at the same reduction. The ratio of reduction used is usually indicated at the beginning of the work or can be ascertained by comparing the incipit to the first notes of the first phrase. The reader should interpret 'fast notes' in this rule to mean the fastest moving note values in any particular composition.
4 For a discussion of some exceptions see Perkins *Text* 103, 104.
5 Harrán *Text*

6 This is not described anywhere but would be the same as the known practice of 'telescoping,' in which the singing of the lengthy texts of the Gloria and Credo was shortened by assigning more than one text phrase at a time to be sung simultaneously in the various voice parts. Discussed in Reese *Middle* 421, and Reese *Renaissance* 41 and 126.

7 McKinnon *Representations*, Wright *Cambrai*

8 For this observation I am indebted to Thomas Binkley.

9 For the modern performer familiar with early notation a detailed discussion of tempo can be found in several books where the topic is presented with all of its complexities. See Apel *Notation*, Bank *Tactus*, Gullo *Tempo*, Parrish *Notation*, Rastall *Notation*, and Sachs *Rhythm*.

10 Ramis *Musica*

11 For further discussion see Mendel *Triple* and Sachs *Rhythm*.

12 Milán *Maestro*

13 See Jacobs *Tempo* 17–19 and Milán *Maestro* 296.

14 Quoted in Donington *Interpretation* 363

15 Translated in Strunk *Source* 377–92; also in Caccini *Nuove* 43–56

CHAPTER 4

1 Finck *Practica*, Maffei *Lettere*, Conrad *Modo*

2 Ganassi *Fontegara*

3 Caccini *Nuove*

4 Zacconi *Prattica*

5 As in Apel *French* vol. 1

6 See ch. 11, section 1.9.

7 See ch. 11, sections 1.4 and 1.7 for bibliographical references.

8 Crane *Extant*

9 Periodicals containing recent research on instruments can be found in ch. 11, section 1.7, expecialy *GSJ* and *AMIS J*.

10 Baines *Woodwind* 210

11 Bowles *Haut*

12 Polk *Dufay* 61. Typical ensembles in England are given in Rastall *Consort*.

13 Reported in Bowles *Instruments* 47

14 For further discussion of the variety of bagpipes see Marcuse *Survey* 673–7.

15 See Zippel *Suonatori*.

16 Polk *Dufay* 64; see Bowles *Processions* for details.

17 *EDM* 7 contains early trumpet fanfares including military signals from ca 1600.

18 For further discussion see Bowles *Iconography*, Brown *Voices*, Polk *Dufay*, and Polk *Ensemble*.

19 Polk *Dufay* 61
20 Brown *Voices* 100–1
21 Ibid. 97–102
22 For works with specific instrumentation and an enlightening discussion of musical life in Italy during the sixteenth century, see Brown *Instrumentation*.

CHAPTER 5

1 Repertory is listed in ch. 11, section 2.1 and the listings by national style.
2 Werf *Troubadours* 19, 20
3 Discussed below, pp. 190–7
4 Preludes are discussed below, pp. 115–16 and 187–9.
5 See Werf *Trouvère*, Werf *Measurability*, and the introduction by Alejandro Planchart in Wardell *Troubadours*.
6 For discussion of various types see Hoppin *Medieval*; for repertory see ch. 11, section 2.1, Waite *Rhythm*, and Thurston *Perotin*.
7 *CMY* 6 and Anderson *Conductus*
8 See ch. 11, section 2.3b.
9 *RRM* 2–7
10 Ch. 11, listings by national style and by particular composer
11 Hughes *Polyphony*
12 Bukofzer *Studies* 176–89
13 Completely instrumental performances will be discussed later in the chapter.
14 *MB* 4
15 Ch. 11, sections 2.1 and 2.3c
16 See Hughes *Polyphony*.
17 *PMF* 6–11, Pirrotta *Fourteenth*, Marrocco *Cacce*
18 Finck *Practica*
19 *Liber*
20 Brown *Instrumentation* chs. 3, 6, Broder *Orchestra*
21 Brown *Instrumentation* ch. 3
22 Prizer *Frottola*
23 Ch. 11 under all national styles, sixteenth-century list
24 Apel *French*, Reaney *Fifteenth*
25 For an interesting discussion of the significance of the fermata in such instances, see Warren *Punctus*.
26 For a discussion of these fixed forms see Hoppin *Medieval* chs. 11, 12, 13, 17, 18 or Reese *Medieval* chs. 7, 8, 12, 14.
27 *CW* 43 and *AER* 186
28 Brown *Instrumentation* ch. 3

29 For further discussion see Polk *Dufay* 65, 66.
30 Aubry *Estampies*, Bokum *Dansen*, McGee *Medieval*, Wolf *Tänze*; also entries in ch. 11, section 2.6
31 See Blades *Percussion*.
32 See Howard Ferguson 'Preludes' in Grove *Dictionary* vol. 15, 210–12.
33 Bokum *Dansen*, McGee *Medieval*, Wolf *Tänze*
34 See ch. 11, section 2.4.
35 See ch. 11, section 2.2. Also, individual examples can be found in various collections of medieval polyphonic repertory.
36 See ch. 11, section 2.4.
37 See ch. 11, section 2.2 and national lists.
38 Marix *Bourgogne*
39 Brown *Renaissance* 94; also see Brown *Florentine*, text volume, ch. 12.
40 See note 21 above.
41 For information on krummhorns see Boydell *Crumhorn* and Meyer *Crumhorn*.
42 CEKM 1, Plamenac *Faenza*
43 EDM 37, 38, 39
44 Benvenuto *Cavezzoni*
45 Oxenbury *Intabolatura*
46 Ferguson *Keyboard* 20
47 Quoted in Strunk *Source* and MacClintock *Readings* 133–4
48 Fuller *Fitzwilliam*
49 Additional repertory for keyboard is listed in ch. 11, section 2.6, and extensive discussions and lists of sources can be found in Apel *Keyboard*, Ferguson *Keyboard*, and Bedbrook *Keyboard*.
50 Dissertori *Bossinensis*, Schlick *Tabulaturen*, Gombosi *Capirola*
51 JLS, LSJ
52 Romano *Duorum*, RRR 16, 17, Smet *Viola*
53 Modern editions are listed in ch. 11, section 2.2.
54 A variety of early instrumental music is also published by LPM and MSEP.

CHAPTER 6

1 D'Accone *Chapels*, D'Accone *Performance*, D'Accone *Singers*, Polk *Dufay*, and Wright *Cambrai*
2 Wright *Cambrai* 310
3 McKinnon *Representations*, Wright *Cambrai*; but see Bachmann *Bowing* 121–2.
4 Harrison *Britain* 205, 206
5 EDM 37–9, Rokseth *Orgue*
6 Giovanni Gabrieli *Omnia Opera* ed. D. Arnold, AIM vol. 5, x

7 Hughes *Old Hall,* MB 10–12
8 See ch. 11, section 2.4.
9 Bottrigari *Desiderio* 44, 45
10 On the use of music in English mystery plays see Dutka *Mystery.*
11 See ch. 11, section 2.5.
12 See McGee *Dialogue.*
13 *Processionale*
14 See transcription in Hollman *Maastricht.*
15 Gennrich *Robin*
16 Brown *Theatrical*
17 MB 18
18 Brown *Instrumentation*
19 See ch. 11, section 2.5.
20 Werf *Troubadours* 134–8
21 Incorrectly edited in *Opera Omnia* ed. Besseler, vol. 6, 76
22 Pirrotta *Fourteenth*, Marrocco *Cacce*
23 Wilkins *Adam*
24 CPS, all vols

CHAPTER 7

1 See ch. 11, section 1.6. Especially helpful for improvisation is the forthcoming Aarset *Improvisation.*
2 Brown *Embellishing*
3 Ibid. 6, 7
4 CEKM I
5 Plamenac *Faenza*
6 See discussion below, pp. 211–12.
7 There is some controversy over this point. Willi Apel in *Notation* 39–40 states that signs in the Robertsbridge Codex indicate graces. More recent research by Margaret Bent (not yet published) suggests that the signs refer to mensuration.
8 See list of sources in ch. 11, section 1.6.
9 Brown *Embellishing* 63, 64
10 Ganassi *Rubertina* ch. 2
11 All known Italian examples written between 1553 and 1638 are edited and published in Erig *Diminutions.*
12 MacClintock *Readings* 3–7
13 See Speck *Relationships.*
14 Reported in Brown *Embellishing* 56, 57
15 Translation quoted in Stevens *Cathedral* 167
16 See Brown *Embellishing* ch. 6.

CHAPTER 8

1 See Pirrotta *Orfei* ch. 1 for date and discussion.
2 Extensive discussion of improvisation is found in the articles by Ernest T. Ferand cited in ch. 11, section 1.6. The information here is largely drawn from these publications by Ferand and Polk *Foundations*.
3 Ferand *Vocal* 138, 139
4 Readers interested in the more complex forms of improvisation are directed to the special studies cited in ch. 11, section 1.6.
5 See ch. 11, section 2.6.
6 This subject is more fully discussed in Polk *Foundations*.
7 Polk *Foundations* 18
8 Crane *Materials*, WE 6
9 Crane *Materials* 62–6; Bukofzer *Studies* 199–200

CHAPTER 9

1 Ganassi *Fontegara*, Dalla Casa *Modo*, Cardanus *Musica*, Agricola *Musica*, Arbeau *Orchésographie*, Rognioni *Selve*, Rogniono *Passaggi*, Mersenne *Harmonie*
2 Detailed discussion may be found in Brown *Embellishing*, Erig *Diminutions*, Horsley *Techniques*, and Houle *Tonguing*.
3 I am grateful to Professor Ross Duffin for this information.
4 Agricola *Musica*, Ortiz *Tratado*, Ganassi *Rubertina*, Cerreto *Prattica*, Mersenne *Harmonie*, Rognioni *Selve*; the subject is discussed in Boyden *Violin*, Erig *Diminutions*, and Woodfield *Viol*.
5 Bermudo *Libro*, Diruta *Transilvano*, Sancta *Libro*, Henestrosa *Libro*
6 This observation is also made in Brown *Embellishing* 10 n. 3.
7 Ganassi *Fontegara* chs. 1, 2, 23, 24, 25
8 See 'Notes inégales' by David Fuller in Grove *Dictionary* vol. 13, 420–7.
9 Poulton *Style*
10 Wolf *Tänz*, Bokum *Dansen*, McGee *Medieval*
11 Plamenac *Faenza*

CHAPTER 10

1 A far more extensive treatment of the practical and organizational aspects of early music performance is given in Kottick *Collegium*. I have limited this discussion to points not covered in that source.

BIBLIOGRAPHY

Aarset *Improvisation* Aarset, Timothy C. *The Art of Improvisation in Renaissance Music* forthcoming

Aarset *Polyphonic* – 'Toward a Definition of Polyphonic Ensemble Improvisation circa 1500' *Fifteenth-Century Studies* IV (1980) 1–16

AER Greenberg, Noah and Paul Maynard, eds *An Anthology of Early Renaissance Music* (New York 1975)
Forty-one transcriptions with translations and performance suggestions

Agricola *Musica* Agricola, Martin *Musica Instrumentalis deudsch* (Wittenberg 1529 and 1545)
Facsimile in PAP 20

AIM American Institute of Musicology
Many publications of medieval and Renaissance music, theorists, studies

Alton *Buche* Alton, J. and Brian Jeffery *Bele buche e bele parleure* (London 1976)
Pronunciation of Early French including Provençal, Picard, and Norman

AMIS American Musical Instrument Society

AMIS J *Journal of the American Musical Instrument Society* (1975–   )

AMM Hoppin, Richard, ed. *Anthology of Medieval Music* (New York 1978)
Seventy-one transcriptions with translations

AMP Feicht, Heironim, ed. *Antiquitates Musicae in Polonia* (Graz and Warsaw 1963–   )

AMP 8 *Pepliner Tabulatur*
Transcription of instrumental compositions from the late sixteenth and early seventeenth centuries à 4

AMP 14   *Sources of Polyphony up to 1500*
Medieval sacred polyphony

AMP 15   *The Organ Tablature of Warsaw Musical Society*
Sixteenth-century sacred music for organ

Anderson *Bamberg*   Anderson, Gordon A., ed. *Compositions of the Bamberg Manuscript* (AIM 1977)
Thirteenth-century motets including translations; same as
Aubry *Motets*

Anderson *Clayette*   – ed. *Motets of the Manuscript La Clayette* (AIM 1975)
Thirteenth-century polyphony

Anderson *Conductus*   – ed. *Notre Dame and Related Conductus, Opera Omnia*
10 vols planned (Henryville, Pa 1979–)

Anderson *Huelgas*   – ed. *The Las Huelgas Manuscript* 2 vols (AIM 1982)
Thirteenth-century polyphony; same as Anglès *Huelgas*

Anderson *Latin*   – ed. *The Latin Compositions in Fascicules 7 and 8 of the Notre Dame Manuscript Wolfenbüttel, Helmstadt 1099*
2 vols (Brooklyn 1972–6)
Vol. 1: transcriptions and commentary; vol. 2: transcriptions

Anglès *Cantigas*   Anglès, Higinio, ed. *La música de las cantigas de Santa Maria del Rey Alfonso El Sabio* 3 vols (Barcelona 1943–64)
Thirteenth-century secular monophony

Anglès *Catalunya*   – *La música a Catalunya fins al segle XIII* (Barcelona 1935)

Anglès *Huelgas*   – ed. *El Còdex de Las Huelgas* 3 vols (Barcelona 1931)
Thirteenth- and fourteenth-century polyphony
Transcriptions are in vol. 3, and include sacred polyphony and monophony; same as Anderson *Huelgas*

AOM   Fellerer, Karl G., ed. *Anthology of Music* (Cologne 1959–);
English ed. of *Das Musikwerk* (Cologne 1951–)

AOM 1   *Four Hundred Years of European Keyboard Music*
Four compositions from the fifteenth and sixteenth centuries

AOM 2   *Troubadours, Trouvères, Minnesang and Meistergesang*

AOM 3   *The Sixteenth-Century Part Song in Italy, France and Spain*

AOM 9   *Medieval Polyphony*
Sacred and secular, from France and Italy

AOM 10   *The German Part Song from the Sixteenth Century to the Present Day*
Sacred and secular

AOM 12   *Improvisation in Nine Centuries of Western Music*
Discussion and examples of improvisation

AOM 22   *The Art of the Netherlanders*
Sacred and secular

AOM 27	*The Dance*
	Monophonic and polyphonic
AOM 47	*The Motet*
Apel *French*	Apel, Willi, ed. *French Secular Compositions of the Fourteenth Century* 3 vols (AIM 1970–2)
	Vol. 1 includes a pronunciation guide for medieval French
Apel *Keyboard*	– *The History of Keyboard Music to 1700* Transl. and rev. by Hans Tischler (Bloomington, Ind. and London 1972)
	Includes an extensive bibliography and list of sources
Apel *Notation*	– *The Notation of Polyphonic Music 900-1600* (5th ed., Cambridge, Mass. 1961)
AR	*The American Recorder* (1960–)
Arbeau *Orchésographie*	Arbeau, Thoinot *Orchésographie* (1589); English transl. M. Evans (New York 1967)
	Information about sixteenth-century dance steps
ARS	American Recorder Society Editions
	Continuing collection including much early music edited for recorder
Atlas *Dufay*	Atlas, Allan, ed. *Dufay Quincentenary Conference Papers* (New York 1976)
Atlas *Giulia*	– ed. *The Capella Giulia Chansonnier* 2 vols (Brooklyn 1975)
	Vol. 1: commentary, vol. 2: transcriptions
Atlas *Luchini*	– 'Paolo Luchini's *Della musica*: A Little-Known Source for Text Underlay from the Late Sixteenth Century' *The Journal of Musicology* 2 (1983) 62–80
Aubry *Estampies*	Aubry, Pierre *Estampies et danses royales* (Paris 1907, repr. 1975)
	Thirteenth-century monophonic dances from manuscript Paris Bibl. Nat. Fr. 844; same as Keruzoré *Estampies* and McGee *Medieval*
Aubry *Motets*	– *Cent motets du XIIIe siècle* 3 vols (Paris 1908, repr. New York 1964)
	Same as Anderson *Bamberg*
Bachmann *Bowing*	Bachmann, Werner *The Origins of Bowing*; English transl. N. Deane (London 1969)
Baines *Instruments*	Baines, Anthony *Musical Instruments through the Ages* (New York 1961)
Baines *Tinctoris*	– 'Fifteenth-Century Instruments in Tinctoris' 'De inventione et usu musicae'' *GSJ* 3 (1950) 19–26
Baines *Woodwind*	Baines, Anthony *Woodwind Instruments and Their History* (London 1957)
Bank *Tactus*	Bank, J. A. *Tactus, Tempo and Notation in Mensural Music*

from the Thirteenth to the Seventeenth Century
(Amsterdam 1972)

Bassano *Motetti*   Bassano, Giovanni *Motetti, madrigali et canzoni francese*
(Venice 1591)

Destroyed; description by E. Ferand in *Festschrift Helmuth Osthoff zum 65. Geburtstage* (Tutzing 1961)

Bassano *Ricercare*   – *Ricercare, passaggi et cadentie* (Venice 1585); modern ed. R. Erig (Zürich 1976)

Bedbrook *Italian*   Bedbrook, Gerald S., ed. *Early Italian Keyboard Music* 2 vols (London 1955–6)

Vol. 1 contains four toccatas by Merulo; vol. 2 includes works by Cavazzoni

Bedbrook *Keyboard*   – *Keyboard Music from the Middle Ages to the Beginning of the Baroque* (London 1949); repr. with additional material (New York 1973)

Bédier *Chansons*   Bédier, Joseph and Pierre Aubry *Les chansons de croisade* (Paris 1909)

Secular monophonic

Bent *Diatonic*   Bent, Margaret 'Diatonic Ficta' (working title) in preparation

Bent *Ficta*   – 'Musica Recta and Musica Ficta' *Musica Discipline* 26 (1972) 73–100

Benvenuti *Cavazzoni*   Benvenuti, Giovanni, ed. *M.-A. Cavazzoni, J. Fogliano, J. Segni ed anonimi: Composizioni per organo* (Milan 1941)

Berger *Chromatic*   Berger, Karol *Theories of Chromatic and Enharmonic Music in Late Sixteenth-Century Italy* Studies in Musicology 10 (Ann Arbor 1980)

Bermudo *Libro*   Bermudo, Joan *El libro llamado … ossuna* (1555, facs. ed. Kassel 1957)

Bessaraboff *Ancient*   Bessaraboff, Nicholas *Ancient European Musical Instruments* (Cambridge, Mass. 1941)

Includes discussion, measurements, and diagrams of museum instruments

Blades *Early*   Blades, James and Jeremy Montagu *Early Percussion Instruments from the Middle Ages to the Baroque* (London 1976)

Blades *Percussion*   – *Percussion Instruments and Their History* (rev. ed. London 1975)

Bokum *Dansen*   Bokum, Jan ten, ed. *De dansen van het trecento* (Utrecht 1967)

The fifteen dances from manuscript London, British Library 29987. Same as McGee *Medieval* and Wolf *Tänze*

Bottrigari *Desiderio* Bottrigari, Ercole *Il Desiderio* (Venice 1594, facs. ed. K. Myer 1924); English transl. C. MacClintock (AIM 1962)

Bovicelli *Regole* Bovicelli, Giovanni *Regole, passaggi de musica ...* (Venice 1594, facs. ed. N. Bridgman 1957)

Bowles *Haut* Bowles, Edmund 'Haut and Bas: The Grouping of Musical Instruments in the Middle Ages' *Musica Disciplina* 7 (1954) 115–40

Bowles *Hiérarchie* – 'La hiérarchie des instruments de musique dans l'Europe féodale' *Revue de Musicologie* 42 (1958) 155–69

Bowles *Iconography* – 'Iconography as a Tool for Examining the Loud Consort in the Fifteenth Century' AMIS J 3 (1977) 100–21

Bowles *Instruments* – 'Musical Instruments at the Medieval Banquet' *Revue Belge de Musicologie* 12 (1958) 41–51

Bowles *Musikleben* – *Musikleben und Aufführungspraxis des 15. Jahrhunderts* (Leipzig 1976)
Many reproductions of paintings

Bowles *Processions* – 'Musical Instruments in Civic Processions During the Middle Ages' *Acta Musicologica* 33 (1961) 147–61

Boydell *Crumhorn* Boydell, Barra *The Crumhorn and other Renaissance Windcap Instruments*, (Buren, 1982)

Boyden *Violin* Boyden, David *The History of Violin Playing* (London 1965)

BQ *Brass Quarterly* (1957–65)
Superseded by BWQ

Brainard *Art* Brainard, Ingrid *The Art of Courtly Dancing In the Early Renaissance* (West Newton, Mass. 1981)

Brainard *Court* – *Three Court Dances of the Early Renaissance* (New York 1977)

Broder *Orchestra* Broder, Nathan 'The Beginnings of the Orchestra' JAMS 13 (1960) 174–80

Brown *Embellishing* Brown, Howard M. *Embellishing Sixteenth-Century Music* (London 1976)

Brown *Florentine* – *A Florentine Chansonnier From the Time of Lorenzo the Magnificent* 2 vols, Monuments of Renaissance Music 7 (Chicago and London 1983)
An edition of 268 texted and untexted works from the late fifteenth century

Brown *French* – *Music in the French Secular Theater, 1400–1550* (Cambridge, Mass. 1963)

Brown *Iconography* – and Joan Lascelle *Musical Iconography* (Cambridge, Mass. 1972)

Brown *Instrumentation* – *Sixteenth-Century Instrumentation* (AIM 1973)

Brown *Printed* — *Instrumental Music Printed Before 1600* (Cambridge, Mass. 1965)

Brown *Renaissance* — *Music in the Renaissance* (Englewood Cliffs, NJ 1976)

Brown *Theatrical* — ed. *Theatrical Chansons of the Fifteenth and Early Sixteenth Centuries* (Cambridge, Mass. 1963)
An anthology of sixty chansons

Brown *Voice* — 'Instruments and Voices in the Fifteenth-Century Chanson' *Current Thought in Musicology* ed. J.W. Grubbs et al. (Austin and London 1976) 89–137

Brunelli *Esercitii* Brunelli, Antonio *Varii esercitii* (1614); modern ed. R. Erig (Zürich 1977)
Diminutions and variations on various intervals; exercises for one and two voices

Bukofzer *Studies* Bukofzer, Manfred *Studies in Medieval and Renaissance Music* (New York 1950)

BWQ *Brass and Woodwind Quarterly* (1968–   )

Caccini *Nuove* Caccini, Giulio *Le nuove musiche* (1601); modern ed. H.W. Hitchcock (Madison 1970)

Cardanus *Musica* Cardanus, Hieronymus *De musica* (ca 1546) in *Hieronymus Cardanus: Writings on Music* ed. Clement Miller (AIM 1973)

Cattin *Laude* Cattin, Giulio *Italian Laude and Latin Unica in the MS Capetown, Grey 3.b.12* (AIM 1977)
Laude ca 1500

Cauchie *Janequin* Cauchie, Maurice, ed. *Trente chansons de Clément Janequin* (Paris 1928)

Cauchie *Quinze* — *Quinze chansons françaises du XVIe siècle* (Paris 1926)

Cazeaux *French* Cazeaux, Isabelle *French Music in the Fifteenth and Sixteenth Centuries* (Oxford 1975)

CEKM *Corpus of Early Keyboard Music* (AIM 1963–   )
Many volumes of keyboard music of all kinds from the fourteenth to the seventeenth centuries

Cerreto *Prattica* Cerreto, Scipione *Della prattica musica vocale et strumentale* (Napeles 1601, facs. ed. Bologna 1969)

Charles *Handbook* Charles, Sydney R. *A Handbook of Music and Music Literature in Sets and Series* (New York 1972)

Charles *Pepys* — *The Pepys Manuscript 1236* (AIM 1967)
Fifteenth-century English sacred polyphony

Chater *Marenzio* Chater, James *Luca Marenzio and the Italian Madrigal 1577–1593* 2 vols (Ann Arbor 1981)
Transcriptions in vol. 2

Chominski *Polish*   Chominski, Jozef M. and Z. Lissa, eds *Music of the Polish Renaissance* (Cracow 1955)
A collection of instrumental, vocal, sacred, secular works

CMY   *Collegium Musicum* (New Haven 1955–)

CMY 2   *Thirty Chansons for Three and Four Voices from Attaingnant's Collection*

CMY 4   *The Wickhambrook Lute Manuscript*
From the sixteenth century

CMY 5   *Three Caput Masses*

CMY 6   *Thirty-five Conductus for Two and Three Voices*

CO   *Continuo* (1977–)

Coclico *Compendium*   Coclico, Adrian *Compendium musices* (Nuremberg 1552, facs. ed. 1964) English transl. A. Seay (Colorado Springs 1973)

Collins *Medieval*   Collins Jr, Fletcher, ed. *Medieval Church Music-Drama* (Charlottesville 1976)

Collins *Production*   – *The Production of Medieval Church Music-Drama* (Charlottesville 1972)
Discussion with acting and staging suggestions

Conforto *Breve*   Confort, Giovanni *Breve e facile maniera d'essercitarsi ad ogni scolaro ...* (Rome 1593, facs. ed. 1922)

Conrad *Modo*   Zabern, Conrad von *De modo bene cantandi choralem cantum* (Mainz 1474); modern ed. Jul. Richer 'Zwei Schriften von Conrad von Zabern' in *Monatshefte für Musikgeschichte* 20 (1888) 95–108
Excerpt in MacClintock *Readings*

Coover *Records*   Coover, James and Richard Colvig, eds *Medieval and Renaissance Music on Long-Playing Records* (Detroit 1964); *Supplement for 1962–71* (Detroit 1973)

CPS   *Capolavori polifonici del secolo XVI* (Rome 1939–)
A series of madrigal-comedies from the late sixteenth and early seventeenth centuries

Crane *Extant*   Crane, Frederick *Extant Medieval Musical Instruments* (Iowa City 1972)

Crane *Materials*   – *Materials for the Study of the Fifteenth Century Basse Dance* (Brooklyn 1968)
Includes transcriptions of all known French basse dance material from the fifteenth century

Cuesta *Trobadors*   Cuesta, Ismael Fernandez de la, and Robert Lafont, eds *La cançon dels Trobadors* (Tolosa 1979)
Monophonic vocal music with translations; transcriptions without rhythm but including original notation

Curtis *Keyboard*   Curtis, Alan *Dutch Keyboard Music of the Sixteenth and Seventeenth Centuries* Monumenta Musica Neerlandica 3 (Amsterdam 1961)

cw   *Das Chorwerk* (1929–)
A series of vocal part-music issued in small fascicules; see index in Heyer *Sets*

D'Accone *Chapels*   D'Accone, Frank 'The Musical Chapels at the Florentine Cathedral and Baptistry During the First Half of the Sixteenth Century' *JAMS* 24 (1971) 1–50

D'Accone *Florentine*   – *Music of the Florentine Renaissance* (AIM 1966–)
Sacred and secular

D'Accone *Musicians*   – 'Music and Musicians at Santa Maria Del Fiore in the Early Quattrocento' *Scritti in onore di Luigi Ronga* (Milan 1973) 99–126

D'Accone *Performance*   – 'The Performance of Sacred Music in Italy during Josquin's Time, c. 1475–1525' in E. Lowinsky and B. Blackburn, eds *Josquin des Prez: Proceedings of the International Josquin Festival-Conference* (London 1976) 601–18

D'Accone *Singers*   – 'The Singers of San Giovanni in Florence during the Fifteenth Century' *JAMS* 14 (1961) 307–50

Dalla Casa *Modo*   Dalla Casa, Giovanni *Il vero modo di diminuir* 2 vols (Venice 1584, facs. ed. Bologna 1970)

Dart *Interpretation*   Dart, Thurston, ed. *The Interpretation of Music* (London 1954)

Dart *Inviolata*   – ed. *Parthenia In-Violata* (New York 1961)
For virginals and optional base viol ca 1620

Dart *Parthenia*   – ed. *Parthenia* (London 1960)

DDT   *Denkmäler deutscher Tonkunst* 65 vols (1892–1931)

DDT 1   S. Scheidt *Tabulatura nova* (1524)
Psalms, fantasies, etc. for organ

DDT 2   H. Hassler *Werke I, Cantiones sacrae*

DDT 7   H. Hassler *Werke II, Messen*

DDT 16   M. Franck und V. Haussmann *Ausgewählte Instrumentalwerke*

DDT 23   H. Praetorius *Ausgewählte Werke*

DDT 24, 25   H. Hassler *Werke III, Sacri concentus*

DDT 31   P. Dulichius *Prima pars Centuriae* (1607)

DDT 34   *Newe deudsche geistliche Gesenge für die gemeinen Schulen*

DDT 41   P. Dulichius *Secunda pars Centuriae* (1608)

DDT 65   T. Stoltzer *Sämtliche lateinische Hymnen und Psalmen*

Diruta *Transilvano*   Diruta, Girolamo *Il Transilvano* (1593, facs. ed. Bologna
                        1969); English transl. in MacClintock *Readings*
Disertori *Bossinensis*   Disertori, Benvenuto, ed. *Le frottole per canto e liuto
                        intabulate da Franciscus Bossinensis* (Milan 1964)
                        Contains works by Spinacino and Bossinensis for lute and
                        lute and voice, and Antico organ selections
Dittmer *Worcester*   Dittmer, Luther, ed. *The Worcester Fragments* (AIM 1957)
                        Thirteenth- and fourteenth-century sacred polyphony
Dobson   Dobson, Eric J. *English Pronunciation, 1500–1700*
Pronunciation   (London 1937)
                        Very difficult to use
Dodd *Viols*   Dodd, Gordon *Thematic Index of Music for Viols* (n.p. 1980)
Dolmetsch *England*   Dolmetsch, Mabel *Dances of England and France, 1400–1600*
                        (London 1949)
Dolmetsch   Dolmetsch, Arnold *The Interpretation of Music of the
Interpretation*   Seventeenth and Eighteenth Centuries* (London 1915)
Dolmetsch *Spain*   Dolmetsch, Mabel *Dances of Spain and Italy
                        from 1400–1600* (London 1954)
Donington   Donington, Robert *The Interpretation of Early Music*
Interpretation   (London 1963, rev. ed. 1974)
Dronke *Medieval*   Dronke, Peter *The Medieval Lyric* (2nd ed. London 1977)
                        Includes melodies and translations
Droz *Chansonniers*   Droz, Eugénie, Yvonne Rokseth, and Geneviève Thibault,
                        eds *Trois chansonniers français du XVe siècle* (Paris 1927)
DTO   *Denkmäler der Tonkunst in Österreich* (1894–   )
DTO 10, 32   Isaac *Choralis Constantinus Books I and II*
DTO 12, 24, 40, 48,   Handl *Works*
51, 52, 78, 94, 95
DTO 14, 15, 22, 38,   *Trent Codices* (fifteenth century)
53, 61, 76, 120
DTO 28   Isaac *Secular Compositions*
DTO 37   *Austrian Lute Music of the Sixteenth Century*
DTO 41   *Minnesinger Manuscripts*
DTO 71   Neidhard von Reuenthal *Lieder*
DTO 77   *Italian Musicians 1567–1625*
                        Written for the Austrian Imperial Court
DTO 90   *Netherland and Italian Musicians of the Graz Court
                        Orchestra of Karl II 1564–1590*
DTO 98, 100, 103,   Vaet *Complete Works*
104, 108, 198, 113, 114

DTO 123	du Gaucquier *Sämtliche Werke* (sixteenth century)
Dutka *Mystery*	Dutka, Joanna *Music in the English Mystery Plays* (Kalamazoo 1980)
	Lists of music and instruments
EDM	*Das Erbe deutscher Musik* (1935–)
EDM 4, 8, 85, 86	*Das Glogauer Liederbuch*
EDM 5	Senfl *Sieben Missen zu vier bis sechs Stimmen*
EDM 7	*Trumpeterfanfaren, Sonaten und Feldstücke nach Aufzeichnungen deutschen Hoftrompeter des 16/17 Jahrhunderts*
EDM 10, 15	Senfl *Deutsche Lieder*
EDM 13	Senfl *Motetten*
EDM 16	Othmayr *Ausgewählte Werke*
EDM 20	Forster *Friche teutsche Liedlein*
EDM 22	Stoltzer *Ausgewählte Werke*
EDM 23	Dietrich *Ausgewählte Werke*
EDM 37, 38, 39	*Buxheimer Orgelbuch*
EDM 42	Coclico *Consolationes piae musica reservata*
EDM 57	Finck *Ausgewählte Werke*
EECM	*Early English Church Music* (London 1963–79)
	Anthems, Masses, Magnificats, organ music
Einstein *Golden*	Einstein, Alfred, ed. *The Golden Age of the Madrigal* (New York 1942)
	Twelve Italian madrigals
Einstein *Madrigal*	– *The Italian Madrigal* 3 vols (Princeton 1949, repr. 1971)
	Vol. 3 contains transcriptions of frottole and madrigals
EM	*Early Music* (1971–)
EMB	Gleason, Harold, ed. *Examples of Music before 1400* (rev. 2nd ed. New York 1965)
Erig *Diminutions*	Erig, Richard with V. Gutmann *Italian Diminutions* (Zürich 1979)
	Discussion of embellishment, complete edition of all diminutions with the originals from 1553 to 1638 in Italy; also includes a discussion of articulation
Fellows *Lutenist*	Fellows, Edmund H., ed. *The English School of Lutenist Song Writers* 2 series, 32 vols (London 1920–32)
Fellows *Madrigalists*	– ed. *The English Madrigalists* 36 vols (1914–24, rev. ed. London 1958–)
Ferand *Improvisation*	Ferand, Ernest *Die Improvisation in der Musik* (Zürich 1938)
Ferand *Sodaine*	– ' "Sodaine and Unexpected" Music in the Renaissance' *MQ* 37 (1951) 10–27

Ferand *Vocal* — 'Improvised Vocal Counterpoint in the Late Renaissance and Early Baroque' *Annales Musicologiques* 4 (1956) 129–74

Ferguson *Keyboard* Ferguson, Howard *Keyboard Interpretation* (London 1975)
Includes a bibliography of modern editions

Finck *Practica* Finck, Hermann *Practica musica* (Wittenberg 1556); English transl. in MacClintock *Readings*

FM Leuchter, Erwin, ed. *Florilegium musicum; History of Music in 180 Examples from Antiquity to the Eighteenth Century* (Buenos Aires 1964)
Anthology

Froidebise *Orgue* Froidebise, Pierre, ed. *Anthologie de l'orgue des primitifs à la Renaissance* 2 vols (Paris 1957)

Frotscher *Aufführungspraxis* Frotscher, Gotthold *Aufführungspraxis alter Musik* (Locarno 1963)
Information about performance practice

Fuller *Fitzwilliam* Fuller Maitland, J.A. and W. Barclay Squire, eds *The Fitzwilliam Virginal Book* 2 vols (Leipzig 1894–99, repr. New York 1963)

Gabrieli *Edipo* Gabrieli, Andrea and Orsatto Giustiniani *La représentation d'Edipo Tiranno au Teatro Olimpico* (Venice 1585), modern ed. by L. Schrade (Paris 1960)

Ganassi *Fontegara* Ganassi, Sylvestro di *Opera intitulata Fontegara* (Venice 1535, facs. ed. 1934); German transl. H. Peter (1956), English transl. D. Swainson (1959)

Ganassi *Rubertina* — *Regola Rubertina* and *Lettione Seconda* (1542, 1543, facs. ed. 1924)

Gennrich *Lyrik* Gennrich, Friedrich, ed. *Exempla altfranzösicher Lyrik* Musikwissenschaftliche Studienbibliothek 17 (Darmstadt 1958)
Anthology of trouvère songs

Gennrich *Nachlass* — ed. *Der musikalishe Nachlass der Troubadours* Summa Musicae Medii Aevi 3, 4, 15 (Darmstadt 1957–67)
302 sacred and secular troubadour melodies and some polyphonic motets

Gennrich *Robin* — ed. *Adam de la Halle: Le Jeu de Robin et de Marion* Musikwissenschaftliche Studienbibliothek 20 (Langen 1962)

Gennrich *Saber* — ed. *Lo gai saber* Musikwissenschaftliche Studienbibliothek 18/19 (Darmstadt 1959)
Fifty troubadour songs

Ghisi *Feste*   Ghisi, Federico *Feste musicali della Firenze Medicea (1480–1589)* (Florence 1939)
Carnival songs and excerpts from *Intermedii*

Gill *Plucked*   Gill, Donald *Wire-string Plucked Instruments Contemporary with the Lute* The Lute Society Booklets No. 3 (Richmond, Surrey 1977)

GMB   Schering, Arnold, ed. *Geschichte der Musik in Beispielen* (Leipzig 1931)

Gombosi *Capirola*   Gombosi, Otto, ed. *Compositione de Meser Vincenzo Capirola, Lute Book 1517* (Neuilly-sur-Seine 1955)

Greenberg *Daniel*   Greenberg, Noah, ed. *The Play of Daniel* (New York 1959)
Greenberg *Herod*   – ed. *The Play of Herod* (New York 1965)
Grove *Dictionary*   *The New Grove Dictionary of Music and Musicians* ed. S. Sadie, 20 vols (London 1980)

GSJ   *The Galpin Society Journal* (1948–   )

Gullo *Tempo*   Gullo, Salvatore *Das Tempo in der Musik des XIII. und XIV. Jahrhunderts* (Bern 1964)

Günther *Chantilly* Günther, Ursula, ed. *The Motets of the Manuscripts Chantilly, Musée Condé 564 (olim 1047) and Modena, Biblioteca estense α. 5, 24 (olim Lat. 568)* (AIM 1965)
Fourteenth-century polyphony

Hagopian *Italy*   Hagopian, Viola L. *Italian Ars Nova: A Bibliographic Guide to Modern Editions and Related Literature* (2nd rev. ed. Berkeley 1973)

HAM   Davidson, Archibald and Willi Apel, eds *Historical Anthology of Music* 2 vols (Cambridge, Mass. 1949)
Vol. 1 includes medieval and Renaissance music

Harrán *Light*   Harrán, Don 'New Light on the Question of Text Underlay Prior to Zarlino' *Acta Musicologica* 45 (1973) 24–56

Harrán *Text*   – 'In Pursuit of Origins: The Earliest Writing on Text Underlay (c. 1440)' *Acta Musicologica* 50 (1978) 217–40

Harrison *Britain*   Harrison, Frank Ll. *Music in Medieval Britain* (2nd ed. New York 1963)

Harrison *Songs*   – and Eric Dobson, eds *Medieval English Songs* (Cambridge 1979)
Secular, monophonic, and polyphonic

Hatto *Neidhart*   Hatto, Arthur and Ronald Taylor, eds *The Songs of Neidhart von Reuental* (Manchester 1958)
Seventeen minnesinger melodies

Heartz *Attaingnant*   Heartz, Daniel, ed. *Preludes, Chansons and Dances for Lute Published by Pierre Attaingnant, Paris 1529–1530* (Neuilly-sur-Seine 1964)

Henestrosa *Libro*   Henestrosa, Luis Venegas de *Libro de Cifra Nueva ...* (1557); transcription in MME 2
Early Spanish keyboard music

Hewitt *Canti B*   Hewitt, Helen, ed. *Ottaviano Petrucci Canti B Numero Cinquanta* Monuments of Renaissance Music 2, ed. E. Lowinsky (Chicago 1967)
Fifty-one chansons by various composers ca 1500, mostly à 4

Hewitt *Odhecaton*   – ed. *Harmonice Musices Odhecaton A* (Cambridge, Mass. 1946)
Ninety-six sacred and secular works from 1501 Petrucci print à 3, 4

Heyer *Sets*   Heyer, Anna Harriet *Historical Sets, Collected Editions and Monuments of Music* 2 vols (3rd ed. Chicago 1980)

Hilton *Index*   Hilton, Ruth *An Index to Early Music in Selected Anthologies* (Clifton, NY 1978)
Lists works in GMB, HAM, MM, TEM, EMB, OMM, MBA, SSM, NS, SS, SSA, FM, and other anthologies

Hollman *Maastricht*   Hollman, Wilbur W. *The Maastricht Easter Play* (New York 1966)

Hoppin *Cypriot*   Hoppin, Richard, ed. *The Cypriot-French Repertory of the Manuscript Torino, Biblioteca Nazionale, J. II. 9* 4 vols (AIM 1960–3)
Anonymous early fifteenth-century polyphony, sacred and secular

Hoppin *Medieval*   – *Medieval Music* (New York 1978)

Horsley *Diminutions*   Horsley, Imogene 'The Diminutions in Composition and Theory of Composition' *Acta Musicologica* 35 (1963) 124–53

Horsley *Improvised*   – 'Improvised Embellishment in the Performance of Renaissance Polyphonic Music' *JAMS* 4 (1951) 3–19

Horsley *Techniques*   – 'Wind Techniques in the Sixteenth and Early Seventeenth Centuries' *BQ* 4 (1960) 49–63

Houle *Tonguing*   Houle, George 'Tonguing and Rhythmic Patterns in Early Music' *AR* 6 (1965) 4–13

Hughes *Accidentals*   Hughes, Andrew *Manuscript Accidentals: Ficta in Focus 1350–1450* (AIM 1972)

Hughes *Old Hall*   – and Margaret Bent, eds *The Old Hall Manuscript* 3 vols (AIM 1969–73)
English sacred polyphony 1350–1450

Hughes *Polyphony* — 'Mensural Polyphony for Choir in Fifteenth Century England' *JAMS* 19 (1966) 352–69

Hughes *Sixth* — *Medieval Music: The Sixth Liberal Art* (Toronto 1974)
Annotated bibliography

Hunt *Recorder* Hunt, Edgar *The Recorder and Its Music* (rev. ed. 1977 London)

Jacobs *Tempo* Jacobs, Charles *Tempo Notation in Renaissance Spain* (Brooklyn 1964)

Jammers *Minnesangs* Jammers, Ewald, ed. *Ausgewählte Melodien des Minnesangs* (Tübingen 1963)

JAMS *Journal of the American Musicological Society* (1948–)

Jeppesen *Copenhagen* Jeppesen, Knud *The Copehagen Chansonnier* (Copenhagen and Leipzig 1927, repr. New York 1965)
Fifteenth-century secular vocal and instrumental

Jeppesen *Frottola* — *La Frottola* 3 vols (Copenhagen 1968–70)
Transcriptions in vol. 3

Jeppesen *Laude* — *Die Mehrstimmige italienische Laude um 1500* (Leipzig 1935)
Polyphonic laude from Petrucci's two vols

Jeppesen *Orgelmusik* — *Die italienische Orgelmusik am Anfang des Cinquecento* 2 vols (Copenhagen 1960)
Vol. 2 contains works by Cavazzoni, Fogliano, Modena, and Brumel

Jerome *Musica* Jerome of Moravia *Tractatus de Musica* ed. S.M. Cserba *Hieronymus de Moravia, O.P.: Tractatus de musica* (Regensburg 1935); excerpt in English transl. in MacClintock *Readings*

JLS *Journal of the Lute Society of America* (1968–)

JVG *Journal of the Viola da Gamba Society* (1963–)

Kemp *Escorial* Kemp, Walter *The Anonymous Pieces in MS Escorial Bibl. del Monasterio, v. III. 24.* (AIM 1980–)
Forty-six chansons à 3 from the fifteenth century

Keruzoré *Estampies* Keruzoré, Alain, ed. *Estampies et danses royales* (Paris 1973)
Edition of all danses in MS Paris BN 844; same repertory as Aubry *Estampies*

Kinkeldey *Dance* Kinkeldey, Otto 'Dance Tunes of the Fifteenth Century' *Instrumental Music* ed. David Hughes (Cambridge, Mass. 1959, repr. 1972) 3–30, 89–152

Kökeritz *Chaucer* Kökeritz, Helge *The Pronunciation of Chaucer's English* (repr. Toronto 1979)

Kottick *Collegium* Kottick, Edward L. *The Collegium: A Handbook*

(Stonington, Conn. 1977)
A basic manual for establishing a collegium program in an American university

Kottick *Cordeform*   – *The Unica in Chansonnier Cordeform* (AIM 1967)

Lanfranco *Scintille*   Lanfranco, Giovanni M. *Scintille di musica* (1533)

Le Huray *Reformation*   Le Huray, Peter *Music and the Reformation in England 1549–1660* (London 1967)

Lesure *Parisienne*   Lesure, François et al, eds *Anthologie de la chanson parisienne au XVIe siècle* (Monaco 1953)
Forty-eight chansons

Liber   *The Liber Usualis with Introduction and Rubrics in English* (New York 1952)

Liuzzi *Lauda*   Liuzzi, Fernando *La lauda e i primordi della melodia italiana* 2 vols (Rome 1935)
Monophonic laude from the thirteenth and fourteenth centuries

Lockwood *Dispute*   Lockwood, Lewis 'A dispute on Accidentals in Sixteenth-Century Rome' *Analecta Musicologica* 2 (1965) 24–40

Lockwood *Ficta*   – 'A Sample Problem of *Musica Ficta*: Willaert's *Pater noster*' *Studies in Music History* ed. Harold Powers (Princeton 1968) 161–82

Lowinsky *Medici*   Lowinsky, Edward *The Medici Codex of 1518* 3 vols, Monuments of Renaissance Music 3, 4, 5 (Chicago 1968)
Fifty-three motets transcribed in vol. 3

Lowinsky *Text*   – 'A Treatise on Text Underlay by a German Disciple of Francisco de Salinas' *Festschrift Heinrich Besseler* (Leipzig 1962) 231–51

Loyan *Trent*   Loyan, Richard *Canons in the Trent Codices* (AIM 1967)
Fifteenth century

LP   *Le Pupitre* (1967–)

LP 2   Le Jeune *Missa ad placitum*

LP 5   *Chansons françaises pour orgue vers 1550*

LP 9   Attaingnant *Danseries à 4* (1547)

LP 10   Gastoldi *Balletti à 5* (1591)

LP 27   Gabrieli *Canzoni e sonate*

LPM   London Pro Musica Editions
Many series for vocal and instrumental music in modern edition

LSJ   *The Lute Society Journal* (1959–)

Lyons *Lute*   Lyons, David *Lute, Vihuela, Guitar to 1800: A Bibliography* Detroit Studies in Music Bibliography 40 (Detroit 1978)
Includes cittern and general biographies of composers and performers

MacClintock *Balet* MacClintock, Carol and Lander MacClintock, eds *Le balet comique de la royne* (1581, AIM 1971)
Transcription and translation of the entire performance

MacClintock *Readings* MacClintock, Carol, ed. *Readings in the History of Music in Performance* (Bloomington 1979)

McGee *Dialogue* McGee, Timothy J. 'The Role of the *Quem Quaeritis* Dialogue in the History of Western Drama' *Renaissance Drama* new series 7 (1976) 177–91

McGee *Medieval* – *Medieval Dances* forthcoming

McKinnon *Instruments* McKinnon, James 'Musical Instruments in Medieval Psalm Commentaries and Psalters' *JAMS* 21 (1968) 3–20

McKinnon *Representations* – 'Representations of the Mass in Medieval and Renaissance Art' *JAMS* 31 (1978) 21–52

McPeek *Egerton* McPeek, Gwynn S. *The British Museum Manuscript Egerton 3307* (London 1963)
Mostly sacred polyphony

Maffei *Lettere* Maffei, Giovanni *Delle lettere* ... (Naples 1562) modern ed. of letters concerning singing in N. Bridgman 'Giovanni Camillo Maffei et sa lettre sur le chant' *Revue de Musicologie* 38 (1956) 10–34. English transl. in MacClintock *Readings*

Maillard *Trouvères* Maillard, Jean and Jacques Chailley, eds *Anthologie de chants de trouvères* (Paris 1967)

Mairy *Chansons* Mairy, A., Lionel de la Laurencie, and Geneviève Thibault, eds *Chansons au luth et airs de cour français du xvie siècle* (Paris 1934)

Marcuse *Dictionary* Marcuse, Sibyl *Musical Instruments: A Comprehensive Dictionary* (New York 1964)

Marcuse *Survey* – *A Survey of Musical Instruments* (New York 1975)

Marix *Bourgogne* Marix, Jeanne, ed. *Les musiciens de la cour de Bourgogne au xve siècle, 1420–1467* (Paris 1937)

Marrocco *Cacce* Marrocco, William T., ed. *Fourteenth-Century Italian Cacce* (2nd rev. ed. Cambridge, Mass. 1961)

Marx *Tabulaturen* Marx, Hans, ed. *Tabulaturen des XVI. Jahrhunderts* Schweizerische Musikdenkmäler 6, 7 (Basel 1967, 1970)
Tabulature transcriptions of instrumental and vocal compositions from 1490 to 1520

Masson *Carnival* Masson, Paul, ed. *Chants de carnaval florentins* (Paris 1913)
Twenty carnival songs from ca 1490 to 1520

Maurer *Lieder* Maurer, Friedrich, ed. *Die Lieder Walthers von der Vogelweide* 2 vols (Tübingen 1960, 1962)

MB
Musica Britannica (1951–   )
Many volumes of medieval and Renaissance, vocal and instrumental, sacred and secular

MBA
Hamburg, Otto, ed. *Musikgeschichte in Beispielen, von Antike bis Johann Sebastian Bach* (Wilhelmshaven 1976)
Anthology

Mendel *Triple*
Mendel, Arthur 'A Brief Note on Triple Proportion In Scheutz' *MQ* 46 (1960) 67–70

Merian *Tanz*
Merian, Wilhelm *Der Tanz in den deutschen Tabulaturbüchern* (1927, repr. Hildesheim 1968)
Sixteenth and seventeenth centuries

Merritt *Motets*
Merritt, A. Tilman, ed. *Quatorzième livre de motets composés par Pierre de Manchecourt parus chez Pierre Attaignant (1539)* (Monaco 1964)

Mersenne *Harmonie*
Mersenne, Marin *L'harmonie universelle* (Paris 1636)
English transl. R. Chapman *The Book on Instruments* (The Hague 1957)

Meyer *Crumhorn*
Meyer, Kenton T. *The Crumhorn, Its History, Design, Repertory, and Technique* Studies in Musicology 66 (Ann Arbor 1981)

Milán *Maestro*
Milán, Luis de *El Maestro* (1536); English transl. and transcription C. Jacobs (University Park, Pa. 1971)
Same as *PAM 2*

Minor *Renaissance*
Minor, Andrew and Bonner Mitchell *A Renaissance Entertainment* (Columbia, Mo. 1968)
Description and transcriptions of music from 1539 festivities in Florence for the marriage of Cosimo I

MM
Parrish, Carl and John Ohl, eds *Masterpieces of Music Before 1750* (New York 1951)

MME
Monumentos de la Música expañola (Barcelona 1941–   )
Sacred and secular, vocal and instrumental

MMF
Expert, Henri ed. *Les monuments de la musique française au temps de la Renaissance* 15 vols (1924–30)
Sacred and secular vocal

MMR
– ed. *Les maîtres musiciens de la Renaissance française* 23 vols (1894–1908)
Sacred and secular, vocal and instrumental

Monkmeyer *Antwerpener*
Monkmeyer, Helmut, ed. 'Antwerpener Tanzbuch': *Galliarden, Balli, Allemanden zu vier Stimmen (1583)* 2 vols (1962)
Four-part dances published by Pierre Phalese

Monkmeyer *Löwener* – ed. *'Löwener Tanzbuch': Fantasien, Pavanen, Galliarden zu vier Stimmen (1571)* 2 vols (1962)
Four-part dances published by Pierre Phalese

Montagu *Instruments* Montagu, Jeremy *The World of Medieval and Renaissance Musical Instruments* (London 1976)

Monterosso *Frottole* Monterosso, Raffaello and Benvenuto Disertori, eds *Le frottole nel' edizione principe di Ottaviano Petrucci* (Cremona 1954)
First three Petrucci frottola books

MQ *The Musical Quarterly* (1915–   )

MSEP Musica Sacra et profana
Many publications of early music for voice and instruments

Munrow *Instruments* Munrow, David *Instruments of the Middle Ages and Renaissance* (London 1978)

NAWM Palisca, Claude, ed. *Norton Anthology of Western Music* 2 vols (New York 1980)
Vol. 1 has sixty-two transcriptions of medieval and Renaissance compositions with translations

Newcomb *Ferrara* Newcomb, Anthony *The Madrigal at Ferrara 1579–1597* 2 vols (Princeton 1980)
Vol 2 has twenty-seven madrigals

Newcombe *Erart* Newcombe, Terence, ed. *Jehan Erart, Thirteenth Century Trouvère d'Arras* (AIM 1975)

Newman *Dances* Newman, Joel, ed. *Sixteenth Century Italian Dances* Penn State Music Series 12 (1966)
Instrumental dances à 4

NOHM *The New Oxford History of Music* (London 1954–   )

NOHM 2 *Early Medieval Music Up to 1300*

NOHM 3 *Ars Nova and the Renaissance, 1300–1540*

NOHM 4 *The Age of Humanism, 1540–1630*

NS Kamien, Roger, ed. *The Norton Scores* 2 vols (3rd ed. New York 1977)

OMM Marrocco, William T. and Nicholas Sandon, eds. *Medieval Music* (Oxford 1977)
106 transcriptions, translations, and commentary; monophony, polyphony, sacred, and secular

Ortiz *Tratado* Ortiz, Diego *Tratado de glosas sobre clausulas ...* (Rome 1553); German transl. M. Schneider (Cassel 1961), English transl. P. Farrell *JVG* 4 (1967) 5–9

Oxenbury *Intabolatura*	Oxenbury, William and Thurston Dart, eds *Intabolatura nova de balli* (London 1965)
	Italian dances from 1551
PAM	*Publikationen Alterer Musik* 11 vols (Leipzig 1926–40, repr. Hildesheim 1967–8)
PAM 1^1, 3^1, 4^2	Machaut *Musicalische Werke*
PAM 1^2	Ockeghem *Messen 1–8*
PAM 2	Milán *Libro de música de vihuela de mano intitulado El Maestro*
	Same as Milán *Maestro*
PAM 4^1, 6	Marenzio *Six Books of Five-part Madrigals*
PAM 8	Petrucci *Frottole Books 1 and 4*
PAM 9	Willaert *Motets*
PAM 11	*Notre Dame Organa for Three and Four Voices*
Panum *Stringed*	Panum, Hortense *Stringed Instruments of the Middle Ages* (1940, rev. ed. J. Pulver London 1971)
PAP	*Publikationen älterer praktischer und theoretischer Musikwerke* 29 vols (Berlin 1873–1905)
PAP 1, 2, 3, 4	*Mehrstimmiges deutsches Liederbuch von 1544*
PAP 6	Josquin *Ausgewählte Kompositionen*
PAP 7	Walther *Wittenbergisch Gesangbuch von 1524*
PAP 8	Finck *Ausgewählte Kompositionen*
PAP 9	Erhart Oeglin *Liederbuch zu vier Stimmen*
	Includes Hofheimer, Isaac, etc.
PAP 15	Hans Leo Hassler *Lustgarten, 1601*
PAP 20	Martin Agricola *Musica instrumentalis deudsch*
PAP 23	*Sechzig chansons zu vier Stimmen*
PAP 24	Dressler *Siebzehn Motetten*
PAP 25	Langius *Eine ausgewählte Sammlung Motetten*
PAP 26	Vecchi *L'amfiparnasso*
	Same as CPS 5
PAP 29	Forster *Kurzweilige ... Liedlein*
Parrish *Notation*	Parrish, Carl *The Notation of Medieval Music* (rev. ed. New York 1959)
Perkins *Mellon*	Perkins, Leeman and Howard Garey *The Mellon Chansonnier* 2 vols (New Haven 1979)
	Vol. 1: transcriptions and facsimiles, vol. 2: commentary and translations
Perkins *Text*	– 'Toward a Rational Approach to Text Placement In the Secular Music of Dufay's Time' in Atlas *Dufay* 102–14
Picker *Chanson*	Picker, Martin *The Chanson Albums of Marguerite of Austria*

	(Berkeley and Los Angeles 1965)
	Eighty-two chansons and a few motets à 4 and 5, all from ca 1500
Pirrotta *Fourteenth*	Pirrotta, Nino, ed. *The Music of Fourteenth-Century Italy* 5 vols (AIM 1954–64)
Pirrotta *Orfei*	– and Elena Povoledo *Li due Orfei* (Torino 1969); English rev. ed. *Music and Theatre from Poliziano to Monteverdi* (Cambridge 1982)
Plamenac *Faenza*	Plamenac, Dragan *Keyboard Music of the Late Middle Ages in Codex Faenza 117* (AIM 1972)
	Ornamented fourteenth-century sacred and secular
PMF	*Polyphonic Music of the Fourteenth Century* (Monaco 1956–)
	Includes sacred and secular, vocal and instrumental music from France, Italy, and England
Polk *Bands*	Polk, Keith 'Wind Bands of Medieval Flemish Cities' BWG 1 (1968) 93–113
Polk *Dufay*	– 'Ensemble Performance in Dufay's Time' in Atlas *Dufay* 61–75
Polk *Ensemble*	– 'Ensemble Instrumental Music In Flanders, 1450–1550' *Journal of Band Research* 2 (1975) 12–27
Polk *Flemish*	– 'Flemish Wind Bands in the Late Middle Ages: A Study of Improvisatory Instrumental Practices' unpublished PHD dissertation (University of California 1966)
Polk *Foundations*	– 'The Foundations of Ensemble Improvisation in the Late Fifteenth Century' unpublished article
Polk *Wind*	– 'Municipal Wind Music in Flanders in the Late Middle Ages' BWQ 2 (1969) 1–15
Pope *Manuscript*	Pope, Isabel and Masakata Kanazawa *The Musical Manuscript Montecassino 871* (Oxford 1978)
	141 transcriptions of mid-fifteenth-century French, Italian, and Spanish sacred and secular polyphony from Naples
Poulton *Graces*	Poulton, Diana 'Graces to Play in Renaissance Lute Music' EM 3 (1975) 107–14
Poulton *Style*	– ' "How to Play with Good Style" By Thomas De Sancta Maria' LSJ 12 (1970) 23–30
Prizer *Courtly*	Prizer, William *Courtly Pastimes: The Frottole of Marchetto Cara* (Ann Arbor 1979)
Prizer *Frottola*	– 'Performance practices in the Frottola' EM 3 (1975) 227–35
Processionale	*Processionale Monasticum* (1893)
Ramis *Musica*	Ramis de Pareja *Musica practica* (1482, facs. ed. Bologna 1969); modern ed. J. Wolf (Leipzig 1901)

Rastall *Consort*   Rastall, Richard 'Some English Consort-Groupings of the
                     Late Middle Ages' *Music and Letters* 55 (1974) 179–202
Rastall *Notation*   – *The Notation of Western Music: An Introduction*
                     (London 1982)
Reaney *Fifteenth*   Reaney, Gilbert *Early Fifteenth-Century Music* (AIM 1955–)
                     Vols 1, 2, 3, and 4: French sacred and secular polyphony; vols 5, 6,
                     and 7: Italian sacred and secular polyphony
Reese *Middle*   Reese, Gustave *Music in the Middle Ages* (New York 1940)
Reese *Renaissance* Reese, Gustave *Music in the Renaissance* (rev. ed. New York
                     1954)
Remnant *Rebec*   Remnant, Mary 'Rebec, Fiddle and Crowd in England'
                     Proceedings of the Royal Musical Association 95 (1969) 15–28
RI*d*IM   Répertoire international d'iconographie musicale
Rognioni *Selve*   Rognioni, Francesco *Selve de varii passaggi* (Milan 1620,
                     facs. ed. Bologna 1970)
Rogniono *Passaggi* Rogniono, Richardo *Passaggi per potersi essercitare nel
                     diminuire* (Venice 1592)
Rokseth *Motets*   Rokseth, Yvonne, ed. *Treize motets et un prélude pour orgue
                     édités par Pierre Attaingnant (1531)* (Paris 1930)
                     Volume 7 of Attaingnant's earliest keyboard prints
Rokseth *Orgue*   – ed. *Deux livres d'orgue parus en 1531: Pierre Attaingnant*
                     (repr. Paris 1967)
                     Contains organ alternatim for Mass Ordinary
Rokseth *Polyphonies* – *Polyphonies du XIIIe siècle* 4 vols (Paris 1935–9)
                     Thirteenth-century motets from the Montpellier Codex; same as
                     RRM 2–7
Romano *Duorum*   Romano, Eustachio *Musica Duorum* (1521); modern ed.
                     H. David, Monuments of Renaissance Music 6 (Chicago 1975)
                     Duets for instruments of various pitches
RRM   *Recent Researches in Music of the Late Middle Ages and Early
                     Renaissance* (Madison 1975–)
                     Large collection of vocal and instrumental music from all locations
RRR   *Recent Researches in Music of the Renaissance*
                     (Madison 1964–)
                     Large collection of vocal and instrumental music from all locations
Sachs *Instruments* Sachs, Curt *The History of Musical Instruments* (New York
                     1940)
Sachs *Rhythm*   – *Rhythm and Tempo* (New York 1953)
Sancta *Libro*   Sancta Maria, Tomás de *Libro llamado arte de tañer fantasia*
                     (Valladolid 1565)
SCA   *Smith College Archives* (Northampton, Mass. 1935–)

SCA 4	*Canzoni, sonetti, strambotti et frottole, Libro Tertio, Andrea Antico, 1517*
SCA 5	Arcadelt *Chansons*
SCA 6	Rore *Madrigals for Three and Four Voices*
SCA 8	Galilei *Contrapunti a due voci (1584)*
Schlick *Tabulaturen*	Schlick, Arnolt *Tabulaturen etlicher Lobgesang und Liedlein* (Mainz 1512); modern ed. G. Harms (1924)
	For solo keyboard, solo lute, voice and lute
Schwartz *Petrucci*	Schwartz, Rudolf, ed. *Ottaviano Petrucci: Frottole I und IV* (Leipzig 1935)
Seay *Chansons*	Seay, Albert, ed. *Transcriptions of Chansons for Keyboard* (AIM 1961)
	Vols 1–3 of Attaingnant's earliest keyboard prints
Seay *Medieval*	– *Music in the Medieval World* (2nd ed. Englewood Cliffs 1975)
Slim *Madrigals*	Slim, H. Colin, ed. *A Gift of Madrigals and Motets* 2 vols (Chicago 1972)
	Transcriptions of thirty motets and thirty madrigals in vol. 2
Slim *Nova*	– ed. *Musica Nova* Monuments of Renaissance Music 1 (Chicago 1964)
	Twenty-one ricercari mostly à 4, published in 1540
Smet *Viola*	Smet, Robin de *Published Music for the Viola da Gamba and Other Viols* Detroit Studies in Music Bibliography 18 (Detroit 1971)
Smijers *Motets*	Smijers, Albert and A. Tillman Merritt, eds *Treize livres de motets parus chez Pierre Attaingnant en 1534 et 1535* (Monaco 1934–63)
	Thirteen motet books
Smijers *Ockeghem*	– ed. *Van Ockeghem tot Sweelinck* (Amsterdam 1939–)
	Sacred and secular, fifteenth and sixteenth centuries
Smoldon *Music*	Smoldon, William *The Music of the Medieval Church Dramas* ed. Cynthia Bourgeault (Oxford 1980)
Smoldon *Pastorum*	– ed. *Officium Pastorum* (London 1967)
Smoldon *Perigrinus*	– ed. *Peregrinus* (London 1965)
Smoldon *Planctus*	– ed. *Planctus Maria* (London 1965)
Smoldon *Visitatio*	– ed. *Visitatio Sepulchri* (London 1964)
Southern *Escorial*	Southern, Eileen, ed. *Anonymous Pieces in the MS Escorial IV.a.24* (AIM 1981)
	Sixty-four chansons and frottole, mostly à 3
Speck *Relationships*	Speck, Linda J. *Relationships Between Music and Text in Late*

Thirteenth Century Motets unpublished PH D dissertation (University of Michigan 1977)
Discusses variant readings as evidence of improvisatory practices

SS   Godwin, Joscelyn, ed. *Schirmer Scores* (New York 1975)
Anthology

SSA   Wolf, Johannes, ed. *Sing- und Spielmusik aus älterer Zeit* (Leipzig 1931)
Anthology

SSM   Lerner, Edward, comp. *Study Scores of Musical Styles* (New York 1968)
Anthology

Stäblein *Mass*   Stäblein-Harder, H. *Fourteenth-Century Mass Music in France* (AIM 1962)
Polyphonic, sacred

Sterne *Getron*   Sterne, Colin, ed. *The Son of Getron* (Pittsburgh 1962)

Stevens *Court*   Stevens, John *Music and Poetry in the Early Tudor Court* (London 1961)

Stevens *Tudor*   Stevens, Denis *Tudor Church Music* (London 1961)

Stevenson *Antologia*   Stevenson, Robert *Antologia de polifonia Portuguesa 1490–1680* Portugaliae Musica 37 (Lisbon 1982)
Twenty-seven transcriptions of vocal polyphony for three to eight voices

Stevenson *Cathedral*   – *Spanish Cathedral Music in the Golden Age* (Berkeley and Los Angeles 1960)

Stevenson *Columbus*   – *Spanish Music in the Age of Columbus* (repr. The Hague 1964)

Strunk *Source*   Strunk, Oliver *Source Readings in Music History* (New York 1950)

Susato *Danserye*   Susato, Tielman *Danserye zeer lustich ... 1551* ed. F. Giesbert, 2 vols (1936)
Fifty-seven dances à 4

Taylor *Melodien*   Taylor, Ronald *Die Melodien der weltlichen Lieder des Mittelalters* 2 vols (Stuttgart 1964)
Monophonic

Taylor *Minnesinger*   – *The Art of the Minnesinger* 2 vols (Cardiff 1968)

TCM   *Tudor Church Music* 10 vols (London 1922–9)

TECM   Knight, Gerald and Will Reed, eds *Treasury of English Church Music* 5 vols (London 1965)

TECM 1   *1100–1500*

TECM 2   *1545–1650*

TEM   Parrish, Carl, ed. *A Treasury of Early Music* (New York 1958)

Thurston *Perotin*   Thurston, Ethel, ed. *The Works of Perotin* (New York 1970)

Tintori   Tintori, Giampiero, ed. *Sacre rappresentazioni nel manuscritto*
Rappresentazioni   *201 della Biblioteca Municipale di Orleans* (Cremona 1958)
All liturgical dramas from this manuscript; rhythmic transcription is fanciful but photo of original is included

Tischler *Motets*   Tischler, Hans *The Earliest Motets (to ca 1270)* (in preparation)

Torchi *L'Arte*   Torchi, Luigi *L'arte musicale in Italia* 7 vols (1877–1908, repr. 1968)
Vol. 1: fourteenth- to sixteenth-century sacred and secular polyphony; vol. 2: sixteenth-century sacred and secular; vol. 3: fifteenth- to seventeenth-century organ

Tyler *Guitar*   Tyler, James *The Early Guitar: A History and Handbook* (Oxford 1980)

Vaccaro *Luth*   Vaccaro, Jean-Michel *La musique de luth en France au XVIe siècle* (Paris 1981)

Vicentino *Musica*   Vicentino, Nicola *L'antico musica ridotta alla moderna prattica* (1555, facs. ed. E. Lowinsky in Documenta Musicologica 1959)

Virgiliano *Dolcimelo*   Virgiliano, Aurelio *Il Dolcimelo* (ca 1600)

Waite *Rhythm*   Waite, William *The Rhythm of Twelfth-Century Polyphony* (New Haven 1954)

Walker *Pellegrina*   Walker, Daniel P. et al., eds *Musique des intermèdes de 'la Pellegrina'* (Paris 1963)
Edition of the 1589 *intermedii* from Florence

Wangermée *Flemish*   Wangermée, Robert *Flemish Music*; English transl. R. Wolf (Praeger 1968)

Wardell *Troubadours*   Wardell, Thomas *The Music of the Troubadours* (Santa Barbara, 1979)

Warner *Performance*   Warner, Thomas 'Indications of Performance Practice in Woodwind Instruction Books of the Seventeenth and Eighteenth Centuries' unpublished PHD dissertation (New York University 1964)

Warren *Punctus*   Warren, Charles W. 'Punctus Organi and Cantus Coronatus in the Music of Dufay' in Atlas *Dufay* 128–43

WE   *The Wellesley Edition* (1950–   )

WE 3   *The Dublin Virginal Manuscript*

WE 6   *Fifteenth Century Basse Dances*

WE 8   *The Bottegari Lutebook*

Werf *Measurability*   Werf, Hendrik van der 'Concerning the Measurability of
                        Medieval Music' *Current Musicology* 10 (1970) 69–73
Werf *Troubadours*   – *The Chansons of the Troubadours and Trouvères* (Utrecht
                        1972)
Werf *Trouvère*   – 'The Trouvère Chansons as Creations of a Notationless
                        Culture' *Current Musicology* 1 (1965) 61–82
Whitehill *Calixtinus* Whitehill, Walter, G. Prado, and J. Garcia, eds *Liber Sancti
                        Jacobi, Codex Calixtinus* 3 vols (Santiago de Compostela 1944)
                        Twelfth-century secular polyphony
Whitwell *Wind*   Whitwell, David *The Renaissance Wind Band and Wind
                        Ensemble* (Northridge, Calif. 1983)
Wilkins *Adam*   Wilkins, Nigel, ed. *The Lyric Works of Adam de la Hale*
                        (AIM 1967)
                        Chanson, jeux-partis, and motets
Wilkins *Chaucer*   – *Music in the Age of Chaucer* (Cambridge 1979)
                        A discussion of fourteenth-century styles and repertory
Wilkins *Reina*   – ed. *A Fourteenth Century Repertory from the Codex Reina*
                        (AIM 1966)
                        Fifty-two polyphonic ballades, virelais, and rondeaux
Wilkins *Repertory*   – ed. *A Fifteenth Century Repertory from the Codex Reina*
                        (AIM 1966)
                        Secular French 1410–50
Winternitz   Winternitz, Emanual *Musical Instruments of the Western
Instruments   World* (New York 1967)
Winternitz *Symbolism* – *Musical Symbolism in Western Art* (London 1967)
Wolf *Squarcialupi*   Wolf, Johannes, ed. *Der Squarcialupi Codex* (Lippstadt 1955)
                        Fourteenth-century Italian
Wolf *Tänze*   – 'Die Tänze des Mittelalters' *Archiv für Musikwissenschaft* 1
                        (1918–19) 24–42
                        Transcriptions of medieval dances; some errors; same as McGee
                        Medieval
Woodfield *Viol*   Woodfield, Ian 'Viol Playing Techniques in the Mid-Sixteenth
                        Century: A Survey of Ganassi's Fingering Instructions' *EM* 6
                        (1978) 544–9
Wright *Cambrai*   Wright, Craig 'Performance Practices at the Cathedral of
                        Cambrai 1475–1550' *MQ* 64 (1978) 295–328
Young *Drama*   Young, Karl *The Drama of the Medieval Church* 2 vols
                        (Oxford 1933)
Zabern *Modo*   Zabern, Conrad von *De modo bene cantandi* (1474); partial
                        English transl. in MacClintock *Readings*

Zacconi *Prattica*   Zacconi, Ludovico *Prattica di musica* 2 vols (Venice 1592, repr. Bologna, n.d.); English transl. in MacClintock *Readings*

Zarlino *Istitutioni*   Zarlino, Gioseffo *Istitutioni harmoniche* (1558, repr. New York 1965)

Zaslaw *Performance*   Zaslaw, Neil and Mary Vinquist *Performance Practice: A Bibliography* (New York 1971)

Zippel *Suonatori*   Zippel, Giovanni *I suonatori della Signori di Firenze* (Trent 1892)

INDEX

References to musical examples are in boldface type.